Sixth Edition

INTRODUCTION
TO
EDUCATIONAL
ADMINISTRATION

Roald F. Campbell   *University of Utah*

John E. Corbally   *John D. and Catherine T.
MacArthur Foundation*

Raphael O. Nystrand   *University of Louisville*

ALLYN AND BACON, INC.
Boston   London   Sydney   Toronto

9133/52

LIBRARY OF CONGRESS CATALOGING IN PUBLICATION DATA
Campbell, Roald Fay, 1905–
    Introduction to educational administration.

    Includes index.
    1. School management and organization.   I. Corbally, John E., 1924–   II. Nystrand, Raphael O.
III. Title.
LB2805.C25   1983   371.2   82-24475
ISBN 0-205-07983-0

PRINTED IN THE UNITED STATES OF AMERICA
10 9 8 7 6   88

TO MARGARET, MARGUERITE, AND SUE

CONTENTS

PREFACE

This is a new book in educational administration, in spite of the fact that it appears as the sixth edition and bears the same title as its predecessors. We are grateful for the reception that earlier editions under this title received but we thought it was time to wipe the slate clean. This has permitted us to make a new assessment of the field of educational administration—its practice and its study—and to decide once again what should be said as an introduction to the field. Readers familiar with preceding editions will recognize that the challenges presented in the final chapter are similar to those set forth in earlier editions, but the analysis of schools and school administration that precedes this chapter is almost entirely new.

Our purposes remain the same as in the previous editions. First, we seek to orient readers by providing an overview of the field and helping them consider a career in that field. We continue to believe that the book can help individuals make realistic assessments about whether they wish to become administrators. A second purpose is to help teachers to (1) understand the role of administrators in schools and (2) participate more effectively in administration. Certain sections may also be useful to practicing administrators, school board members, and lay citizens: these readers may discover new perspectives that enlarge their context for understanding the practice of educational administration.

As with previous editions, our intention is to provide an *introduction to*, not a *survey of*, the field; the field is too comprehensive to be surveyed adequately. Educational administration covers a wide range of positions in school systems and other agencies. In order to provide an adequate concept of educational administration, we deal first with the nature and purposes of administration, the setting in which it takes place, and its demands on administrators as people. We then examine a series of topics that represent recurring themes or problem areas in administrative life—decision making, leadership, communication, resource allocation, conflict management, change, and appraisal. Finally, we discuss our position that competent administrative leadership is crucial to the perpetuation of the democratic way of life in the United States.

Our starting point in preparing this edition was to ask what schools are like and what issues concern those who administer them. We prepared a brief prospectus outlining our thoughts about these questions and sought the reactions of a number of school administrators in diverse settings. We asked them to tell us which topics are most germane to prospective administrators and why. We also invited them to provide us with brief anecdotes of experiences that highlight particular problems. Their responses helped focus our efforts on school events in the real world.

As in previous editions, we have included some discussion of theory and research from other disciplines, which is based upon institutions other than schools. In doing so, however, we have attempted to draw only from literature that has implications for school administration, and we have done our best to be explicit regarding these implications. We believe the result is a practical book— one that introduces students to the field of educational administration by addressing the actual concerns of administrators, and by demonstrating the applicability of selected theory and research to these concerns.

With this edition John E. Corbally, Jr. returns to the writing team. Along with Roald F. Campbell and John A. Ramseyer, he was an author of the first three editions. When Corbally became president of Syracuse University and Ramseyer died, Edwin M. Bridges and Raphael O. Nystrand were invited to join the writing team. Campbell, Bridges, and Nystrand prepared the fifth edition and had planned the sixth when Bridges elected to drop out of the project. At this point Corbally, who had recently become President Emeritus at the University of Illinois and returned to a faculty position, accepted an invitation to participate in the sixth edition.

We are indebted to many individuals whose willingness to share their ideas and react to ours has influenced the nature of this book. Foremost among these persons is Edwin Bridges, who was coauthor of the fourth and fifth editions and who helped design the approach to this edition. We appreciate the consultation of the many school administrators who have helped us to understand the issues that concern them, and who suggested concepts and illustrations for our use. We have also benefited from the insights of our colleagues and students—most recently at the universities of Utah, Illinois, and Louisville but also at other institutions we have served. In this regard, the Ohio State University warrants special mention, for the book originated there and each of us enjoyed several years of stimulating and supportive colleagueship as members of its faculty of educational administration.

R. F. C.
J. E. C.
R. O. N.

CHAPTER 1

INTRODUCTION

In this first chapter we raise basic questions about the nature of educational administration. In so doing we introduce many of the themes that will be developed more fully in succeeding chapters. The questions have to do with a definition of educational administration, a consideration of its purpose, the characteristics of schools, the nature of administrative work, people in administration, preparation for the administrative role, and the current status of the field. We conclude the chapter by describing the plan of this book. At the outset, we make a number of assumptions that should be acknowledged: (1) that organizations are essential in our kind of world; (2) that administrators can perform useful functions in organizations; (3) that a knowledge of organizational behavior, internal and external, can permit an administrator to act more effectively; and (4) that educational organizations and their management have some unique characteristics that deserve treatment. We now proceed with the basic questions and some discussion of each.

Educational administration is the management of institutions designed to foster teaching and learning. These institutions include public schools, school districts, private schools, instructional organizations sponsored by industry, public and private colleges, public and private universities, and many others. While many of these institutions are in the public realm, many, as already suggested,

WHAT IS EDUCATIONAL ADMINISTRATION?

1

are under private, church, association, or industrial auspices. The teaching and learning activities sponsored by these institutions have a wide range of clients, from nursery school children through graduate and professional school students. Particularly for the public schools and colleges, we have developed state and national agencies designed to supervise and coordinate their performance. In a sense, then, these agencies also are engaged in educational administration.

A Field of Practice and of Study   The management of the broad range of institutions noted above clearly supports the notion that educational administration is a field of practice. As such, it has some aspects in common with other fields of management such as public administration, hospital administration, and business management. While we recognize some common elements between administration in the public realm and management in the private realm, we do not wish to overstate the case. We contend that there are also some unique aspects to public administration and particularly to educational administration.

Not only is educational administration a field of practice; it is also a field of study. It is mostly in this century that the study of educational administration emerged; first at the Teachers College of Columbia University and followed shortly thereafter by graduate programs at Stanford University, the University of Chicago, and other institutions. In study as well as in practice there are elements common to educational administration and administration in other arenas. We see much value in recognizing these elements but we think they frequently have been accepted without critical examination and without testing in educational organizations. It is primarily since the 1950s that educational administration has become a field of study in its own right.[1]

We should note that educational administration is an applied field and not a discipline in the sense that chemistry and history are disciplines. As an applied field, educational administration has much in common with other applied fields such as engineering and medicine. Just as engineering must build upon such disciplines as mathematics and physics and medicine upon such disciplines as anatomy and biology, educational administration must build upon a number of basic disciplines such as psychology, sociology, political science, and economics. But the concepts of these disciplines cannot be borrowed indiscriminately; they must be adapted and tested in educational organizations. For instance, studies in leadership have been well summarized elsewhere but the applicability of these studies to educational organizations needs more examination. It is this kind of examination and application to which this book is addressed.

Since educational administration is a broad field of practice and of study there are numerous career positions in the field. On the practice side, at the school level, these positions include school principals, school supervisors, school superintendents, and many others. At the college level, these positions include department chairpersons, deans, and presidents. In addition, there are many state and national agency personnel such as division chairpersons, directors, superintendents, commissioners, and so forth. On the study side of the field there are researchers in universities, in private research firms, and in governmental agencies. There are also professors in colleges and universities who make it their business to study the field, organize its concepts, and transmit information to prospective and practicing administrators. Many of these professors also engage in field relationships with practitioners and some of them conduct field studies and do other research.[2]

We have defined educational administration as a broad field of practice and of study. We have also alluded to many of the career positions found in the field. For this book, however, we will delimit our discussion to the direction and management of schools and school districts. We have decided on this focus for two reasons. First, we think it will permit us to deal more specifically with the problems confronting schools and school districts. Second, most people choosing careers in educational administration will probably begin them in schools and school districts. Each of these reasons deserves some elaboration.

Focus on Schools and School Districts

Our desire to deal with the problems of schools and school districts should not be misunderstood. There is no way that we can write a cook book to be used by school principals and district superintendents. The problems in the field are too varied, too dependent on local conditions both in and out of the schools, too much affected by the people involved in particular organizations, to permit the spinning out of recipes. At the same time, we take the position that some problems occur often in schools and school districts and that a consideration of these problems is a good way to examine the practice of educational administration. Thus, in Chapters 6 through 12 we deal with some of the problems and issues that frequently confront schools and school districts. The categories we have developed come not only from our own experience with schools and school districts, but also represent the judgments of many school administrators with whom we have conferred. We hope to bring to each of these problem or issue areas the appropriate conceptual formulations and the empirical findings of the field while keeping the spotlight on the problems and issues. With respect to knowledge in the field we will try to be guided by the ever pertinent question, "So what?"

Let us now be more explicit about the people for whom this book is probably most germane. Many of these, we suspect, are aspiring administrators currently engaged as teachers in the schools. As teachers they have already encountered many of the problems and issues covered in Chapters 6 through 12. They have become aware of such problems and issues as decision making, leadership, and communication *from the standpoint of teachers*. Part of our task, then, is to help teachers view these problems and issues from a new perspective: that of the administrator who must see the organization as a whole, and not just as one teacher in the organization.

Much of what we say about schools and school districts has some application to the administration of other educational organizations. For instance, resources must be allocated in all organizations. Conflict should be managed in all organizations as well. Our illustrations, however, are usually drawn from schools and school districts. We trust that the generalizability of such treatment to other types of educational administration will not be ignored.

Why are there administrators in schools and school districts? Or, to be more specific, what useful functions do principals, superintendents, and other school administrators perform? These questions are sometimes raised by parents, teachers, school board members, and at times by school administrators themselves.

The basic purpose of administration is to enhance teaching and learning. In short, administration serves an instrumental and not a primary purpose. Since schools exist for teaching and learning, people who work in schools and school systems should contribute to that overriding purpose. Teachers deal directly with students; hence it is relatively easy to see how they may contribute to teaching and learning. Since many administrative activities do not deal directly with students, the relationships of these activities to teaching and learning are not always apparent. Nonetheless, the varied activities of administrators should in the end be designed to enhance teaching and learning. This charge is not always easy to implement, as will be shown.

Some researchers who have studied the work of administrators, specifically that of school principals, have become greatly concerned about the routine tasks of the job. They contend that meetings, reports, and a thousand and one things, with little or no apparent relationship to the instructional program of the school, demand too much of principals' time. Some of these critics suggest that the way out of this morass is to make principals the instructional leaders of their schools. Frequently this seems to mean that principals should become curriculum specialists; that they should devote their time to the development of instructional programs; that they should request that teachers implement these programs; that they should visit classrooms to check on the implementation of such programs; and that they should confer with teachers after such visits about ways to improve the teaching of such programs.

We have no quarrel with having principals perform many activities related to instruction. We do take exception to the idea that these activities constitute the complete role. Principals are the formally appointed leaders of their schools. They are line officers in the school system. As such principals take responsibility for what happens in their schools. To be sure, principals have many others, notably teachers, who can and should help them with the task of running the school, and this support should be enlisted. But in the end principals should be held responsible for seeing that an appropriate learning environment is established and maintained. To do that they must exercise leadership in many areas, and not only in the curriculum activities listed above.

Let us be more specific and illustrate the range of activities that principals may be called upon to perform. They may find it necessary to help a group of parents understand that more time should be devoted to the teaching of reading. They may find it necessary to seek the help of the mathematics specialist in the central office to work with a group of teachers who are attempting to improve their mathematics instruction. They may find it necessary to delegate certain record-keeping and reporting activities to a competent clerk so that more time can be devoted to other duties. They may find it necessary to support and justify the budget needs of their schools with the central office. They may find it necessary to explain and represent the position of their schools on an issue such as sex education to a group within the community. They may find it necessary to monitor closely the performance of teachers who may or may not be continued as members of the teaching staff. These and many other activities can ultimately enhance teaching and learning. The range of these activities obviously goes beyond the curriculum-centered tasks noted above.

We also take exception to the concept of principals as instructional leaders on other grounds. First, there is no way that principals can remain highly competent in all instructional areas. We also question whether principals can be *as* competent in reading as the best reading teachers in their buildings. We also question whether principals can be as competent in curriculum development as the best curriculum development staff member in the central office. Thus we see principals as generalists needing and relying on the expertise of others. Indeed, the expertise of principals becomes that of fitting the pieces together so that the total program of teaching and learning, whether in the more formal arena of the classroom or in the school regimen itself, is the best that can be devised. In short, principals must help shape the environment so that teaching and learning are fostered.

This brings us to another reservation we have to the concept of principals as instructional leaders. Fostering a desirable environment requires a wide range of activities on the part of principals. At times they must work with teachers, at times with students, at times with parents, at times with central office representatives, at times with interest groups in the community, and at times with professional organizations, among others. Only the principal is in a strategic position to recognize and to respond to the concerns of each group. In many cases, neglect of these concerns will lead in the end to a less effective organization, one that is less able to enhance teaching and learning. Our position is that principals and other school administrators should manage their organizations so that teaching and learning are enhanced whether such managerial activities are related to improved instruction immediately or in the future.

To advocate such a purpose for educational administration is one thing, to implement it is quite another. Organizations provide a milieu in which personal goals often supercede organizational goals. Etzioni and others have researched this phenomenon, called goal displacement.[3] People in organizations frequently become more concerned with preserving and building up the organization than in helping it serve its stated or obvious purposes. Indeed, some believe that schools tend to become welfare organizations conducted more for the welfare of teachers than for the instruction of students. We need not accept such a proposition in full to detect some tendency in that direction. Administrators, no less than teachers, may find in the organization ways of realizing personal goals. For instance, being head of an organization may bring a status that is satisfying to the administrator. Or, using an administrative post in one organization as a stepping stone to the next administrative post may become an obsession with some administrators. Or, the administrator may enjoy the deference received from other members of the organization and even find it difficult to differentiate between that deference and genuine respect or friendship. The spouse of the administrator, as well, may come to enjoy the deference of organizational members and confuse it with respect or friendship. While there is probably no way of setting aside such social-psychological phenomena as status, ambition, and deference, administrators need to be alert to such distractions and prevent them from distorting their stated goals.

Functions of Administration   Let us be more specific about the distinctive functions administrators should perform to enhance teaching and learning. We suggest the following:

1. *The administrator should discern and influence the development of goals and policies for the schools.* The goals may reside in the culture of the community and of the school and if so, they should be identified and perhaps made explicit. If the administrator becomes convinced that the goals and policies now extant are inadequate or incomplete, he or she then has the obligation to exert influence to see that they are developed. To be sure, the administrator cannot achieve this function alone; other people—board members, lay citizens—should be involved in this process. But it is the administrator's job to see that some direction is given to this development.

2. *The administrator should stimulate and direct the development of programs to achieve the goals and purposes.* Here again, many others are involved and few administrators can dictate this process. But the administrator can elicit the help of appropriate people, can give some direction to the steps needed in such development, can support those who carry the development forward, and can make it clear that this activity is basic to the operation of the organization.

3. *The administrator should establish and coordinate an organization to implement the programs.* Central to this function is the determination of staff requirements, the employment of competent persons to fill the positions, and the establishment of necessary relationships among staff members. As far as is possible, assignments and expectations should be clear. Staff members should know what the formal organi-

zation of the system is and what the procedures are for questioning the arrangements. This function too requires a great deal of interaction among different people, a process the administrator attempts to keep healthy.

4. *The administrator should procure and manage the resources needed to support the organization and its programs.* Implicit in this function are the processes of budgeting—the projection of expenditures and revenues; and of accounting—keeping track of where monies have gone. But to budget properly there must be some conception of programs and of how money can be used to make them effective. In addition, to secure money from the larger environment—the district, the state, the national government, and even from private sources—a case for the programs must be made and appropriately presented.

5. *The administrator should represent the organization to groups in the local or larger community, and when necessary, mediate among these groups.* This is perhaps the most forthright political function that the administrator is called upon to perform. There are many groups in the community and even in the school itself and they frequently have diverse perceptions of the organization and of its performance. In representing the organization the administrator must cope with these diverse perceptions. Moreover, in many situations, the administrator must help organizations with diverse views of the school and its procedures reach enough agreement to permit the school to continue to operate. This often thrusts the administrator into the broker role, one demanding political skills of a high order.

6. *The administrator should appraise the effectiveness and efficiency of these operations.* We use the term effectiveness to mean the achievement of the goals and we use the term efficiency to mean at lowest possible cost. Feedback and appraisal should occur as the functions are performed. How well were goals established? How well were programs developed? How effective has the organization been? In addition to answering these questions, the administrator should address the larger concern—have the programs been effective and efficient? As with many other functions, the administrator will need staff help to perform the appraisal function adequately, but it is the administrator's task to see that it is done.

It might strengthen our case if we could present research to demonstrate that the performance of each of these functions by the administrator does indeed improve learning in the school or school district. Recently, the State of Georgia sought such evidence as it attempted to revise its school standards. In the area of management strategies, for instance, state officials asked Knezevich to review the research for evidence of relationships between management strategies and student outcomes. Knezevich began by expressing doubt that research could "provide direct guidance" to the revision of the standards. His paper confirmed, in large part, his doubts.[4] Campbell,[5] who was asked to critique the Knezevich paper, pointed out that to seek empirically derived relationships between management strategies and educational outcomes may, at least for now, be asking for the impossible. Few studies to date have dealt with such relationships and future studies will find the terrain difficult. It is hard to find relationships between *teaching* strategies and educational outcomes due in part to the many other variables found in the teaching/learning process. To determine relationships between *management* strategies and educational outcomes is obviously still more difficult. All the variables found in teaching, in home background, in socio-economic class, in student abilities and attitudes, and more, are involved. At present there may be no way that all of these variables can be held steady while we look at the relationships between administrative strategy and pupil learning. We can make some reasonable assumptions about these relationships, but empirical evidence, except for bits and pieces, is not yet available. The functions enumerated above, then, represent reasonable assumptions.

WHAT ARE THE CHARACTERISTICS OF SCHOOL ORGANIZATIONS?

Since most of us have had additional first-hand experience with schools as teachers and parents, we might assume that we already know all about the characteristics of school organizations. We surely know some things about schools and school districts but we may have been so close to these organizations that we failed to note some of their salient characteristics. If we are to examine problems and issues in school organizations, as we do in Chapters 6–12, it seems most desirable to suggest the nature of the organizations in which those matters take place. While Chapters 2 and 3 deal more specifically with school organizations and their environments, an overview is presented here.

To begin with, schools and school districts are social institutions. Within the organizations there are students, teachers, administrators, and many kinds of service personnel including clerks and custodians. Members of each of these groups occupy distinctive positions and are expected to behave in certain ways. For instance, the role expectations held for students are different from those held for teachers. Similarly, the norms ordinarily ascribed to principals are different from those ascribed to custodians. Clearly, the relationships among the many kinds of people found in schools and school districts are varied and complex. Only if those relationships are understood and generally accepted can the organization function effectively.

But as social institutions schools and school districts do not exist in isolation. They are very much a part of the larger environment or social system. For each school district there is a board of education, most often elected by the voters of the district. The board is sometimes seen as half in and half out of the organization, an interstitial body. While the board of education may not be entirely within the environment of schools and school districts, many other persons and organizations are clearly within that environment. The parents of the students are an important part of the environment. Parents may act as individuals or they may join one or more organizations that serve as their representatives. Some of the organizations, such as the Parent Teachers Association, are inclined to support schools; others are formed to object strenuously to some school policies, particularly in such areas as text book selection and sex education. Frequently, the community or the school district also contains one or more organizations interested in reducing taxes or at least seeing that they are not increased.

In addition to the local organizations found in the school environment, only a few of which have been mentioned, there are many state and national groups. These include official bodies such as the legislature and the state board of education at the state level, and the Congress and the Department of Education at the national level. In addition, there are many unofficial or voluntary groups such as the state and national teachers organizations, state and national labor organizations, and state and national business organizations. All are part of the school environment and affect schools and school districts.[6] Thus, the complex internal social relationships in schools are made even more complex by the interactions between schools and their environments.

A second important characteristic is size, and schools vary greatly in this respect. A few one-room schools offering as many as eight grades of elementary instruction still exist. On the other hand, in many city school districts enrollments exceed 600 students in elementary schools and 2,000 students in high schools. Despite the fact that most large cities such as New York, Chicago, and Los Angeles comprise a single school district, about 75 percent of the school districts enroll fewer than 2,500 students.[7] Even in large city school districts individual school organizations, when compared to many other types of organizations, tend to be small in size. For instance, in a school of 500 students there may be 20 to 25 teachers, one principal, an assistant principal, one or two clerks, two custodians, and two or three lunch workers. In addition to these, there may be resource people on call in the central office of the school district. While most school and school district organizations are small in size, the wide variability among these organizations should not be overlooked.

A third characteristic of schools and school districts is that they are hierarchical organizations. The board of education is usually placed at the top of the hierarchy, followed by the superintendent, the principals, and the teachers. In terms of responsibility, students are responsible to teachers, teachers responsible to principals, principals responsible to the superintendent, and the superintendent responsible to the board of education. While these hierarchical arrangements do exist in schools and school districts, the actual relationships among levels are quite complex. Frequently communication among levels, up or down, is relatively easy. Further, many administrators are reluctant to simply give orders; they prefer to appropriately involve other members of the staff in decision making.

March has concluded that educational organizations are organized anarchies.[8] He uses the term to describe organizations in which goals are ambiguous, technologies unclear, and participation fluid. One has to acknowledge that all of those conditions occur to some extent in educational organizations. Noting these, Weick may have suggested a more useful concept: he characterizes educational organizations as loosely coupled. For Weick loose coupling may refer to organizations where conditions such as the following obtain: resources exceed demands; any one of several means will achieve the same end; influence is slow to spread; there is little coordination; there are few regulations; and there are infrequent inspections of activities in the system.[9] These two concepts will be discussed further in Chapter 3.

Finally, we should note that educational organizations are people intensive. Every twenty to thirty students require a teacher, every ten to fifteen teachers require a principal, and every few principals require a superintendent. Further, every new program, whether in the education of the poor, bilingual education, or education of the handicapped, needs one or more supervisors and directors in the school district office. While audiovisual aids have long been used in schools and there has been experimentation with computer-based instruction, the technological displacement of school personnel has not gone very far. Indeed, even the use of paraprofessionals to assist teachers has met resistance in many quarters.

These conditions have not stilled the voices of those who demand more productivity in education. Among many, familiar with the application of technology in industry, the schools are often seen as downright resistant to change. A few hardy professionals are persistent in their research efforts to identify those teaching and administrative strategies that appear to make a difference in student achievement.[10] As these efforts help us identify more clearly which strategies and even which people affect most positively the learning outcomes of students, there will be real gains. However, it seems doubtful at this point that the intensive use of people in educational organizations will be altered appreciably.

WHAT IS THE NATURE OF ADMINISTRATIVE WORK?

In schools, as in other organizations, there is frequently some question about what administrators do. One could simply say that administrators perform the functions enumerated earlier in this chapter. But that performance is frequently invisible to school patrons and sometimes even to teachers. For instance, decision making with respect to the employment of teachers or the allocation of items in the budget are activities not easily discerned by the casual observer. Moreover, the list of administrative functions offered above, like many other formulations, suggests what administrators ought to do, and not necessarily what they really do. Further, the functions set forth represent categories of duties, not specific activities. If we are to understand administrative work, we must obviously go beyond a conceptualization of administrative functions.

Sometimes administrators are challenged to be expert at statecraft, to show the way the schools should go to both professionals and laypeople. We hope that administrators have some capacity to sense the purposes of the school in our kind of culture and to let that insight guide them as they work with others to implement those purposes. At the same time, we recognize that administrators are not heroes but down-to-earth workers. After his analysis of educational administration, March concluded that "much of the job of an educational administrator involves the mundane work of making a bureaucracy work. It is filled with activities quite distant from those implied by a conception of administration as heroic leadership. It profits from elementary competence."[11]

One of the problems in describing administrative work is that there have been few studies based on the observation of administrators at work. There have been studies in which administrators were asked to report what they do. But these self-report studies may be contaminated by what administrators think they ought to do. As one notable exception to self-reports, Mintzberg[12] has described the work of five chief executives he observed over a period of time. Three of these managers were in business, the fourth was the director of a hospital, and the fifth was a superintendent of schools. With a sample of this kind we can not be certain that Mintzberg's findings describe accurately the work of school administrators but they are at least suggestive.

Mintzberg concludes, among other things, that administrative work is fast paced, fragmented, often requires a superficial response, focuses more on action than on thought, and emphasizes verbal communication. In short, the administrator is required to make numerous decisions over a day, many of them mundane in nature, and frequently has little time to consider alternative courses of action or to generate data supporting these alternatives. On the face of the matter it sounds as though the administrator leads a rather hectic existence.

We have checked this characterization of administrative work with a number of school administrators and they ascribe considerable validity to it. There will be further attention to this topic in Chapter 4. We hope that we can help prospective administrators assess the nature of administrative work realistically.

ARE PERSONAL CHARACTERISTICS AND ADMINISTRATIVE ROLES COMPATIBLE?

As indicated earlier, school administrators are responsible for the operation of a school or school district. They cannot meet that responsibility without the help of many other people, but it is the administrators who must elicit the cooperation of others and direct them in a common enterprise. To perform this function they must accept the goals of the organization and the role of stimulating others to accept those goals as legitimate demands on their time and energy. In a sense, each administrator must become the "organization man." Administrators take action because it is good for the organization, even when such action is not entirely compatible with their dispositions.

For instance, the principal of a school may find, after using all possible remedies, that a teacher is not performing adequately and should not be retained on the faculty. Personally, the principal may be very sympathetic with the teacher. The principal may even find it repugnant that one person in an organization has the power to alter the career of another person. In keeping with these personal dispositions the principal will probably consider less severe alternatives. Perhaps the teacher should be given another trial year. Deep down, however, the principal is convinced that the teacher in question will not make it in the present situation. Then the principal may be tempted to recommend that the teacher be transferred to another school. While this strategy is often used and sometimes makes a difference in teacher performance, the principal finally recognizes that such action is merely "passing the buck." The teacher's performance has not been adequate, response to remedial suggestions has been minimal, and for the good of the organization the teacher cannot be recommended for continued employment. Personal dispositions aside, the principal must confront the teacher with such a decision, review the evidence leading to the decision, and counsel the teacher regarding some other type of employment. This decision must also be transmitted to the central office with appropriate supporting evidence. In taking these actions, the principal has been able to place organizational imperatives above personal dispositions.

Organizational imperatives and personal dispositions are important dimensions in understanding organizational behavior. Getzels and his colleagues[13] have developed a model depicting the school as a social system in which these two dimensions are central. The organizational imperatives are referred to as the normative dimension and the personal dispositions as the personal dimension. The normative dimension consists of the roles of personnel in the school and the expectations held for each role. The personal dimension consists of the personality characteristics of the personnel and their need-dispositions. Some organizations, such as the military, expect a high degree of role conformity. Other organizations, such as an artist colony, allow and even encourage great personality divergence. In most school organizations there is probably a fair balance between the role and personality dimensions.

For those who are already in an administrative post, the social-systems way of thinking about an organization has implications for satisfaction with the administrative role. In the conflict between the normative and the personal dimensions, if the personal tends to overwhelm the normative the administrator will probably experience more dissatisfaction than satisfaction in the role. If, on the other hand, one can recognize this conflict but see the importance of the normative in organizational achievement, the administrative role can bring considerable satisfaction. One need not wait to become an administrator to determine the compatibility of the role: every teacher is apt to be called upon to chair a committee, a department, a grade-level organization, or some other group effort where the goals of the organization (or the normative dimension) will assume added importance. These experiences can be used to determine one's compatibility with the administrative role. A more extended treatment of this and related matters is provided in Chapter 5.

We have contended above that the work of the school administrator should enhance teaching and learning. To comprehend and perform in such a role, the prospective administrator should have a strong background in liberal education, training in education as a broad field of study, and finally, training in educational administration itself. We stress a liberal education background because the public school is an important institution in our culture and we believe that the administrative officer of the school should understand both the culture and the role of the school in it. If there be deficiencies in the liberal education background of the prospective administrator, they should receive some attention as part of the graduate program.

While we are not certain that every school administrator must first be a teacher, we are convinced that school administrators need some knowledge about American education, its purposes, procedures, organization, history, and current problems. With understandings of this kind, school administrators will be in a position to comprehend more fully the organizations for which they are responsible, and to determine which practices should be sustained and supported and which should be improved or eliminated. In short, we take the position that administrators must have some knowledge about the institution under their direction. At present, nearly all administrators are drawn from the ranks of teachers. In preparing to teach much of the necessary education background may be acquired. In some cases, however, extensive preparation in a content area may prevent the prospective teacher from a broad consideration of school purposes and procedures. Where such deficiencies exist they should be corrected as part of the graduate program.

The third important component of the background of the prospective administrator is training in educational administration itself. This is not the place to discuss in detail the specific elements of a preparation program, but we do wish to stress several points. We recommend, first, that such programs begin with a set of recruitment and selection procedures. Some people, as suggested above, should not consider nor be considered for a career in administration; these people should be discouraged from entering a program. On the other side, people who appear to have the personal qualities and the professional interest and commitment needed in administration should be sought out and encouraged to enter a program. We place considerable importance on recruitment and selection because we believe that selection of suitable administrative candidates is fully as important as any training program in the preparation of competent administrators. People entering administrative training have already developed, over a period of twenty-five to thirty years, most of what they will be even after an additional year or two of training in administration. Training in administration should build on strengths already acquired and demonstrated.

Second, we suggest a sequence of certain courses. Again, these should vary somewhat depending on what each candidate has done previously. We would expect candidates to have some understanding of educational organizations and the people who work in them; of relationships between schools and school districts to the larger society; of curriculum and instruction; of supervision and evaluation of instruction; and of school business management. In addition, a few courses in such basic disciplines as psychology, sociology, and political science may be useful.

Third, the prospective administrator should have a number of clinical experiences. Some of these, particularly the observation variety, might come as part of the formal courses suggested above. In addition, it would be most helpful for each administrative candidate to serve an internship where there is actually an opportunity to perform, under supervision, in the administrative role. An important part of that experience would involve responsibility for real administrative tasks.

A fourth aspect of the program is many informal opportunities for candidates to interact with their instructors, with practicing administrators, and with each other. Indeed, prospective administrators may learn more from each other than they do in their formal courses. There is little opportunity for these informal interactions where courses are all of the drive-in kind offered in later afternoon and evening. At least a portion of the graduate program should be offered under more relaxed circumstances. The total training program is designed to extend understanding, change attitudes, and sharpen skills. Only when attention is given to all elements—selection, course structure, clinical experience, and informal relationships—would such outcomes be likely.

The traditional route to administration has placed much emphasis on experience. Candidates first have experience in teaching and sometimes in quasi-administrative positions. Some of these persons may be encouraged to do graduate work in administration and to secure administrative certificates. When vacancies develop they are then moved into administrative posts. Over time, an assistant principal may become a principal, a principal may become a central office director, a director may become an assistant superintendent, and an assistant superintendent may become a superintendent. Not many who follow this route become superintendents and those who succeed arrive at the position after many years of experience.

In recent years, an alternative route has been used to some extent. More emphasis is placed on graduate study and less on long-term administrative experience. Frequently this has meant both completion of a doctoral program in administration and a willingness to be mobile when seeking a position. The graduate study route has permitted some people, at least, to reach a superintendency or other top administrative post at a relatively young age. Which route to stress is in the end an individual decision and involves personal as well as professional considerations.

WHAT IS THE PRESENT STATUS OF THE FIELD? In some ways these are not the happiest of times for education and educational administrators. Education is affected by many of the problems of the larger society, such as concern about our purpose and direction as a nation and the realization that we have entered an economy of scarcity. These and related problems have crept up on us. For most of our history we were an expanding society, bigger was better, and we seemed to have abundant resources. As a nation and largely as individuals we felt in control of our own destiny. Now we find ourselves dependent on other nations for much of our oil; new and emerging nations do not necessarily accept our leadership; and at home we are challenged to make a pluralistic society work. These are not conditions that can be changed easily or quickly. Most of the dilemmas of the larger society affect the schools and some deserve discussion in more detail here.

First, the school is a declining industry. After decades of an expanding school population we find that in most states school enrollments are on the decline. For the nation as a whole elementary school enrollments peaked in 1970 and secondary enrollments in 1977. Decreases begun after those years are expected to continue at least through 1983, when enrollments in the primary grades are expected to be 15 percent lower than in the peak year.[14] But these figures tell only part of the story. In some states, particularly in the South and the West, school enrollments are actually increasing. This means that the decrease is more severe than national figures suggest in many of the states of the East and Midwest. Even in these states, however, there are great variations among school districts.

Enrollment decline itself is not really the problem; rather it is the concomitants of that decline, and they are serious. As March[15] has noted, when enrollments go down there are fewer teaching and administrative vacancies; hence school personnel become older. The stimulation provided by new and younger associates is missing. As jobs become scarce, those already employed remain in place as a matter of security even when they must teach or perform other services in areas for which they are not prepared. In many cases enrollment declines have been so severe that schools, in the interest of economy, have had to be closed. Each school closing has required major adjustments on the part of teachers, parents, and entire neighborhoods. These conditions clearly make more difficult the task of any school administrator who attempts to stimulate and coordinate the efforts of a faculty.

A second problem is that there seems to be increasing concern on the part of the public with the purposes and outcomes of the schools. In a sense, the schools are affected by the current general disenchantment with all public agencies. There is skepticism about welfare agencies, the courts, and even government itself. Possibly, too, the schools have been seen as a panacea—agencies that could take on any challenge, whether it be to overcome poverty or promote moral behavior. Such unrealistic expectations may at times have obscured the purposes to which the schools might reasonably address themselves. In any case, clarification of what schools can and should do is needed by professionals and the public alike. This examination might also consider alternatives to the present public school system. Coons and Sugarman,[16] for example, have made a case for family control of schools by means of a voucher system (discussed further in Chapter 2).

As part of the uncertainty about the purpose of the school, there has also been growing concern about its outcomes. Some critics contend that schools do not make much difference anyway.[17] Many believe, however, and some recent research[18] suggests that schools can make a great difference. In any case, many schools do not appear to be living up to their potential. Evidence for deficiencies includes declining test scores and poor performance of graduates on the job. Closely related to demands for better results is the insistence by some critics that schools become more productive. Here the increased use of technology in industry is often used as an analog. The limitations as well as the possibilities in making the schools more productive need more understanding, as does the clarification of school purposes.

The formation of teachers' unions over the past decade or so has emerged as a third problem. At one time organizations for teachers, school administrators, and school boards, frequently with the help of such groups as the Parent Teacher Association, were able to form coalitions and exert considerable political influence over the state legislature and other groups. With the development of teacher bargaining most of those coalitions have been shattered. Teachers still have considerable political clout because of their numbers but their exercise of that influence sometimes backfires.[19] Many parents and other citizens have not quite reconciled the political activism of teachers with the need for informed and dedicated educators in the classroom. Perhaps even more serious, the role of teachers' unions in the management of the school has not yet been defined or accepted. For instance, the issue of which problems require union consideration and which are the prerogative of management produces controversy in many school systems.[20]

Finally, there is the ever-present problem of how to pay for the schools. When enrollments go down, costs do not decrease proportionately; unless buildings are closed altogether, charges for building maintenance do not go down along with enrollment decreases, for instance. It is also difficult to make faculty reductions correspond neatly to enrollment declines. Even with some reductions in personnel and facilities, inflation has put great stress on school budgets. When all of these problems are accompanied by efforts to limit taxes the problem of financial support for the public schools is indeed a thorny one.

Problems such as those listed above may discourage some from becoming school administrators. On the other hand, there is no lack of challenge or opportunity in the field today. Those who believe they can help in the clarification of public purpose may try their hand. Those who think they have the skills to help teachers collaborate in a common endeavor may wish to accept the challenge. Those who believe they can help parents and communities understand why schools are worth paying for may welcome the opportunity.

To this point we have dealt with the status of the field in terms of the practice of administration. What about the study of administration? For the past twenty to thirty years emphasis on the development of theory and research in educational administration has increased. We think our understanding of educational organizations and the people who work in them has increased. Even so, there is much to be done. For example, academic programs in administration have long included courses in organizational analysis. More recently, many of those programs also have included courses on the politics of education. In recent years researchers have begun to synthesize the two approaches on the theory that the functioning of schools and school districts cannot be understood unless they are viewed both internally and externally. In other words, the operation of the school is affected by both relationships within it and interactions between it and the environment. Immegart and Boyd have suggested that the key to understanding this new approach is the study of how educational policy is formulated.[21]

WHAT IS THE PLAN OF THIS BOOK?

The book is organized into three sections. Chapters 2 through 5 deal with the setting or context for school administration, and cover school environments, organizational characteristics, the work of administrators, and administrators as people. In Chapters 6 through 12 we discuss many of the problems, issues, and functions of school administrators, from decision making to appraisal. The book ends by suggesting some of the challenges of the field.

The book is intended to serve as an introduction to the field, and as such, covers broad areas of concern. Reference will be made to concerns such as curriculum development, school finance, and the legal aspects of education but there is no way we can treat the topics definitively. Some books, in the author's desire to encompass the whole field, have dealt so extensively with some of the concrete tasks of administration that they have missed its essence: to give direction to and to facilitate the planning, implementation, and evaluation of educational programs by professionals and the public. We have tried to avoid that mistake.

Our treatment of the work of administrators is also general, in that it concentrates on those responsibilities and issues faced by many or most schools. Unfortunately, we are unable to deal in a book of this scope with problems that are unique to one administrator or one school. It is our hope, however, that our general treatment will provide a solid grounding in the basic knowledge, skill, and understanding that should be brought to a career in educational administration.

ENDNOTES

1. For example, see Luvern L. Cunningham et al., eds., *Educational Administration: The Developing Decades* (Berkeley, Cal.: McCutchan Publishing, 1977) and William L. Boyd and Robert L. Crowson, "The Changing Concepting and Practice of Public School Administration," in David C. Berliner, ed., *Review of Research in Education* vol. 9 (Washington, D. C.: American Educational Research Assn., 1981).
2. For a description of professors see Roald F. Campbell and L. Jackson Newell, *A Study of Professors of Educational Administration* (Columbus, Oh.: University Council for Educational Administration, 1973).
3. Amitai Etzioni, *Modern Organizations* (Englewood Cliffs, N.J.: Prentice-Hall, 1964), p. 10.
4. Stephen J. Knezevich, "Management Strategies" in H.J. Walberg, ed., *Research and State Standards* (Berkeley, Cal.: McCutchan Publishing).

5.   Roald F. Campbell, "Critique of Management Strategies," in H.J. Walberg, ed., *Research*.

6.   For instance, see Roald F. Campbell et al., *The Organization and Control of American Schools*, 4th ed. (Columbus, Oh.: Charles E. Merrill, 1980), Chs. 13 and 14.

7.   National Center for Eduction Statistics, *The Condition of Education, 1979 Edition* (Washington, D.C.: U.S. Government Printing Office, 1979), p. 78.

8.   James G. March, "American Public School Administration: A Short Analysis," *School Review* 86(February 1978):223.

9.   Karl E. Weick, "Educational Organizations as Loosely Coupled Systems," *Administrative Science Quarterly* 21(March 1976):5.

10. For instance, see J. Alan Thomas et al., "Educational Administration: A Multilevel Perspective," *Administrator's Notebook* 27(1978–79).

11. James G. March, "American Public School Administration," p. 233.

12. Henry Mintzberg, *The Nature of Managerial Work* (New York: Harper and Row, 1973).

13. See J.W. Getzels et al., *Educational Administration as a Social Process* (New York: Harper and Row, 1968).

14. National Center for Education Statistics, *The Condition of Education*, p. 45.

15. James G. March, "Analytical Skills and the University Training of Educational Administrators," *Journal of Educational Administration* 12(May 1974).

16. John E. Coons and Stephen D. Sugarman, *Education by Choice* (Berkeley: University of California Press, 1978).

17. For instance, see Christopher Jencks, *Inequality* (New York: Basic Books, 1972).

18. M. Rutter et al., *Fifteen Thousand Hours: Secondary Schools and Their Effects on Children* (Cambridge, Mass.: Harvard University Press, 1979).

19. See Stanley M. Elam, "The National Education Association: Political Powerhouse or Paper Tiger?" *Phi Delta Kappan* 63(November 1981):169–174.

20. For instance, see A.M. Cresswell and M.J. Murphy, *Teachers, Unions, and Collective Bargaining in Public Education* (Berkeley, Cal.: McCutchan Publishing, 1980).

21. Glenn L. Immegart and William L. Boyd, eds., *Problem Finding in Educational Administration: Trends in Research and Theory* (Lexington, Mass.: D.C. Heath, 1979), Ch. 14.

CHAPTER 2

THE ENVIRONMENT OF SCHOOLS

In this chapter we examine the environment within which schools and school districts operate. While there is no simple definition of what constitutes the environment of schools, we will discuss the matter under the following categories: student population, organizational arrangements, citizen attitudes, teachers' organizations, legal constraints, and financial resources. Clearly, schools and school districts are part of the larger society, or as some would say, the larger social system. As such, schools receive financial and moral support from the larger society and affect the larger society by providing both individual and social benefits. Schools can and should influence society; society, in turn, sets the boundaries within which schools and school districts work. Thus it is most important that school administrators understand their environments and learn to cope with the factors comprising them.

One additional point needs to be made: the environments of particular schools and school districts vary greatly from one another. Some environments are urban, others rural; citizens in one school district are supportive of schools, in another district they are not; some school districts are rich, others are poor; and so forth. There are no rules of thumb concerning relationships between schools and their environments. Each administrator must be able to assess the environment in which he or she works, and learn to deal with that specific environment. We hope the categories suggested here can provide a framework for beginning such an assessment.

DIVERSE STUDENT POPULATION

In one sense, students are an internal part of schools and school districts; in another sense, they are part of the external environment. Because the numbers and distribution of students and their interests and attitudes affect schools and school districts in many ways we have chosen to treat students as part of the environment.

Numbers and Distribution of Students

There are some 48 million students enrolled in K through grade 12 in the schools of the United States. Approximately 43 million are enrolled in public schools and 5 million in nonpublic schools.[1] These enrollments are spread among 16,000 public school districts, in which there are, according to the National Center for Education Statistics, about 64,000 elementary schools (grades K–8) and 24,000 high schools (grades 9–12). In addition, there are so me 14,000 nonpublic elementary schools and 5,000 nonpublic secondary schools.[2] These schools, public and nonpublic alike, vary greatly in terms of student enrollment. There are still a few one-room schools in rural areas where as few as a dozen students in grades 1 through 8 are enrolled. In urban areas and consolidated rural areas elementary schools frequently have enrollments of 300 to 600 students, but there are many variations from these figures. High school enrollments frequently run from 200 to 2000 students, but again many high schools vary from these figures. Our point is a simple one: the manager of each school needs to begin by taking account of how many students and potential students reside in the attendance area of that school.

A school attendance area is simply the geographical area established by the board of education as that part of a school district to be served by a single school. In small communities where there is but one elementary school or one high school attendance areas and district boundaries are coterminous. In larger school districts several attendance areas are usually designated.[3] In a number of larger school districts an open enrollment plan (usually for high schools) has been established. Under this arrangement students apply to and can attend, if space permits, any school in the district. Open enrollment plans are often accompanied by differentiation between the instructional programs among the schools in the district. Under this system an assessment of potential student enrollment is obviously more difficult to make.

A second complication of assessing potential enrollment has resulted from attempts to desegregate schools. Whether desegregation plans are court-ordered or voluntary they frequently mean that the neighborhood school has to be altered, often by busing students from one attendance area to another in order to achieve a better racial balance in the district. Clearly, where such desegregation efforts are underway the assessment of potential student enrollment is still further complicated. Open enrollment and desegregation arrangements have other implications for school operation, as will be noted later.

A third consideration in making an assessment of potential student enrollment is the percentage of the total age group likely to be enrolled in the school. The percentage of sixteen- and seventeen-year-olds enrolled in school for 1979 in the United States is illustrative. That year 89 percent of the whites and 91 percent of the blacks were enrolled. In 1970 the figures were 91 percent for whites and 86 percent for blacks.[4] Again, the national figures say little about individual schools and school districts; to the extent possible, figures for each jurisdiction should be obtained. The figures, of course, represent only the beginning of assessment. If most of the age group is enrolled, school managers might then ask how well instructional programs are serving the students. If a substantial part of the age group is not enrolled, school people might seek the reasons for the low enrollment. In general, as the enrollment of any age group approaches 100 percent the diversity of the student population increases. That diversity is partially tied to the interests and attitudes of students, a matter to which we now turn.

Percent of Age Group Enrolled

Children and youth vary greatly in their interests. Some are interested in academic programs; some are not. Many are interested in athletics and other school activities; others are not. Nearly all children and youth spend a great deal of time watching TV, often the more sensational programs. Some young people become interested in work and hold jobs during summer vacations or part time during the academic year. Most children and youth are interested in their peers and peer approval is of great significance to adolescents. Recent studies suggest that young people are much more precocious sexually than they once were. Part of this precocity seems to come from the onset of puberty at an earlier age; an average of 12.5 years for girls and 13 years for boys.[5] Not only are young people more aware of sex than before, but many of them are sexually active. Indeed, one survey reports that nearly half of the Nation's fifteen- to nineteen-year-old girls have had premarital sex, and that the numbers are still climbing.[6]

Interests, Attitudes, and Peer Influences

The attitudes of children and youth also vary greatly. Young people frequently reflect the attitudes and beliefs of their parents and other adults in the community. Young voters, for instance, tend to vote essentially as their parents do. While some young people pay little attention to broad social issues, others show great interest. With ready access to the media, particularly television, those who do become interested in public questions are frequently much more sophisticated about these matters than was once the case. Some young people become disturbed by the apparent differences between our public and private morality. They may, for example, have come to expect honesty from people who hold positions of public trust and then become very critical when they find that some are less than honest. Like their elders, many youth are confused by a world where values seem to be in transition.

As noted above, peer influence is particularly strong during the adolescent years. Frequently during a student's high school years the influence of parents, teachers, church leaders, and other adults take second place to peer influence. Dress, interests, and attitudes are often molded by the need for peer approval. One of the major motivations for sexual activity among adolescents, is the argument that "everybody is doing it."

Transition to Adulthood

Coleman and his colleagues point out that high schools and colleges are now the dominant institutions for youth, replacing work settings common in the past.[7] They also note that the transition of youth to adulthood in our society is beset with a number of problems. Some of the problems or issues, particularly as they relate to high schools, are the following: the segregation of youth from adults; the segregation of youth from children; the relationship of learning activities to productive activities; and the appropriate role of the school with respect to academic and nonacademic functions.

To alleviate these and related problems Coleman and others make a number of recommendations, including the development of more specialized schools, a reduction in the size of high schools, and a mixture of part-time work and part-time school. These suggestions run counter to general practice and the common folklore surrounding high schools. For example, specialized schools conflict with the general commitment to comprehensive high schools; advocacy of small schools conflicts with attempts to benefit from economy of scale by establishing large schools; a mixture of work and study obviously expands on the current purpose of the high school and makes its operation much more complex.

Whether or not the high schools of the nation accept new directions, they cannot escape the fact that they must address the problems of the youth who attend them, and these problems have long-range social consequences as well as immediate academic importance. In short, the nature of youth, their strivings, their confusions, their attempts to grow up are all part of the school environment.

STRAINED ORGANIZATIONAL ARRANGEMENTS

Another important part of the environment of schools is the organizational arrangements. We refer here to those aspects of the environment that are straining current systems and tend to make the operation of schools complex and difficult. Among these are declining enrollments, the issue of autonomy for single schools, increased state control, and the status of national influences.

Declining Enrollments

During the past decade or so declining school enrollment has become a familiar phenomenon. In terms of K–12 enrollments in the Nation as a whole, 49,891,000 students were enrolled in 1967; 47,611,000 in 1978; and projections for 1984 are 43,591,000.[8] In many states, particularly in the Northeast and Midwest, enrollment declines have exceeded the national average. For instance, in terms of preprimary to grade 8 enrollments, Illinois went from 1,687,909 in 1970 down to 1,395,192 in 1978. Comparable figures for Michigan were

1,604,997 to 1,252,965; and for New York, 2,448,403 to 2,000,069.[9] Even in these states the declines do not fall evenly on all school districts. Some large city districts have actually lost as much as half of their student enrollment over the past decade or two. Frequently, suburban districts have gained enrollment in these population shifts.

While most states have experienced enrollment declines the intermountain states as well as Texas, Florida, Rhode Island, and Alaska have had enrollment increases over the last decade, and projections suggest further increases are to come. As with declines, enrollment increases do not pertain to all districts alike. And as in the East, so in the West there may be actual enrollment declines in larger cities, while in suburban and some rural districts—particularly those affected by energy developments—there may be sharp increases.

Despite these differences among states and school districts, for many school districts of the nation student enrollment decline is a fact of life. Upon first confronting such a phenomenon one might ask why enrollment decline is a problem. Indeed, decrease in enrollment might be more of a boon than a bane; schools might require less money, and teaching loads reduced. Over time, these advantages may accrue but the immediate consequences have made school operation difficult.

With enrollment declines, particularly in the inner cities, it has been necessary to close a number of schools. This process runs counter to many of our cultural norms. In this country school and lay people alike have been committed, consciously or unconsciously, to the "bigger and better" syndrome. We have had centuries of growth and expansion, we have seldom had to confront the idea that "smaller might be better." Even more significant than our general acceptance of growth as the normal state of affairs is the fact that the closing of a particular school means in the minds of many people the destruction, or at least the beginning of the destruction, of the neighborhood. Whether or not schools are that important to the preservation of the neighborhood is beside the point. Many think the school is that important and they act on that belief. What have been the results? Many schools have closed, parents have prevented others from closing, a number of superintendents have lost their jobs in their attempt to close schools, school board members who advocated school closings have been replaced, and community and school dissension has frequently developed. The consequences of school closings, real or potential, are an aspect of the environment that school people must confront.

Declining enrollments have other deleterious effects on school organizations. As March[10] pointed out, in a declining industry management is locked into place by the lack of promotion opportunities and thus tends to age. This frequently leads to a decline in managerial vitality. March continues: "There are fewer chances for advancement. There are fewer resources. There are fewer occasions of success. The aging of employees (not just management) tips the cynicism scale further in the direction of doubt about the utility of commitment. Organizational goals and personal self-interest diverge."[11]

**Single School
Autonomy**

Another strain on organizational arrangements is the emerging controversy over the degree of autonomy that should be granted to individual schools in a district. Tyack[12] has dealt extensively with what he calls the establishment of "the one best system" in this country. He shows that consolidation of single schools into large school districts began in the cities and then extended to the rural areas. These consolidation efforts, covering much of this century, have been impressive. As late as 1948 there were 103,000 local school districts[13]; today there are 16,000. Large school districts tended to adopt the corporate model of management. Many functions were centralized in the name of efficiency. Supervisors in school district offices multiplied in order to direct these functions. Thus, in the larger districts, associate superintendents for business and for instruction evolved. In addition, there emerged directors and supervisors of elementary education, secondary education, guidance, personnel, and so on. This focus on district or centralized control frequently meant that little autonomy was given to the principal and staff of a single school. Like branch managers in many businesses, principals were to implement the policies and programs of the district board of education and the central administration. Little credence was given to the idea that the staff of a single school might be innovative and develop the differentiated program most suitable to its own neighborhood.

This push toward centralization and standardization seems to have run its course. By law in some states, notably California and Florida, school site management has been mandated. Even without benefit of law many other school districts have recognized the desirability of extending additional autonomy to single schools. This movement has been spearheaded, in large part, by lay citizens. The legislatures of California and Florida went so far as to require that lay citizens in school attendance areas be involved with principals and teachers in the management of their schools. Lay citizens in other school districts have made similar demands even in the absence of legal requirements.

At least three circumstances have accentuated this movement. The first is the controversy surrounding the closing of schools described above. Second, the problems surrounding desegregation of schools, particularly in our larger cities, have increased citizen involvement. Third, the recent widespread disenchantment with schools (dealt with in more detail later) has spurred many citizens to action.

There has also been stimulus from professionals for placing more emphasis on the single school as a strategic unit. As a result of his long experience with a league of cooperating schools, Goodlad concluded: "First, the optimal unit for educational change is the single school with its pupils, teachers, principal—those who live there every day—as primary participants."[14] Other students of school operation have noted the key role the principal can play in setting the climate in the school and establishing the expectations for teachers and students.[15] Thus, both lay citizens and professionals increasingly advocate substantial autonomy for each school.

This shift from centralized control to single-school autonomy does not come easily. In the first place, centralized bureaucracies would like to stay put.

Second, many school principals, accustomed to the centralized pattern, are not prepared for more autonomy and added responsibility. Clearly, granting more autonomy will result in more diversity among schools. This diversity could show up in instructional programs, personnel policies, business practices, and parent participation. A lack of standardization is likely to make school district management more complex and more difficult; it may also make it cost more. Thus, there is always the question of what and how much autonomy should be delegated to single schools. These concerns, particularly when augmented by growing public participation, add appreciably to organizational strain.

Another strain on organizational arrangements is found in increased control of education at the state level.[16] State legislatures and state education agencies set standards for many aspects of school district operation, including instruction, personnel, finance, and safety and health. School districts obviously have no choice but to operate within the standards.

Increased State Control

The amount of money available to school districts is also subject to state law. This is especially the case when most school revenue comes from state rather than local sources. Even in those states where override elections are possible, however, the provisions for such elections are usually specified in state law. Frequently, too, the accounting and reporting of school expenditures are set forth in state codes. As with standards, state jurisdiction over school finances has increased in recent years.[17]

One of the reasons for increased state jurisdiction has been the disposition of Congress and the national education agencies to require states to act as federal proxies. In many federal programs, including those for the disadvantaged, the handicapped, and vocational education, specific requirements are placed on the state by federal guidelines. If these stipulations are not met there is always the threat of the withdrawal of federal funds. In order to meet federal mandates most state education agencies are supported by federal funds in amounts sufficient to pay from one-half to two-thirds of the salaries of agency staff members. In effect, each state education agency has become an outpost of the federal government. While we recognize the importance of many federal programs and the necessity for some state supervision of them, such control seriously constrains the operation of schools and school districts, making increased state control an important part of the environment.

Schools have had a long relationship with the federal government.[18] From 1950 to about 1970 federal influence increased sharply. During that period federal dollars were made available, often aimed at the reform of school practices. In addition, money was provided from programs designed to address deep-seated social problems such as poverty and segregation. The 1970s appeared to be a period of reappraisal of federal roles, but before the decade was out there was even more federal involvement in the life of the schools. This control is illustrated by Title IX regulations concerning sex discrimination in the schools; more detailed legislation on vocational education; and Public Law 94–142 con-

National Influences

cerning the education of the handicapped. Much of the legislation of this period was tied to the movements to guarantee civil rights to women and the handicapped, with the federal government acting as the leader of social reform, making sure that schools carried out that reform.

With the election of Ronald Reagan to the Presidency, the whole question of federal relationships to the states is once again under scrutiny. The Congress appears to be taking another look at school desegregation programs, particularly mandated school busing. Regulations pertaining to bilingual education, prepared at the end of the Carter administration, were withdrawn by the Reagan administration and replaced by new ones. Conservative members of Congress with a majority in both the House and the Senate consolidated federal education programs and made more use of block grants to the states. In their effort to reduce the rate of growth of the federal budget, the conservatives also reduced funds for education and other social programs. In a sense, recent events suggest some retreat from a federal presence in school operation.

But national influences, governmental and nongovernmental, still impinge upon the schools. For one thing, there is still a substantial body of federal statutes pertaining to the schools. For another, school cases are frequently tried in federal courts. The federal government also still funds a national assessment of education program even though it is administered by the Education Commission of the States. In terms of nongovernmental influences, the national media, particularly the television networks and the weekly news magazines, continue to analyze and report on conditions in the schools. When such reports dramatize problems in distant schools, some people are prone to ascribing the same problems to local schools and to join with others in demanding reform. Some of the media coverage makes extensive use of studies made by scholars of national repute who may advocate tuition tax-credit schemes and voucher plans, both of which are thought by many to threaten the survival of the public schools.

CHANGING CITIZEN ATTITUDES

Any program of public education stands or falls largely on how citizens view it. In recent decades citizens' attitudes toward schools have undergone changes and we now consider some expressions of those changes.

A Pluralistic Culture

Our nation is composed primarily of peoples who migrated here from other countries, and for much of our history we were enamoured with the notion of the melting pot. We expected to mold all newcomers, whether from Europe, Asia, or Africa, into Americans relatively homogeneous in customs, language, and attitudes. For a time we came close to succeeding in that effort. We then recognized that in the homogenizing process we destroyed aspects of the varied cultures that should have been preserved. Moreover, we saw that in addition to destroying parts of the old cultures we frequently did little to help people participate in the new one.

Our diversity shows up dramatically in the populations of many school districts in our large cities. In several there are more blacks than whites enrolled. In some there are more Spanish-speaking than English-speaking students. In recent years enrollment in the public schools has come to include refugees from East Asia and many other places. Clearly, the stereotype of Americans as white, Anglo-Saxon, and Protestant is gone. In schools and in our society as a whole we must come to terms with the need for elements of unity within great diversity.

Creating a sense of common purpose is necessary to public education, but it is no easy achievement. The emergence of assertive and activist ideological groups, whether in the political or the religious arena, makes this doubly difficult.

For example, it is written in the Bill of Rights that there must remain in this country freedom of religion (and by implication, nonreligion). In the last few years, however, a number of groups have formed to pressure schools to teach a religiously based concept as an alternative "scientific" explanation of the origin of humankind. Within the context of religious faith some parents and some churches may wish to teach such concepts, and their right to do so should be protected. But for parents or church groups to insist that their religious views be promulgated as scientific views in the public schools leads to divisiveness in our culture.

The U.S. Supreme Court has confirmed in a number of cases[19] that public schools must remain neutral on questions of religious doctrine. Schools may teach *about* religious and moral issues, but they may not advocate one view over another.

Consequently, administrators today find themselves challenged to mediate between groups that are in strong opposition to one another, as they attempt at the same time to uphold the spirit and letter of the law. Similar controversies can arise from disagreements on political ideologies, racial lines, national origins, sexual differences, economic circumstances, and in other ways. These cleavages can create chaos in a school, or at least decrease support for it. Clearly, the pluralism of our culture is an important part of the environment, and school people must understand it and devise ways of dealing effectively with it.

Over most of our history public schools have been held in almost sacred esteem. People generally assumed that public schools were needed and that most teachers and school administrators were competent and dedicated public servants. To be sure, these attitudes did not always translate into generous salaries for school workers. Nor did these perceptions necessarily prevent the development of school teacher stereotypes. At the same time, most teachers and school administrators were respected members of society.

Reasons for this respect are not hard to find. School personnel shared in the dominant views of the culture of our past. For example, in speaking of the history of school superintendency Tyack has this to say:

From Faith to Skepticism

> I suggest that superintendents in the nineteenth century conceived of their
> task in part as an evangelical enterprise, a search for organizational means to

realize the goal of creating a "redeemer nation." As aristocrats of character in their own idealized self-conception, they were certified not so much by professional training as by church membership and a shared earnestness. In short, they were quintessential Victorians: evangelical Protestant, British-American, bourgeois. Although this tradition became much attenuated by newer sources of ideology in the twentieth century, it nonetheless left behind a legacy of millenial optimism and an ideal of heroic leadership.[20]

The idea that superintendents were giving "heroic leadership" to an important institution not only persisted in the minds of superintendents but also in the minds of many citizens until about two decades ago.

As recent Gallup polls suggest, the basic faith once held in the public schools has given way to skepticism on the part of many people. In one poll, 9 percent of those sampled gave the schools an A rating, 27 percent a B rating, 34 percent a C rating, 13 percent a D rating, 7 percent a Fail rating, and 10 percent did not know.[21] There is other evidence of waning public confidence in the public schools. Many school elections for the passage of bond issues and override operating levies now fail, whereas at one time most of such issues passed. As well, the news media have found examination of school performance—with an emphasis on failures—good copy. *Newsweek,* for instance, recently provided an extensive summary of public school performance in a three-part series.[22] On the whole, the coverage was accurate and fair. At the same time, the first heading, "Why Public Schools Fail," was apparently designed to catch the eye of those who are already skeptical.

The skepticism on the part of many lay citizens is not without foundation. To begin with, schools have taken on too many functions. Schools alone cannot cure poverty, effect integration, reduce unemployment, and instill moral behavior in our citizenry. Many or all of these tasks have sometimes been thrust upon the schools, particularly in the reform efforts of the 1960s. In the attempt to do too much, schools often did not do well those functions which they might reasonably be expected to do. We turn next to some examination of this problem.

Stress on School Outcomes   During the 1960s and 1970s *accountability* became a key word in American education. Not only were more tasks thrust upon the schools but additional efforts were made to hold schools accountable for the achievement of those tasks. Federal funding contributed to this state of mind. Congress and the U.S. Office of Education found it necessary to evaluate programs receiving federal money in order to justify continuation of their support. Federal officials also determined what was meant by evaluation by specifying that a particular evaluation model be applied to programs using federal grants.

Another aspect of the emphasis on school outcomes is found in the development and implementation of the National Assessment of Educational Progress (NAEP). This program was encouraged by Francis Keppel, then U.S. Commissioner of Education, as early as 1963. The first to chair the exploratory program was Ralph W. Tyler, then director of the Center for the Study of the Behavioral Sciences at Stanford, California. In time, implementation of the program was shifted from federal agencies to the Education Commission of the States but federal funding was continued. Now in operation for more than a decade, the program tests learning in reading, writing, science, mathematics, social studies, citizenship, music, literature, vocational education, and art. The responses of the students in the NAEP sample are analyzed by age level, sex, geographic region, level of parent education, size and type of community, and race. Assessments are staggered by subject and made in each subject at intervals of four or five years. As a result of the NAEP program much more can be said about what children and young people know and what they can do. Ahmann concludes his thoughtful discussion of the program with these words:

> Surveys such as NAEP are not designed to investigate causal relationships directly. Instead, they serve as a means for generating hypotheses with respect to possible causes of achievement patterns, which can then be studied more intensively by designing appropriate experiments or conducting thorough case studies. In a very real way large-scale assessment programs are beginning points, not end points, in our search for answers with regard to the improvement of student achievement in our schools.[23]

While NAEP has been careful not to identify assessment results by state or school district, this has not prevented some states and many school districts from making their own assessments of educational progress.

Perhaps even more influential than the results of the NAEP have been the declining test scores of high school seniors. In the eleven-year period, 1966–67 to 1976–77, mean test scores for high school seniors on the verbal section of the Scholastic Aptitude Test (SAT) declined from 466 to 429. On the mathematical section, the decline was from 492 to 470.[24] The reasons behind these declines were sought by an advisory panel to the College Entrance Examination Board. While a number of probable causes were given, the most logical explanations appear to be (1) an increased percentage of the age group in school and (2) an expanded curriculum resulting in students spending less time on the basic subjects covered by the SAT.

An interesting twist on this concern with school outcomes has been the research reports of certain scholars. Coleman[25] and Jencks,[26] for instance, have suggested or implied that the school one attends makes relatively little difference to achievement. These researchers seem to hold that most learning can be ascribed to the home, peers, and other cultural influences rather than the school. These conclusions may have been overstated by some who did not read Coleman and Jencks carefully. Moreover, other scholars have pointed out limitations in the studies themselves. Our point here, however, is that the dissemination of such findings has cast further doubt upon the schools' ability to teach effectively.

Consideration of Alternatives

Greater awareness of the pluralism of our culture, the shift in attitude from faith to skepticism about the schools, and the increasing attention given school outcomes have led to an increased consideration of alternatives to present school arrangements. Such alternatives include nonpublic schools, alternative schools in a public school system, voucher plans, and tuition tax credits for parents. Enrollments in nonpublic schools, ordinarily about 10 percent of public school enrollments in the nation at large, appear to be experiencing some increase. Many large school systems have established alternative schools within the system. Some alternative schools stress the basics; others the humanities, the sciences, or the individual development of students. In a number of school districts these alternative arrangements are well supported.[27]

For the most part, voucher plans and tuition tax credits for parents are still in the proposal stage. Basically, the voucher is an arrangement whereby a parent is provided by the state with a voucher, or promise to pay, the average per capita cost of schooling in the state. This voucher can be presented to any school, public or private, the parent chooses. Only one district—Alum Rock, California—has tried a version of the voucher plan and the results there have not been conclusive.[28] Even so, the voucher idea has been convincingly articulated in a book, *Education By Choice*, by Coons and Sugarman.[29] These and other supporters of the plan reportedly still expect to have the voucher plan submitted to public referendum in California. Should vouchers receive public approval in one state, other states might well follow.

The tuition tax credit plan is a simple idea. A parent pays tuition to a private school. The federal government, in turn, would allow a credit against taxes owed by the parent for a portion of the tuition paid. Plans now being considered often suggest that such credit be limited to $500.00 per student per year. No one can predict what the allowance might become over a period of years if such a plan were adopted. Catterall[30] has raised a number of issues about tuition tax credits such as the effects on public school costs, equity among income groups, and the legal status of such plans. The present climate of skepticism about the effectiveness of public schools provides a context for favorable consideration of tuition tax credit arrangements.

ASSERTIVE TEACHERS' ORGANIZATIONS

To this point we have shown that components in the environment of schools include diverse student populations, a number of constraining organizational influences, and the changing attitudes of citizens. We now suggest that assertive teachers organizations are another important aspect.

The NEA and AFT

The National Education Association was organized in 1857 and initially drew its membership from teachers and school administrators. For most of its history the NEA was concerned primarily with professional problems and only secondarily with teacher welfare. For example, it was the NEA in collaboration with the American Association of School Administrators that established the Educational Policies Commission in 1936. This Commission gave leadership to the reconstruction of American education after the ravages of the depression of the 1930s. One important result of this effort was publication of *The Purposes of Education in American Democracy.*[31]

In recent decades the NEA has changed its priorities and made the welfare of teachers its primary concern.[32] A number of factors—such as competition with the American Federation of Teachers, the growing influence of the labor movement, an attempt to develop a more realistic approach to political power, and perhaps inept school management—seem to have prompted this change in organizational outlook. In any case, the NEA, with its state and local affiliates, has become a powerful special interest group at national, state, and local levels.

The American Federation of Teachers was organized in 1916 as a component of the American Federation of Labor and remains today an affiliate of the AFL–CIO. The AFT has had its greatest success in large city school districts and at the national level. In many states the AFT has little or no influence. From the beginning, chief school administrators were not eligible for membership in AFT and its leadership, therefore, resided with teachers themselves. In recent decades, many state administrator groups, once a component of NEA affiliates, have severed relationships with such organizations. This division has resulted in teachers assuming leadership in the NEA and its state and local affiliates to a much greater extent than was once the case. Thus, in the original tradition of AFT and in the new stance of NEA, the division between management and labor, prominent in the labor movement, has been transferred to school district operation.

Both NEA and AFT groups have increased their political activities. For example, in the twelve states included in the Educational Governance Project, teachers' organizations, usually NEA affiliates, were viewed as being the most influential interest groups in the legislative arena.[33] Teacher groups had and used their great resources such as numbers of members, dollars, staff expertise, and political action strategies to influence legislative action.

Increased Political Activity

Nor is political activity limited to the state level. Some twenty states have provisions in their state codes that give or imply official recognition of teacher negotiations.[34] Thus bargaining between teachers' organizations and management is a recognized activity. In most of the other states teacher negotiations go on without the sanction of state law. In most school districts teachers are prepared to employ all of the steps found in industrial labor relations, including strikes, if necessary, to achieve their ends. In a recent year some 275 teacher strikes at the district level were reported.[35]

Another development among teachers' organizations has been a disposition to enlarge the scope of bargaining. Most school boards and administrators have come to recognize the reasons why teachers must negotiate salary and other welfare benefits. Formal or informal negotiations with teachers about welfare issues makes school operation more difficult, but it is generally recognized as necessary. However, when teachers' organizations attempt to extend the scope of negotiations to include questions of curriculum and instruction, school managers often resist. Such extensions may be seen as encroachment upon managerial functions. Differences in perception on the part of teachers' organizations and school managers as to their roles and authority represent still another aspect of the environment with which school administrators must cope.

Possible New Relationships   Some modifications in the relationship between teachers' organizations and school district management may be emerging. At one time teachers', school boards', and school administrators' organizations were in most states joined in coalitions with parent groups and others in support of the schools, but many of those coalitions have broken up.[36] The labor-management approach of teacher negotiations has driven the two groups apart. This split plays into the hands of the skeptical public, a fact that both teachers and school managers may be starting to recognize.

It may be that some teachers' organizations have overplayed their hands and begun to provoke a backlash. Elam, a long-time educational observer, for example, editorialized in a recent *Phi Delta Kappan*[37] regarding the National Education Association. Citing a *New Republic* article, Elam writes, ". . .veteran power brokers have been pushed aside by a relative newcomer to the hurly-burly of Capitol politics: the National Education Association." In the last four years, the article notes the NEA has helped elect a President, almost singlehandedly forced a Department of Education down Congress's throat, and lobbied successfully for dramatic increases in federal spending on education. Elam then reviews the current goals of the NEA and concludes:

> I also believe that the NEA will never reach its goals if it relies heavily on callous pressure politics. Public support is too precious and too fragile to risk with Teamster tactics. Teachers must build coalitions, not play the ultimately self-defeating special-interest game, the bane of modern American politics.[38]

Not all agree with Elam. At the same time, it should become apparent to teachers' organizations and school managers alike that they have many common interests. Schools cannot be effective institutions unless they command public confidence and public resources. To achieve these ends teachers and school managers will need to collaborate on many fronts. If teachers and administrators begin once again to collaborate, it will represent another interesting aspect of the school environment.

GROWING LEGAL CONSTRAINTS   Another part of the environment of schools and school districts is the growing body of school litigation, particularly in the federal courts. The constitutional basis for much of this litigation resides in the First, Fifth, and Fourteenth amendments. The First Amendment deals with freedom of speech, religion, press, and other matters; the Fifth Amendment provides protection against self-incrimination; and the Fourteenth Amendment extends citizen rights, including due process and equal protection, to the states.[39] To illustrate, we will describe recent cases concerning desegregation, school finance reform, and the civil rights of students.

Perhaps no single court decision has affected schools more than *Brown* v. *The Board of Education* in 1954.[40] Declaring that segregation of school students by race was unconstitutional, it—and a long line of subsequent court decisions—has required drastic changes in school operation in hundreds of school districts across the country. Moreover, the changes often spilled over from the school into the local community, frequently prompting intense political activity on the part of the citizens and sometimes provoking rancor and dissension.

Desegregation

For more than a decade following the Brown decision there was much resistance in the South against dismantling the dual school systems. The U.S. Supreme Court upheld lower court decisions concerning the enforcement of Brown. In other rulings the Court also held that state legislative, executive, or judicial authorities were not permitted to set aside the constitutional rights set forth in Brown.[41] In time the segregated school systems of the South were eliminated. In the process, many groups of parents established nonpublic schools or academies and withdrew their children from the public schools. In more recent years, some of these academies have closed and children enrolled once again in the public system.

In time, the courts also found northern cities engaging in practices contrary to the Brown decision. While the northern states had not established dual school systems by law, segregated housing patterns did result in many all-black and all-white schools. In the far-reaching Keyes[42] decision the Court recognized the distinction between de facto and de jure segregation, contending that, even in school systems not segregated under law, there can be the "*purpose* or *intent* to segregate.*" However, Justice Powell issued a separate opinion suggesting that the distinction between de jure and de facto segregation was no longer useful. Powell also indicated in his decision that there might be some limitations on the responsibility of officials to desegregate their schools.

Some of these limitations were given specific expression in the Detroit case.[43] In this instance, the federal district court had ordered a metropolitan plan of cross-district busing, and the plan was upheld in the appeals court. The U.S. Supreme Court struck down the plan by a vote of 5 to 4. The Court maintained that there was no proof of segregative action by the eighty-five suburban districts and thus an interdistrict remedy should not be imposed upon them.

As of this writing we seem to have entered a period of reconsideration, at least at the state level, of court-ordered desegregation programs. Court-ordered busing in Los Angeles has been halted. The U.S. Attorney General has indicated that he is opposed to court-ordered busing of students to achieve racial balance. Questions are being raised about the extent to which desegregated schools have contributed to improved learning. Indeed, some observers have concluded that court orders may result in "equalized busing" but have little to do with equal educational opportunity. These doubts may spur new legislation and even some modification of past judicial decisions. Even so, it is unlikely that school districts will be allowed to do as they please without judicial involvement.

Any school district confronted with a court order regarding desegregation will find it a pervasive part of the environment. Even though courts, legislative bodies, and law enforcement officials may be reappraising desegregation plans and their results, no school district can afford to ignore the deleterious effects of segregated schools or the possibility of loss of federal funding for noncompliance with the law. Regardless of viewpoint, citizens have become aware of some of the problems resulting from segregation.

School Finance   Education in this country has historically been a legal responsibility of the state. Despite local and federal involvement in policies and operations, both state codes and case law make it clear that the states have primary jurisdiction over education. This applies to school finance as well as other areas. Most state codes determine the limits within which local boards of education may set or recommend tax levies for current operating expenses for capital improvements. Some states permit local districts, by vote of the electors, to go beyond state mandates but those options are usually limited and specified by state law.

All states provide some state aid to the school districts. In some states, such as Alaska, Delaware, and Hawaii, state revenues constitute a large proportion of per-pupil revenues. In other states, such as Nebraska, New Hampshire, and South Dakota, state revenues are a minor part of available monies. In distributing state aid to local school districts, most states have established some plan of equalization. These plans usually attempt to provide more aid to poor districts and less to wealthy ones. Wealth, often determined by assessed valuation per pupil, can vary greatly among school districts. Equalization plans are frequently designed to equalize tax burdens as well as to equalize, at least to a degree, available revenues per pupil.

In the Serrano case of 1971 the California Supreme Court declared the school finance program of that state unconstitutional.[44] The court found that the California system led to wide disparities in expenditures and educational opportunities among school districts in the state. Following Serrano, over thirty cases were filed to challenge schemes of school finance in other states.[45] These cases were about evenly divided between federal and state courts. The Rodriquez case filed in the federal district court in Texas finally reached the U.S. Supreme Court.[46] There, by a split decision, education was declared not a fundamental interest because it is not a right "explicitly or implicitly guaranteed by the Constitution."

This action upheld the position that education is essentially a state function and that finance remedies should be sought in state legislatures and state courts. Such action has gone forward in several states. Notable among these is New Jersey, where the State Supreme Court struck down a school finance system for violation of a constitutional provision requiring that the legislature "provide for the maintenance and support of a thorough and efficient system of free public schools."[47]

In addition to determining the amount and distribution of revenues, most states also determine the purposes for which these revenues may be expended. States also frequently stipulate the nature of the reporting and auditing practices that school districts must follow. These financial arrangements are an ever-present part of the school environment.

For most of our history the teacher and the school were seen as acting *in loco parentis*, or "standing in place of the parent." Since parents were thought to have the right to administer reasonable punishment to their children, teachers and principals were also thought to have that right. Moreover, if teachers and other school officials were alleged to have administered undue punishment to students such cases were tried in state courts.

Student Rights

With the Tinker[48] case both the doctrine of *in loco parentis* and the jurisdiction of state courts seem to have been brought into question. Tinker was a high school student who, with his sister and a friend, wore black armbands to school in protest of the Vietnam War. Because they refused to remove the armbands upon request, the three were suspended in accordance with school regulations. The students filed a suit seeking an injunction restraining the school authorities from enforcing such disciplinary action. The federal district court dismissed their complaint on the grounds that the school action was reasonable in order to maintain school discipline, but the U.S. Supreme Court reversed the decision. According to the majority opinion of the Court, "School officials do not possess absolute authority over their students. Students in school as well as out of school are 'persons' under our Constitution. They are possessed of fundamental rights which the state must respect, just as they themselves must respect their obligations to the state."[49]

A related case, *Goss* v. *Lopez*,[50] also reached the U.S. Supreme Court. In this instance, at issue was a state law empowering a school principal to suspend a student for misconduct for a period up to ten days provided certain procedures were followed. The court struck down the law and took the position that suspension for ten days was a "serious event in the life of the suspended child" and that the procedures followed were arbitrary and inadequate. Since then, Ohio has modified its law and many school officials elsewhere have modified their procedures governing suspension. Goss, Tinker, and related cases in federal and state courts have been instrumental in changing the context within which schools and school districts operate.

RESTRICTED
FINANCIAL
RESOURCES

Still another aspect of the environment of schools and school districts is that of restricted financial resources. The realities of the situation are found in the growing salary demands of school employees, the disposition of citizens to turn down levy and bond proposals, the development of tax revolts in many states, and the reduction of federal programs.

Salary Demands

School district employees, like employees elsewhere, believe that their salaries should keep up with rises in the cost of living. High inflation rates, characteristic of recent years, make the need for regular salary increases even more critical. The chief reason for the increasing number of teacher strikes noted above the is the fact that in a time of high inflation revenues frequently do not keep pace. Figures compiled by the Utah Education Association illustrate the problem. As shown in *Table 2–1*, average teachers' salaries in Utah began at $6,634 in 1967–68 and rose to $17,442 in 1980–81. In terms of constant dollars the picture is quite different; at the end of the thirteen-year period salaries stood at $7,029, a gain of $375 or 5.7 percent.

These figures reveal a slight gain in purchasing power over the period, hence should not be disturbing until one examines pay scales in other occupations. Beginning salaries for college graduates for 1980 are shown in *Table 2–2*.

With other college graduates commanding, on the average, half again as much as Utah classroom teachers, the teacher shortage in Utah and the salary demands of the Utah teachers are easier to understand.

Citizen Resistance

In spite of the fact that teachers make relatively low salaries and that teacher shortages have developed in some states (particularly in the fields of science and math), citizens are loathe to provide more money for schools. This reluctance is clearly demonstrated in the record of school bond elections over the past several years, as shown in *Table 2–3*. In 1962 and in earlier years approximately three-fourths of all bond elections carried. In recent years such measures passed only

TABLE 2–1
Average teacher salary
analysis for Utah

School year	Consumer price index	Purchasing power of dollar	Average teacher salary	Constant dollars	Dollars lost to inflation
1967–68	100.5	1.000	$ 6,634	$6,634	$ —
1972–73	125.7	.800	8,928	7,142	1,786
1977–78	183.3	.548	13,497	7,896	5,601
1978–79	197.8	.508	14,605	7,419	7,186
1979–80	221.5	.454	15,645	7,102	8,543
1980–81	249.4	.403	17,442	7,029	10,413

Source: Utah Education Association.

Occupation	Beginning salaries 1980	Index relationship
Engineering	$20,136	171.6
Accounting	15,720	133.9
Sales-Marketing	15,936	135.8
Business Administration	14,100	120.1
Liberal Arts	13,296	113.3
Chemistry	17,124	145.9
Mathematics-Statistics	17,604	150.0
Economics-Finance	14,472	123.3
Computer Science	17,712	150.9
Other	17,544	149.5
Average, all fields	17,232	146.8
Utah classroom teachers	11,736	100.0

TABLE 2–2
Beginning salaries for college graduates in the U.S., 1980

Source: Frank S. Endicott, *Trends in Employment of College and University Graduates in Business and Industry, Thirty-fourth Annual Report* (Evanston, Ill.: The Author, Northwestern University, 1980) and earlier reports.

about half the time. National figures for school levy elections do not seem to be available, but fragmentary reports suggest that requests for additional operating funds have done little better than have the bond elections.

Some of the possible explanations of voter behavior at the polls were dealt with above. As long as voters are skeptical about school effectiveness, their approval of more money for current operation or capital improvements will be hard

Year	% Approved
1962	72.2
1967	66.6
1972	47.0
1973	56.5
1974	56.2
1975	46.3
1976	50.8

TABLE 2–3
Outcome of school bond elections in the United States, 1962–1976

Source: National Center for Education Statistics, *Bond Sales for Public School Purposes* (Washington, D.C.: U.S. Government Printing Office, 1978) and earlier reports.

to come by. Then, too, there is the additional fact that many voters, particularly those on fixed incomes, have their own problems because of inflation. Under these circumstances, when given the option at the polls, many citizens tend to say "No."

Tax Revolts   In June, 1978 the California voters approved a referendum, Proposition 13, limiting property taxes to one percent of the 1975 assessed valuation. At the same time, they imposed a two-thirds voter-approval requirement for future taxes. Relatively speaking, property taxes were very high in California and it is not difficult to understand why the voters of that state were ready to revolt. The impact of Proposition 13 in California was not felt immediately, for the state had a large surplus and by the use of additional state aid school districts and other local units of government, ordinarily largely dependent on property taxes, were able to maintain most of their services over the next year or two. Since that time the full impact of Proposition 13 has become clear: in many districts teaching staffs have been reduced and some instructional programs eliminated.

The tax revolt has not been limited to California. Even in states where property tax payments are lower than those in California, the tax revolt fever has caught on. Pipho reported in 1981 that seventeen states had adopted either constitutional or statutory limits on taxation or spending.[51] Many states, unlike the federal government, have constitutional provisions forbidding deficits and these provisions often exacerbate the impact of tax limitations. Whether or not a state has enacted a tax limitation provision, the disposition of the public to favor one is frequently a part of the climate surrounding administrators.

National Pullback   Not only is there reluctance to provide more money at the local level and tax revolt at the state level, but there is also a genuine pullback in school revenues at the federal level. The Congress approved rescissions recommended by the Reagan administration for fiscal year 1981, and deep cuts mandated for education programs in fiscal year 1982. To make matters worse, the Office of Management and Budget has reportedly told federal departments, including the Education Department, that an additional cut of 15 percent must be made for fiscal year 1983.[52] These cuts are not minor adjustments: even the 1981 rescissions represent substantial reductions, particularly in view of inflation. For example, the continuing resolution of the Congress for 1981 established basic grants to the states for Title I programs at $2.8 billion. In the final funding for 1981 that figure was reduced to $2.5 billion. Comparable figures for the education of the handicapped were $922 million, reduced to $874 million. For grants to the states for vocational education the figures were $562 million reduced to $518 million.[53] These are the 1981 reductions only; 1982 and 1983 reductions were still to follow. Again in September, 1982, with a new fiscal year approaching and regular appropriation bills not passed, Congress adopted another continuing resolution to keep the Government in business until December 15,

1982. In this bill, federal education programs were to receive the same amounts of money as they did in fiscal 1982.[54]

SUMMARY

We have shown that schools and school districts operate in a complex environment. The components of this environment include a diverse student population, strained organizational arrangements, changing citizen attitudes, assertive teachers' organizations, growing legal constraints, and restricted financial resources. Since the precise nature of these components varies from school to school and district to district, each school manager should appropriately assess these components to see how they affect his or her school. Clearly, the success of school programs is largely determined by a constructive interaction between the school and its environment. This interaction is a reciprocal one: the school, within limits, can affect the culture, and the culture does affect the school. In the end, the school can be no better than the culture will let it be. In Chapters 6 through 12 we will be more specific about the effect of school environment on administrative practice.

ENDNOTES

1. National Center for Education Statistics, *The Condition of Education, 1980 ed.* (Washington, D.C.: U.S. Government Printing Office, 1980), p. 56.
2. Bureau of the Census, *Statistical Abstract of the United States, 1980* (Washington, D.C.: U.S. Government Printing Office, 1980), p. 138.
3. For more elaboration see Roald F. Campbell et al., *The Organization and Control of American Schools* 4th ed. (Columbus, Oh.: Charles E. Merrill, 1980), Ch. 6.
4. Bureau of Census, *Statistical Abstract of the United States, 1980*, p. 145.
5. "The Games Teen-Agers Play," *Newsweek*, 1 September 1980, p. 51.
6. "Games Teen-Agers Play," p. 48.
7. James S. Coleman et al., *Youth: Transition to Adulthood.* Report of the Panel on Youth of the President's Science Advisory Committee, Washington, D.C.: U.S. Government Printing Office, 1973.
8. National Center for Education Statistics, *Condition of Education*, p. 56.
9. National Center for Education Statistics, *Condition of Education*, p. 58.
10. James G. March, "Analytical Skills and the University Training of Administrators," *The Journal of Educational Administration* 12 (May 1974):17–44.
11. March, "Analytical Skills," p. 19.
12. David B. Tyack, *The One Best System* (Cambridge, Mass.: Harvard University Press, 1974).
13. The National Commission on School District Reorganization, *Your School District* (Washington, D.C.: National Education Association, 1948), p. 15.
14. John I. Goodlad, *The Dynamics of Educational Change* (New York: McGraw Hill, 1975), p. 175.
15. For instance, see Seymour B. Sarason, *The Culture of the School and the Problem of Change* (Boston: Allyn and Bacon, 1971).
16. See Campbell et al., *Organization and Control*, Ch. 3 for more detail.
17. Roald F. Campbell and Tim L. Mazzoni, Jr., *State Policy Making for the Public Schools* (Berkeley, Cal.: McCutchan Publishing, 1976).
18. Campbell et al., *Organization and Control*, Ch. 2.
19. For instance, see Abington School District v. Schempp, 374 U.S. 203 (1963).

20. David B. Tyack, "Pilgrims Progress: Toward a Social History of the School Superintendency, 1860–1960," *History of Education Quarterly* 16(Fall 1976): 258.

21. George H. Gallup, "The 13th Annual Gallup Poll of the Public's Attitudes Toward the Public Schools," *Phi Delta Kappan* 63(September 1981): 35.

22. *Newsweek.* "Why Schools Fail," 20 April 1981, pp. 22–73; "Teachers Are in Trouble," 27 April 1981, pp. 67–83; "Hope for the Schools," 4 May 1981, pp. 66–72.

23. J. Stanley Ahmann, "National Achievement Profiles in Ten Learning Areas," *Educational Studies* 9(Winter 1979):363.

24. Willard Wirtz et al., *On Further Examination.* Report of the Advisory Panel on the Scholastic Aptitude Test Score Decline (New York: College Entrance Examination Board, 1977), p. 6.

25. James S. Coleman et al., *Equality of Educational Opportunity* (Washington, D.C.: U.S. Government Printing Office, 1966).

26. Christopher Jencks, *Inequality* (New York: Basic Books, 1972).

27. Campbell et al., *Organization and Control,* Ch. 17.

28. Jim Warren, "Alum Rock Voucher Project," *Educational Researcher* 5(March 1976): 13–15.

29. John E. Coons and Stephen D. Sugarman, *Education by Choice* (Berkeley: University of California Press, 1978).

30. James Catterall, "Tuition Tax Credits for Schools—A Federal Priority for the 1980's?" *IFG Policy Perspectives.* Institute for Research on Educational Finance and Governance, Stanford University, not dated.

31. Education Policies Commission, *The Purposes of Education in American Democracy* (Washington, D.C.: National Education Association, 1938).

32. Anthony M. Cresswell and Michael J. Murphy, *Teachers, Unions, and Collective Bargaining in Public Education* (Berkeley, Cal.: McCutchan Publishing, 1980), Ch. 3.

33. J. Alan Aufderheide, "Educational Interest Groups and the State Legislature," in Campbell and Mazzoni, *State Policy Making,* Ch. 5.

34. Cresswell and Murphy, *Teachers, Unions and Collective Bargaining,* p. 174.

35. Cresswell and Murphy, *Teachers, Unions and Collective Bargaining,* p. 344.

36. Aufderheide, "Educational Interest Groups," pp. 214–215.

37. Stanley M. Elam, "NEA Pressure Politics and the Public Interest," *Phi Delta Kappan* 62(December 1980): 234–235.

38. Elam, "NEA Pressure Politics," p. 235.

39. For a more complete discussion of the courts see Campbell et al., *Organization and Control,* Ch. 7.

40. Brown v. Board of Education, 347 U.S. 483 (1954).

41. Cooper v. Aaron, 358 U.S. 1 (1958).

42. Keyes v. School District No. 1 Denver, Colorado, 413 U.S. 189 (1973).

43. Bradley v. Milliken, 418 U.S. 717 (1974).

44. Serrano v. Priest, 5 Cal. 3rd 584 (1971).

45. *A Summary of Statewide School Finance Cases.* Washington, D.C.: Lawyers Committee for Civil Rights Under Law, 1974.

46. San Antonio Independent School District v. Rodriquez, 411 U.S. 1 (1973).

47. Robinson v. Cahill, 62 N.J. 473 (1973).

48. Tinker v. Des Moines Independent School District, 393 U.S. 503 (1969).

49. Tinker v. Des Moines, p. 511.

50. Goss v. Lopez, 419 U.S. 565 (1975).

51. Chris Pipho, "Rich States, Poor States," *Phi Delta Kappan* 62(June 1981): 722.

52. *Education Times,* 8 June 1981, p. 1.

53. *Education Times,* pp. 4–5.

54. *Education Times,* 27 September 1982.

CHAPTER 3

ORGANIZATIONAL CHARACTERISTICS OF SCHOOLS

Organizations prescribe many of the activities of individuals who participate in them. Consider the daily activities of an elementary teacher. She (or he) comes to school at a particular time and works with a specific group of students in an assigned room. She teaches a variety of subjects, some of which are prescribed by state law and all of which are approved by the local board of education. Depending upon other actions of the board, she may share the instruction of students in her class with other faculty members. From time to time she consults with the principal, a counselor, another specialist, or parents about student progress. She takes attendance, keeps other records, and submits required reports. She may attend a faculty meeting or some other function after school, but her pattern of activity will be similar each day. Others in the school—students, custodians, cafeteria workers, and administrators—also behave in routine ways. Routines are a central aspect of life in organizations.

Schools began as very simple organizations, often a single teacher, a group of children, and parents with similar expectations. Like many other social units, schools have become more complex. Most are comprised of many classrooms and involve a number of people in nonteaching support functions. Indeed, we now talk about school systems to connote the relationships among several schools and various administrative offices in a given locale. Moreover, local school systems are interrelated with other organizational units, including state and federal agencies, which issue regulations that effect local school routines.

In this chapter, we view schools from an organizational perspective. We discuss some general attributes of organizations and how they pertain to schools. The chapter also treats the manner in which schools are organized and examines some practical and theoretical perspectives which have influenced their development. The concluding section notes that schools are different from other organizations in some important ways, and discusses some of these differences and their implications.

ORGANIZATIONAL ATTRIBUTES

Students of organizational behavior have identified a number of attributes by which organizations may be defined and described. They include (1) goals, (2) technology, (3) division of labor, (4) power centers, and (5) environment.[1] Taken together, these attributes indicate that an organization may be defined as a group of people who work to achieve certain goals in a given setting. As we shall see, organizations vary substantially in their complexity and the degree of formality with which they operate.

Goals

Goals provide meaning and direction to organizations. In the most general sense, they provide reasons for an organization's existence. Thus a manufacturing company is formed to produce certain products at a profit for the owners; the Internal Revenue Service is organized to collect taxes; and schools are intended to provide education for their students. These general goals suggest the activities in which the respective organizations should engage and also indicate criteria by which the organization should be evaluated. Even though goals provide identity and direction for organizations, they usually permit considerable latitude in organizational behavior.

One reason for this is that organizational goals are often so general that they are ambiguous and schools are no exception. The following is a typical statement of school goals:

> WE BELIEVE THAT IT IS THE RESPONSIBILITY OF OUR SCHOOLS . . .
>
> To provide education at the earliest appropriate age and to seek and identify the needs of each individual student on a continuing basis.
> To provide the necessary tools and incentives to assure each student the highest quality of education.
> To provide the necessary programs, training, and qualified and supportive personnel to motivate all students to achieve according to their

individual learning patterns and rates of growth in order to realize their maximum potentials intellectually, economically and socially, culturally and physically.

To provide a climate wherein the uniqueness of the cultures that each individual brings to the classroom setting is positively received.

To provide the structures, policies, and practices that reflect the multi-ethnic nature of our community through the composition of administrative staff, faculties, and student bodies.[2]

This statement is so general that virtually no one would disagree with it. This level of generality provides a basis for widespread public support of schools. It also gives legitimacy to diverse claims for specific school programs and activities. Advocates of *Summerhill* and *McGuffey's Readers* can each read the statement to their liking, as can proponents of instructional television, computerized instruction, sex education, values clarification, moral education, and a host of other ideas. As a result, the process by which these general goals are translated into more specific programs and objectives is likely to become politicized.

Individuals join organizations because they support the goals of the organization. For example, someone who accepts a teaching job ordinarily wants to do the things mentioned in the above goal statement. Like everyone else, however, he (or she) has his own interpretation of the statement, which influences his teaching. He also has some individual goals for participation in the organization. In addition to earning a living, these may include such things as building friendships with fellow teachers, developing a reputation that will lead to a "better" job in another school system, or spending no more time than necessary at school so he may devote as much time as possible to a family business or personal hobby. Such personal goals will influence the manner in which individuals define and contribute to organizational goals.

An important distinction can be made between outcome or performance goals and organizational maintenance goals. Manufacturing products or educating students are performance goals, and most discussions about organizational goals focus upon this type. Less talked about but perhaps more fundamental are organizational maintenance goals.[3] These refer to those activities that are necessary to sustain the organization. The first goal of almost every organization is to survive. Thus, organizational maintenance goals include such aims as attracting clients and resources, maintaining support for the organization among its employees, and sustaining a favorable image with the public. An example of an organizational maintenance activity is preparing the payroll. Teachers assume that they will be paid regularly and school systems make every effort to do this. However, if teachers' paychecks are delayed for some reason, it is likely that the entire system will be disrupted.[4]

An organization designed to achieve certain goals is often structured in subunits, each of which has its own goals subordinate to the general organizational ones. Thus, a small school system may consist of elementary schools, a high school with several departments, and a central office with personnel, business, and instruction divisions reporting to a superintendent. In theory, each of these subunits should pursue its goals to the best of its ability. As they do so, however, there is the possibility of conflict among them. One occasion for conflict involves the allocation of resources; given a limited amount of money each year, we can expect subunit representatives to disagree about allocations. Another kind of conflict concerns the emphasis to be placed on particular programs. For example, an ambitious and capable football coach or band director may make claims upon the time of students that might otherwise be given to academics, or the librarian may restrict access to the library in order to conserve resources. Others in the school will resist such actions and claim they are inconsistent with primary goals.

At times individuals in organizations place such emphasis on achieving subunit goals or maintenance goals that they lose sight of the main goals. This is referred to as goal displacement.[5] One way to think about goal displacement is as a reversal between ends and means. For example, most educators would agree that classroom discipline is essential to teaching and learning. However, a teacher who allows concern for discipline to overshadow teaching or a supervisor who evaluates teachers solely on the basis of their ability to maintain order exhibits goal displacement. At another level, it could be said that a board of education that diverts funds budgeted for instructional improvements to provide larger salary increases for teachers is engaged in goal displacement. Still another form occurs when strict adherance to rules overrides concern for organizational goals; thus a teacher or administrator who insists that a rule be followed, even when it is clear than an exception would be in the best educational interest of a student, is displacing goals.

A related phenomenon is the distortion of organizational goals that may occur because progress toward some is more easily measured than that toward others. An example of this in schools stems from the widespread emphasis on tests of basic achievement spawned by the accountability movement. The fact that students and schools can be compared according to scores on standardized tests has led some schools to modify their curricula in an effort to improve test performances. While agreeing that basic skills are important, many educators believe that the emphasis placed on test results has placed undue pressure on children and teachers and narrowed the curriculum in undesirable ways.

Technology   According to Parsons,[6] organizations function at three levels—technical, managerial, and institutional. The technical level refers to those activities through which the organization achieves its purposes. The managerial level is engaged in supporting the technical level by providing it with resources, coordinating its activities, and mediating between it and the environment. The institutional level provides legitimacy and overall direction to the organization and links it to the broader environment. It is the support of the managerial and institutional levels that enables organizations to develop and implement technologies too complex for individuals to carry out.[7]

The technology of educational organizations is teaching. It involves bringing students, teachers, and materials together to achieve curriculum objectives. This is done most often by dividing students into groups called classes, dividing the curriculum into segments called grades or subjects, and arranging for interaction among them.[8] However, there are substantial variations among schools in the ways they group students, select subject matter, and present it.

In comparison to many other organizations, the technology of schools is uncertain.[9] There is much less that is certain about teaching children than there is about manufacturing computers or even treating cancer. Within general bounds established by state law (of which there are fifty variations) and available textbooks, the curriculum varies from one school system to another. Even at the same school and grade level, teachers in individual classrooms differ substantially in what they teach and how they teach it. Some of this variation is ideological and reflects differences about educational goals. However, much of it stems from a relatively weak knowledge base regarding educational practice.

Division of Labor

The work of an organization is shared among its participants. The pattern according to which this is done is referred to as the division of labor. For small, face-to-face organizations such as two people painting a room, the division of labor is likely to be informal and involve a simple verbal agreement about how to divide the job until it is finished. As organizations become larger and more complex, the division of labor within them is likely to become formalized at several hierarchical levels and across various departments and divisions. The jobs of individuals within these departments and divisions become specialized.

The division of labor in schools involves teachers, administrators, and classified personnel such as custodians, bus drivers, and cafeteria workers. Different responsibilities are associated with each of these positions. These responsibilities and expectations are stated in documents such as policy manuals, position or job descriptions, and teacher contracts. The division of labor differs from school to school. For example, the teachers in one elementary school may be expected to teach art, music, and physical education as well as the basic academic subjects, whereas specialists are employed to teach these subjects in a nearby community. Similarly, teacher aides may be available to help teachers in one school but not in another.

Contemporary school districts, especially large ones, employ many personnel who are not directly involved in teaching. Figure 3–1 portrays the organizational chart of a small city school system. The organizational structure of a large metropolitan school district is shown in Figure 3–2. The charts indicate that both districts employ a number of non-classroom administrative and support personnel. The number of these is substantially greater in the larger district. The larger district also employs more specialists in areas such as curriculum planning, staff development, personnel relations, research, and planning. Comparison of the two figures suggests that the work associated with educating children is divided differently in the respective districts.

FIGURE 3–1   Organizational chart of a small city school system

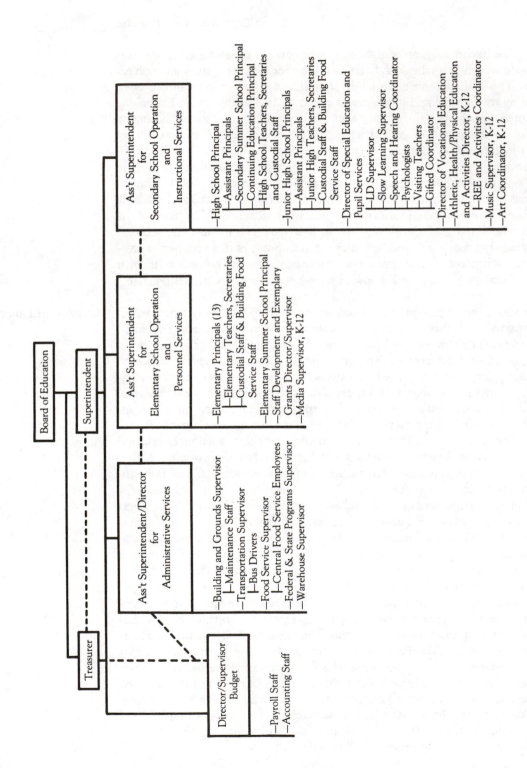

Source: Newark, Ohio City Schools.

The division of labor in an organization is of special concern to administrators. Indeed, it is this division and the resulting need for coordination that creates the need for administrators. Their function is to assure that the efforts of those who report to them are contributing as expected to organizational goals. By coordinating the efforts of others, administrators can help them find satisfaction as individuals as well as achieve expected goals.

Power Centers

Organizations include one or more power centers which establish goals, allocate resources, and monitor progress. They make the decisions that guide the efforts of others in the organization. Power centers are often defined by organizational charters or bylaws. In the case of schools, for example, state statutes prescribe that the local board of education is a power center. Within the bounds of state and federal law, local boards of education have general policy making authority. They are expected to establish local policies governing school matters. In addition, their ministerial responsibilities to the state vest them with certain other powers, such as approval of all personnel appointments, contracts, and purchases.

Other power centers in schools include the superintendents, principals, and classroom teachers. Each of these individuals makes decisions that guide the actions of others. Moreover, because of the positions they hold, others accept the fact that they will do so. For example, teachers expect principals to assign them to classrooms, and students expect teachers to give homework assignments. When individuals act in such ways and their directions are followed, they are exercising authority.

Authority relationships are essential guides to behavior in schools as they are in other organizations. Much of what occurs in a school happens because the superintendent, another administrator, or a teacher says that it should happen. However, the concept of authority involves more than giving orders. It also involves the acceptance of those orders as legitimate and binding by those who receive them.[10] Thus, a teacher exercises authority when he or she announces a test and the students take it. The predictability of such routine activities helps to ensure stability and the continuity of goal-oriented behavior in the organization. Note, however, that the students could refuse to take the teacher's test or even all tests. To do so would be to renounce the authority of the teachers and this would jeopardize the stability of the organization.

Power is generally regarded as the ability of one party to require another to act in a particular way. Authority is then considered legitimate power—that is, power that is consistent with the values of those over whom it is exercised.[11] There are various sources of legitimacy or authority. They include tradition, personality, knowledge, and rational-legal bases. All are present in schools. For example, many decisions go unchallenged simply because they are consistent with the way things have been done in the past. A stereotypic example of authority involves the high school football coach whose personality is so charismatic that his team exerts extraordinary effort to win. Knowledge is a frequently used

FIGURE 3–2
Organizational chart of
a large metropolitan
school district

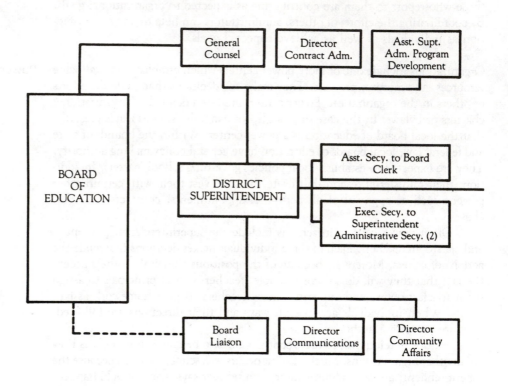

Source: Jefferson County, Kentucky Public Schools.

source of authority for teachers and administrators, especially ín responding to questions from parents and other citizens. It can also be the basis from which to argue for program changes. Rational-legal bases of authority include laws pertaining to schools, board of education policies, and other formal statements.

The rational-legal authority structure is the crux of what is generally referred to as the formal organization of a school system. It includes statements of goals and policies, contractual relationships, and a specified hierarchy of au-

FIGURE 3–2
Continued

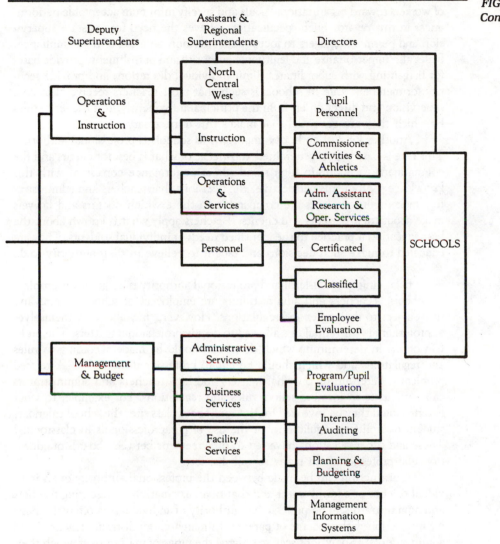

thority. This structure informs a new teacher (or student) of where and when to report and what basic conditions must be observed in order to retain the position. The employee accepts these authority relationships as a condition of having the job.

An important element of rational-legal authority is a body of universal and impersonal rules that spell out the required behaviors at the different levels of the organization. Rules perform a number of functions.[12] They direct the efforts of workers toward organizational goals and specify minimum acceptable performances in this regard. Such specification relieves the need for constant supervision and permits managers to focus their attention on areas of noncompliance. Rules also impersonalize and legitimate authority and punishment, provide bases for bargaining with subordinates, limit individual discretion, and provide security for members. Life in schools is such that most teachers receive classroom supervision and direct orders from the principal infrequently. It is the set of rules by which they are governed that makes this unnecessary.

Another kind of authority important in schools is professional authority. This type is based upon generalized knowledge of what is best for clients and the commitment to maintain high standards of performance consistent with this knowledge.[13] From this perspective, the decisions that teachers and administrators make about students are comparable to those which doctors and lawyers make about their patients and clients. Teachers apply what is known about the best educational practice to the identified needs of individual students. They are educated to make such decisions and taught to believe in their authority to do so.

Balancing rational-legal and professional authority is a significant problem in schools. Teachers and administrators are employees of school systems and thus subject to their rules and regulations. However, they also view themselves as professionals who should be allowed to decide professional matters. The problem occurs in determining which decisions should be made according to rules and regulations and which should be left to professional discretion. A related problem is determining on what matters and how teachers and administrators can participate in forming school rules and regulations. For example, to what extent should they be involved in decisions about class size, the school calendar, student disciplinary regulations, or the use of paraprofessionals in classrooms? These and other questions have led to disagreement between boards of education and professionals in many school districts.

A distinction can be made between the professional authority of an individual teacher or administrator and that of an association representing teachers and administrators. The professional authority of individuals is often the basis for interaction with students or parents. In many school districts, teachers' and administrators' associations seek to enlarge the range of matters over which their members have discretion. The early bargaining efforts of these organizations focused almost entirely on salaries and working conditions. More recently, these organizations have negotiated for the rights of their members to participate more fully in decision making. In this sense, they are attempting to incorporate broader respect for professional authority in the rational-legal authority structure.

In addition to those power centers that are formally recognized as having authority in the organization, there is often an informal power structure as well. In schools, for example, small groups of teachers often assemble informally to discuss events and how to respond to them. A memorandum from the principal requiring that all teachers prepare lesson plans according to a certain format would probably activate these groups. Notwithstanding the principal's rational-legal authority, discussions within informal groups would influence the way teachers respond to this directive.

Informal groups are particularly important in shaping the attitudes of people in the organization, and as such, influence the interpretation of and compliance with rules, regulations, and directives. As anyone who has spent time in a faculty lounge or cafeteria knows, these groups facilitate much communication about school activities. Some of this communication may help clarify responsibilities or directions. It may also serve as a release of tensions provoked by the organization without making an issue of them through formal channels. Of course, if problems remain unsolved, informal groups can also encourage the spread of discontent.

Every organization exists in an environment with which it is interdependent. The nature of the environment for schools was discussed in Chapter 2 and includes forces in the community, state, and nation. As indicated in the preceding chapter, variations in these forces can influence the structure and activities of schools.

Environment

The organizational character of schools has been shaped by a number of practical and theoretical factors. Some of these, such as traditions associated with education and the activities of educators as professionals, are unique to schools. Others, such as the recognition of bureaucracy as an ideal organizational type and the development of management theory, have had an impact on all organizations. Public expectations have influenced schools in both specific and general ways.

PERSPECTIVES THAT HAVE INFLUENCED SCHOOL ORGANIZATION

Tradition is an important factor in school organization. Provisions for public education in the United States date back to the Massachusetts school law of 1647. This act required towns to appoint teachers and established the precedent for free and compulsory education. The compulsory education laws have been an important parameter for the organization of schooling. The requirement that all children of a given age attend school and that such education be available at public expense made school systems dependent upon taxpayers for their support. This has contributed to a tradition wherein decisions about what is taught in schools and who works in them are influenced by local citizen opinions.[14]

Tradition

Decisions about the utilization of time and space for education are also influenced by tradition. Schools are in regular session during the fall, winter, and spring, and in recess during the summer. Instruction is provided to groups of children on a graded basis for a period of twelve years (thirteen if we consider kindergarten). Schools are in session Monday through Friday during the daytime hours. As children progress to the later grades of school, they are asked to do some school work at home as well as in class. All of these things are taken for granted by nearly all school systems and their patrons. The significance of these traditions has been demonstrated in those communities that have considered proposals for year-round school programs: although a few locales have shifted to year-round programs, most have dismissed arguments for better space utilization or accelerating student progress, and retained the traditional school year.

Tradition has also shaped the nature of the workforce in schools. Teaching was seen for many years as an occupation suited primarily to women. As a consequence, women have continued to dominate the ranks of teachers, especially in elementary schools. (There is some evidence that this may change as other careers become more accessible to women.) Tradition has also mandated that individuals have teaching experience as a prerequisite for advancement in school systems. When school buildings were first constructed to house more pupils than single teachers could handle, one of the teachers became the "head teacher" or "principal" teacher. From this early experience, we have come to the point where teaching experience is considered a prerequisite for most, if not all, administrative positions in nearly every school district. In most states, this tradition has been buttressed by laws requiring prior teaching experience of all certified administrators.

Professionalism

The view that education is a profession has had substantial impact on the way schools are organized. The most direct manifestation of this is the broad authority that teachers enjoy in their classroom. The relationship between teachers and their pupils is considered a professional one for which teachers are to be specially educated and certified by the state. State certification requirements purportedly assure that teachers are selected on the basis of competence rather than patronage or personal relationships to employing officials. They also attest that teachers possess the competence to teach effectively. Once holding this certification, teachers enjoy considerable latitude in how they may teach their students. For the most part, students and parents accept this fact. Moreover, teacher authority has been upheld by the courts so long as it is not exercised in conflict with more general rules, policies, laws, or constitutional provisions.

The ideology of professionalism is strong among teachers. They believe that their education and experience provide them with expertise that entitles them to considerable discretion in working with their students. They also believe that this expertise entitles them to a voice in decisions about the curriculum, expectations for students, teaching methods and materials, and many other matters of school policy. In some districts, their participation in such decisions is limited to informal consultation with administrators or advisory committees. In others, these relationships have been formalized through teachers' associations, which negotiate far-reaching contractual agreements with the board of education. The variations among school districts in this regard are substantial. However, the structure of authority in all school districts is influenced to some extent by the professional belief structure of teachers in those districts.

The development of management theory has occurred primarily in the twentieth century.[15] Most of the literature has focused upon the administration of businesses or government agencies. However, the concepts and principles advanced in this literature have been urged upon school officials and are reflected in the organization of school systems. Two of the early and most influential schools of thought involved job analysis and human relations. The structuralist emphasis upon bureaucracy has also been influential. More recent theorists have helped explain the organizational behavior of schools, but they have had less influence on their structure.

Management Theory

The first approach to administration was that of job analysis. We shall note the work of two major contributors to this approach. Frederick Taylor, often called the father of the scientific management movement, was born in 1856. He studied in France, Germany, and Italy in his youth, and later earned an M.E. degree. From 1878 to 1889, he was employed by the Midvale Steel Company, first as a laborer, then as clerk, machinist, foreman, chief draftsman, and finally chief engineer. Taylor noticed that workers were in charge of both planning and performing their jobs, a situation that led, he thought, to much waste and inefficiency. His experience at all levels of industry led him to formulate his principles, which were condensed in *The Principles of Scientific Management*, published in 1911.[16]

Job analysis

His essential points have been summarized by Villers as follows:

1. *Time-study principle.* All productive effort should be measured by accurate time study and a standard time established for all work done in the shop.
2. *Piece-rate principle.* Wages should be proportional to output and their rates based on the standards determined by time study. As a corollary, a worker should be given the highest grade of work of which he is capable.
3. *Separation-of-planning-from-performance principle.* Management should take over from the workers the responsibility for planning the work and making the performance physically possible. Planning should be based on time studies and other data related to production, which are scientifically determined and systematically classified; it should be facilitated by standardization of tools, implements, and methods.
4. *Scientific-methods-of-work principle.* Management should take over from the workers the responsibility for their methods of work, determine scientifically the best methods, and train the workers accordingly.

5. *Managerial-control principle.* Managers should be trained and taught to apply scientific principles of management and control (such as management by exception and comparison with valid standards).
6. *Functional-management principle.* The strict application of military principles should be reconsidered and the industrial organization should be so designed that it best serves the purpose of improving the coordination of activities among the various specialists.[17]

Taylor and other spokesmen of the scientific management movement were influential in seeing many of their principles applied to such firms as Midland Steel Company, Bethlehem Steel Company, Santa Fe Railroad, and Acme Wire Company. Labor, on the other hand, resisted time-and-motion studies and other activities that were perceived as treating men as though they were machines. The whole movement became the object of an investigation by the Social Committee of the House of Representatives in 1912. Following extended hearings, Congress attached a rider to the military appropriation bill prohibiting the use of such funds for time-and-motion studies.

From the perspective of our day, we find that Taylor took a narrow view of management, and that, moreover, he tended to ignore the psychological or personal aspects of mobilizing human effort. At the same time, he did demonstrate that many jobs could be done more efficiently. Even more important, his work stands as a monument to the concept that management can be studied scientifically. No aspect of administration has remained immune to this idea.

Henri Fayol was another major contributor to the job analysis approach to administration. He was born in 1841 of a family of the French School of Mines at St. Etienne. In a sense, he had four careers: twelve years as a mining engineer, sixteen years as a geologist, thirty years as the very able managing director of a large metallurgical firm, and seven years—after retirement at age seventy-seven—as a teacher of administration. In the fourth period, he undertook two main tasks: the first was the formation of the Centre of Administrative Studies; the second was an effort to persuade the French government to pay some attention to the principles of administration.

Although Fayol wrote his book, *Administration Industrielle et Generale,* in 1916, it did not appear in an English translation until 1929, and it was not made generally available in the United States until 1949.[18] Containing the first two parts of the eventual treatise Fayol planned to write, it describes the necessity and the possibility of teaching the principles and elements of management. The now-famous elements were planning, organizing, command, coordination, and control.

In the early stages of the popularization of Fayol's work, attempts were made by some to represent his approach as antithetical to that of Taylor. But at the Second International Congress held at Brussels in 1925, Fayol himself made clear that such interpretations were false. Actually, both men applied the scientific method. Taylor worked primarily at the operative level, or the bottom of the hierarchal structure, while Fayol began with the managing director at the top of the hierarchy. The work of Fayol has been reflected in the thinking and writing of Gulick, Urwick, Sears, and other students of administration.

Both Taylor and Fayol were concerned with industry; both believed that the processes involved in production could be analyzed and studied scientifically. While Taylor concentrated on the worker and Fayol on the manager, both had as an ultimate objective the increased efficiency of industry. To be sure, in his later years Fayol extended the application of his administrative principles to government as well as industry. Even so, both men tended to stress organizational processes and to ignore individuals as such. The time was ripe for a new emphasis, and Mary Parker Follett helped to supply it.

Human relations constituted the second major approach to administration. *Human relations*
Again the work of two major contributors will be noted. Mary Parker Follett was born in 1868. She graduated from Radcliffe College, where she followed a course devoted to economics, government, and philosophy. Throughout her life, she worked to help bring about a better-ordered society in which the individual might live a more satisfying life. This motivation was expressed in her membership on the Boston Committee on the Extended Use of School Buildings from 1909 to 1911, in the help she gave to establish the Department of Vocational Guidance in Boston in 1912, in her service on the Massachusetts Minimum Wage Board for many years, and in her great interest in the League of Nations.

Her book, *Creative Experience*,[19] has been characterized by Metcalf and Urwick as follows:

> . . . mainly psychological in interest and content, [it] marks a definite advance both in the crystallization of thought and in style and phraseology. Its thesis is the reciprocal character—the interpenetration—of all psychological phenomena, from the simplest to the most complex. Human relationships—the ways and work of society and of industry—are at their best when difference is solved through conference and cooperation, when the parties at interest (1) evoke each other's latent ideas based upon the facts of the situation, (2) come to see each other's viewpoints and to understand each other better, and (3) integrate those viewpoints and become united in the pursuit of their common goal.[20]

Follett contended that the fundamental problem of any enterprise, whether it be local government, national government, a business organization, or an educational system, is the building and maintenance of dynamic, yet harmonious, human relationships. She tended to reduce her principles of organizational to four in number, all aspects of what she termed *coordination*. The principles were:

1. Coordination by direct contact of the responsible people concerned.
2. Coordination in the early stages.

3. Coordination as the reciprocal relating of all factors in the situation.
4. Coordination as a continuing process.[21]

Mary Parker Follett might be characterized as a social philosopher with deep psychological insights. She came onto the scene when the process and organizational aspects of administration had been emphasized to the exclusion, perhaps, of the values to be cherished for society as a whole and for the development of individuals in that society. As an academician Follett made a contribution in both the United States and England, but she was also a woman of action. She found much stimulation in the observation of governmental and industrial organizations, and she was welcomed as a consultant by many enterprises.

While Mary Parker Follett became the first great exponent of human relations in administration, it remained for Elton Mayo and his colleagues to supply empirical data in support of such a view. Mayo was born in Adelaide, Australia, in 1880, and received A.B. and M.A. degrees from the University of Adelaide. For twenty years, he served as the senior professor in the Department of Industrial Research of the Harvard Business School. From 1923 to 1932, he and his associates were connected with the now-famous experiments done at the Hawthorne plant of the Western Electric Company, near Chicago.

Industry had long assumed that wages and physical working conditions were the chief factors in employee motivation. The first experiment at Hawthorne (1923–26) was quite simply designed to test the effect of one of these physical conditions—illumination—on worker production. It was found that illumination was not significantly related to production. In the true scientific spirit, the results of the experiment were accepted as proof that the basic assumption needed reconsideration.

A second inquiry was conducted to explore the problem more fully. A group of six operatives were selected for study to determine what factors might be related to their productivity. It was found that whatever factors were changed—whether rest periods, length of day, or methods of payment—and whatever way they were changed (even if the change meant returning to the original conditions), production continued to increase. Moreover, the subjects became more and more satisfied with their jobs, and their attendance continued to show greater regularity. Findings of this nature were secured almost without exception over a five-year period of meticulous experimentation between 1927 and 1932.

Mayo has explained the findings as follows:

> What the Company actually did for the group was to reconstruct entirely its whole industrial situation . . . .
>
> The consequence was that there was a period during which the individual workers and the group had to re-adapt themselves to a new industrial mileu, a mileu in which their own self-determination and their social well-being ranked first, the work was incidental . . . .
>
> The Western Electric experiment was primarily directed not to the external condition but to the inner organization. By strengthening the

"temperamental" inner equilibrium of the workers, the Company enabled them to achieve a mental "steady state" which offered a high resistance to a variety of external conditions.[22]

Clearly, this and similar experiments demonstrated that economic and mechanistic approaches to human relations in industry were inadequate. While wages and working conditions are important to the worker, they rank second to what Mayo called "a method of living in a social relationship." Apparently, the workers in the Hawthorne experiment had gained a sense of playing an important part in a project instead of being mere cogs in a large productive enterprise.

Mayo's work has been subjected to much examination, and some students find two major biases in his experiments.[23] He may have had a management bias, since he was employed by business to help business solve its problems. He may also have had a clinical bias, in that he began with observation and not with theory. Evidently Mayo did have some disdain for theory and had more faith in empiricism. Regardless of these criticisms, however, one must recognize that through long and meticulous experimentation Mayo and his associates collected a large body of data illustrating that what goes on inside the worker is even more significant for production that what goes on outside.

Were one to accept the work of Follett and Mayo uncritically, he or she might assume that adequate human relations is the sum total of administration. Indeed, the so-called "democratic" emphasis in administration of the 1940s and '50s may have sprung from the work of these contributors or, more likely, the inadequate interpretations of some of their disciples.

Structuralism

The development of human relations approaches to management were to some degree a reaction to the mechanistic nature of job analysis. The human relations emphasis was in turn supplanted by a view that gave more emphasis to structural factors. Many authors have contributed to this view, but the seminal work was done by Max Weber. A German sociologist, Weber actually worked at about the same time as Taylor and Fayol. However, because of translation problems, his work had little impact in the United States until the 1940s.

Weber's principal contribution to managerial thought was the definition and elaboration of bureaucracy as an ideal organizational type. Weber identified three kinds of organizations: charismatic organizations built around allegiance to a single leader, who dominated by force of personality; traditional organizations in which leadership was hereditary; and bureaucracies. The latter he considered the superior form because it provided for rational decision making and a high level of efficiency. According to Gross, Weber described bureaucracy as being—

superior to any other form in precision, in stability, in the stringency of its discipline, and in its reliability. It then makes possible a particularly high degree of calculability of results for the head of organizations and for those acting in relation to it. It is finally superior both in internal efficiency and in the scope of its operations and is formally capable of applications to all kinds of administrative tasks.[24]

The essential characteristics of a bureaucracy, according to Weber, are (1) a clear division of labor that permits specialization, (2) a hierarchical structure of authority, (3) a formally established system of written rules and regulations, (4) an impersonal orientation on the part of officials, and (5) opportunities for promotion and career employment in the organization.[25] Anyone familiar with organizational life today recognizes the pervasiveness of these characteristics. However, there are important differences among organizations with respect to each of them. For example, hierarchical authority is more clearly defined in military organizations than it is in universities or hospitals. By comparing organizations with regard to these characteristics, one can say that they are more or less bureaucratic.

In everyday language, the word "bureaucratic" has a pejorative connotation. Our image of a bureaucracy is an organization that is rule-bound, impersonal, and inefficient. We think of bureaucrats as people who shuffle papers, shift responsibility, and impede purposeful action. There is some truth in this view. Just as true, however, is the fact that bureaucracy provides a structure that facilitates the work of complex organizations. For example, the postal service is often referred to as an example of bureaucracy gone awry. While service could be improved, it is impossible to envision an effective alternative to the system that does not incorporate the essential characteristics of bureaucracy. School systems also take on bureaucratic characteristics in order to organize the work of their employees and provide services to large numbers of students.

There are some very real weaknesses of bureaucracy as an organizational type.[26] One is a tendency toward goal displacement, which was discussed in an earlier section of this chapter. A second weakness has to do with the unanticipated consequences of rules.[27]

Rules are intended to clarify expectations for workers so that behavior will meet organizational standards. The presence of rules is also intended to preclude the need for supervisors to intervene directly in the activities of workers, thereby reducing possibilities for interpersonal tensions. However, as *Figure 3–3* indicates, reliance on rules can lead to other, unanticipated consequences.

The explication of rules defines minimum-acceptable behavior. However, this may actually lead to a reduction in performance by persons who formerly exceeded the minimums. As a consequence, administrators may engage in closer supervision, which in turn leads to increased tension. Thus, rules that were intended to standardize performance at a high level and reduce tension may actually lead to reduced performance and increased tension as the rules are enforced. Suppose, for example, that a principal established a rule that all teachers must submit lesson plans to the office in a specified format on a regular basis. The objective may be to provide substitute teachers with appropriate materials. Unanticipated consequences may be the reduction of the quality of lesson plans prepared by many teachers and increased resentment toward the principal.

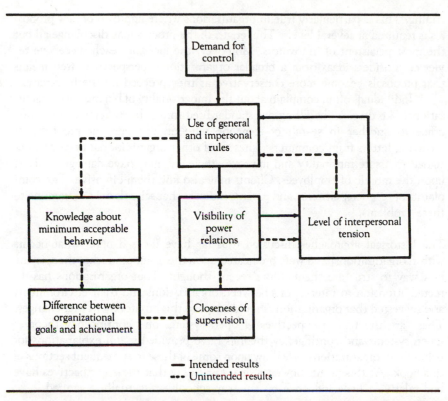

FIGURE 3–3
Consequences of
bureaucratic rules

Source: From J.G. March and H.A. Simon, *Organizations* (New York: John Wiley & Sons, 1958). Used by permission. Based on A.W. Gouldner, *Patterns of Industrial Bureaucracy* (New York: Free Press, 1954).

Another unanticipated consequence of bureaucratic organization is the development of trained incapacity.[28] According to bureaucratic theory, individuals in the organization will be trained as specialists who work according to well-established rules. The fact that their work is routinized allows them to proceed swiftly and without question. However, problems may arise when these specialists are faced with situations that do not fit their well-established rules. Their training may prevent them from assessing the situation properly and dealing with it appropriately. They respond instead with their learned solution to a different problem.

A related problem in bureaucracies is the stifling of creativity and individual initiative.[29] This occurs in two ways. First, as already noted, much behavior is guided by organizational rules. Bureaucrats learn that security in the organization is assured by complying with rules promulgated by the hierarchy. Conversely, actions contrary to the rules or in areas not covered by the rules invite sanctions. Thus, the organization discourages actions that do not have prior approval at higher levels. Second, the process of obtaining such approval is often stifling. This is particularly true in organizations where approval of new proposals is required at several levels. The length of the process may discourage all but the most persistent of innovators. Moreover, the fact that each successive reviewer considers ideas from a broader organizational perspective often means that proposals become more conservative as they proceed up the hierarchy.

Individuals often complain about the impersonality of bureaucratic organizations. We do not like filling out standardized forms, being referred from one office to another in search of someone who understands our problem, or receiving letters from computers. These and other organizational practices, designed to assure rationality and improve efficiency, may have damaging effects upon the morale of employees. Clients may also find them offensive. The complaints of teachers, citizens, and parents indicate that schools are not immune to these problems.

Open systems and contingency theories

The historical approaches discussed thus far have focused upon what occurs within organizations, and were predicated upon the assumption that there is one best way to structure them. More recent thought about organizations has directed attention to interactions between organizations and their environment, and suggested that organizations should adapt to this environment as it changes. These are the basic perspectives of open systems and contingency theory.[30] Open systems and contingency theories have provided useful explanations for behavior in organizations. We draw upon some of these in subsequent sections of this book. At this point, however, it is fair to say that these perspectives have had relatively little influence on the way schools are actually organized.

Public Expectations

The final perspective to be discussed in this section is that of public expectations. Virtually every citizen in our country has attended school. This collective experience shapes the views of schools held by general public and reinforces the traditions discussed above. When changes the public considers dramatic are proposed in school organization, resistance is not uncommon.

In addition to their own school experiences, citizens are influenced in their attitudes toward school organization by their experience in other organizations. In particular, public expectations for schools are influenced heavily by the norms and practices of the business community. Callahan[31] documented the importance of this influence as early as the turn of the century. Demonstrating the impact of "scientific management" upon educational thought and practice, he asserted that schools were too vulnerable to external influence. Nonetheless, the standard of "good business" continues to influence the organization and administration of schools. Public insistence on standards of rationality, efficiency, and accountability for schools is such that administrators worry about publicity portraying schools negatively with regard to these standards.

Public expectations for schools are often communicated through government action. Local boards of education, state legislatures, and the Congress each enact policies and legislation that specify goals and organizational procedures for school districts. These actions may mandate additions to the curriculum, increase or reduce the resources available to schools, encourage particular technologies, or impose operating and reporting regulations, as discussed in Chapter 2. There is also some evidence that the paperwork associated with state and federal reporting requirements has led to the addition of new offices and administrators in many school districts.

To this point, we have discussed general attributes of organizations as they apply to schools, as well as perspectives that have influenced their organizational development. In the concluding section of this chapter, we explain some ways of viewing schools that emphasize their differences from other organizations and help explain why their behavior is often different from that of other organizations.

UNIQUE ASPECTS OF SCHOOL ORGANIZATIONS

As noted above, schools are bureaucratic organizations. However, they differ from many bureaucracies in that those workers at the bottom of the hierarchy, teachers, are highly educated and consider themselves professionals. Their responsibility is to teach children of different backgrounds who learn from various stimuli at different rates. The nature of this responsibility and the fact that it is often carried out in a self-contained classroom means that teachers have great discretion in how they work. In contrast to workers at the lower levels of other bureaucracies, they are more difficult to supervise or to hold to uniform standards of performance. This difficulty is compounded by the ambiguity of school goal structures and the recognition that nonschool factors are important influences on student learning.

Professional Bureaucracies

Lacking the opportunity for close supervision present in other bureaucracies, schools rely on other means to assure that teachers comply with the expectations of those at higher levels in the organization. These include recruitment, screening, and teacher certification requirements as indicators of quality; promulgation of standardized curricula and textbooks; assessment to assure compliance with established procedures; and anecdotal feedback. Although principals observe teachers periodically, their assessment of them is often shaped by the extent to which they perceive that teachers com:py with school rules about such matters as discipline, lesson plans, and the preparation of required reports. Anecdotal feedback from students through parents or other teachers may also be important.

Recognizing the fact that teachers are well-educated professionals whose knowledge of their speciality exceeds that of others in the district, school officials often seek their advice on curriculum and other matters. Thus decision making in schools is often more participative than in other organizations. However, it is not unusual for some tension to exist in schools around the questions of what rules will apply to teachers and who will establish them. To some extent this reflects the tension between bureaucratic and professional values.

Organized Anarchies

Schools belong to a category of organizations that Cohen and March have described as organized anarchies.[32] The principal characteristics of such organizations are unclear goals, uncertain technology, and fluid participation. Decision making in these organizations is marked by ambiguity. As noted earlier, it is difficult to specify goals in educational organizations or to identify technologies that will definitely result in implementation of these goals.

School administrators also face ambiguities related to power, experience, and success. Because they are subject to pressures and sanctions from diverse constituencies, administrators are often uncertain about their power to achieve what they want to do. It is also difficult to learn from and rely on experience as a basis for decision making. Situations are often not what they appear to be, or at least are subject to interpretation from varying perspectives. Thus the natural, learned tendency to act in ways that were successful in what seemed to be similar situations may produce unanticipated and undesirable consequences. For example, many superintendents who learned over the years that it was unnecessary to negotiate with teacher groups have lost their jobs when assertive associations worked to elect boards of education that favor bargaining.

Finally, in organizations where goals and technology are uncertain, administrative success is ambiguous as well. How does one know when the organization is achieving its goals or operating at peak efficiency? Is success for the administrator defined by popularity, promotion, achievement of goals narrow enough to be measured, survival, or any or all of the above?

Domesticated Organizations

Carlson[33] suggested that it is useful to consider whether organizations have control over who enters them and whether clients have control over whether they participate in the organization. Some organizations, which he labeled "domesticated," have no control over who enters them nor do their clients have a choice about attending them. Public schools fall into this category.

The existence of such organizations is guaranteed and they do not need to compete for clients. This may help explain why schools traditionally have been slow to make changes. It also suggests that schools sometimes need to deal with pupils who prefer not to be there—and whom the school would rather not have enrolled. One way that schools have dealt with this problem has been to separate students who are most desirable to deal with for preferential treatment and to segregate those most difficult to deal with in separate classrooms or other activities. Although passage and enforcement of Public Law 94–142 has made this more difficult in recent years, the practice continues in a variety of ways.

Loosely Coupled Systems

A fourth perspective helpful in understanding the unique aspects of schools as organizations is that of loosely coupled systems.[34] Weick uses the phrase loose coupling "to convey the image that coupled events are responsive, *but* that each event also preserves its own identity and some evidence of its physical or logical separateness. Thus, in the case of an educational organization, it may be the case that the counselor's office is loosely coupled to the principal's office. The image is that the principal and the counselor are somehow attached, but that each retains some identity and separateness and that their attachment may be circumscribed, infrequent, weak in its mutual affects, unimportant, and/or slow to respond."[35]

Several conditions are likely to obtain in loosely coupled organizations that would be unusual in highly structured organizations. Loose coupling permits disparate elements of an organization to persist in the face of environmental change, allows for sensitivity to a broader range of environmental changes, allows for localized adaptations, encourages the development and maintenance of novel solutions, permits breakdowns in one part of the system without affecting the other parts, provides more discretion and self-determination for actors within it, and requires relatively small expenditures for coordination.

The relevance of this description to classrooms or schools in the same system is clear. Good teachers may succeed despite the effectiveness of others in their building. Some teachers and principals will sense and respond to changes in public expectations faster than others. They may devise a range of novel approaches to teaching that they employ in their classroom with little effect on events elsewhere in the system. Moreover, it is difficult for the principal or other administrators to control behavior of teachers and others across the system.

SUMMARY

There is a substantial body of literature that discusses the nature of organizations and their behavior. Much of this literature is relevant to schools, which like other organizations involve groups of people working together to achieve certain goals. Schools differ from other organizations, however, with respect to a number of attributes, including goals, technology, division of labor, power centers, and environment. The particular character of school organization has been influenced by a number of factors; among them are tradition, professionalism, management theory, and public expectations. Organizational perspectives that emphasize the unique aspects of schools include professional bureaucracy, organized anarchy, domesticated organization, and loosely coupled systems.

ENDNOTES

1. See, for example, Peter M. Blau and W. Richard Scott, *Formal Organizations* (San Francisco: Chandler Publishing, 1962); Amitai Etzioni, *Modern Organizations* (Englewood Cliffs, N.J.: Prentice-Hall, 1964); and Charles Perrow, *Complex Organizations* 2d ed. (Glenview, Ill.: Scott, Foresman, 1979).
2. Jefferson County Public Schools, *Educational Philosophy*, not dated.
3. See Richard C. Lonsdale, "Maintaining the Organization in Dynamic Equilibrium" in Daniel E. Griffiths ed., *Behavioral Science and Educational Administration*, Sixty Third Yearbook of the National Society for the Study of Education Part II (Chicago: The Society, 1964), pp. 142–177.
4. This fact was demonstrated by the 1979 financial crisis in the Chicago Public Schools.
5. For discussion, see Etzioni, *Modern Organizations*, pp. 10–12.
6. Talcott Parsons, "Some Ingredients of a General Theory of Formal Organization" in Andrew W. Halpin, ed., *Administrative Theory in Education* (Chicago: Midwest Administration Center, University of Chicago, 1958).

7. James D. Thompson, *Organizations in Action* (New York: McGraw-Hill, 1967), p. 15.

8. See W.W. Charters, Jr., "An Approach to the Formal Organization of the School" in Daniel E. Griffiths, ed., *Behavioral Science and Educational Administration*. The Sixty-Third Yearbook of the National Society for the Study of Education, Part II. (Chicago: The Society, 1964), pp. 243–261.

9. James G. March, "American Public School Administration: A Short Analysis," *School Review* 86 (February 1978):217–250. See also John W. Meyer and Brian Rowan, "The Structure of Educational Organizations" in M.W. Meyer et al., *Environments and Organizations* (San Francisco: Jossey Bass, 1978).

10. The concept of authority as an accepted right is explained by Chester Barnard, *The Functions of the Executive* (Cambridge, Mass.: Harvard University Press, 1968).

11. These ideas go back to Max Weber. See the discussion in Etzioni, *Modern Organizations*, pp. 51–57.

12. James G. Anderson, "Bureaucratic Rules: Bearers of Organizational Authority," *Educational Administration Quarterly* 2 (Winter 1966): 7–34.

13. Blau and Scott, *Formal Organizations*, pp. 60–63 and Ronald G. Corwin, "Professional Persons in Public Organizations," *Educational Administration Quarterly* 1 (Fall, 1965): 1–22.

14. See Raymond Callahan, *Education and the Cult of Efficiency* (Chicago: University of Chicago Press, 1962) and Kenneth M. Dolbeare and Phillip E. Hammond, *The School Prayer Decisions* (Chicago: University of Chicago Press, 1971).

15. A brief history is Roald F. Campbell, "A History of Administrative Thought," *Administrator's Notebook* 26 (1977–78), no. 4. Also see Bertam M. Gross, *The Managing of Organizations* (New York: Free Press, 1964), pp. 91–234.

16. This and other works appear in Frederick W. Taylor, *Scientific Management* (New York: Harper and Brothers, 1947).

17. Raymond Villers, *Dynamic Management in Industry* (Englewood Cliffs, N.J.: Prentice-Hall, 1960), p. 29.

18. Henri Fayol, *General and Industrial Management* (London: Sir Isaac Pitman and Sons, 1949).

19. Mary Parker Follett, *Creative Experience* (New York: Longmans, Green, 1924).

20. Henry C. Metcalf and L. Urwick, eds., *Dynamic Administration* (New York: Harper and Brothers, 1942), p. 14. The collected papers of Mary Parker Follett with an introduction by the editors.

21. Metcalf and Urwick, *Dynamic Administration*, p. 297.

22. Elton Mayo, *The Human Problems of an Industrial Civilization* (Boston: Graduate School of Business Administration, Harvard University, 1946), pp. 73, 75.

23. See Delbert C. Miller and William H. Form, *Industrial Sociology*, 2d ed. (New York: Harper and Brothers, 1964), pp. 78–83.

24. Cited in Gross, *The Managing of Organizations*, p. 139.

25. See H.N. Gerth and C. Wright Mills, trans. and eds., *From Max Weber: Essays in Sociology* (New York: Oxford University Press, 1964), pp. 196–204.

26. These are discussed as dysfunctional aspects or unanticipated consequences by H. Randolph Bobbitt, Jr., et al., *Organizational Behavior* 2d ed. (Englewood Cliffs, N.J.: Prentice-Hall, 1978), pp. 79–115. See also Robert K. Merton, *Social Theory and Social Structure* (New York: Free Press, 1968); James G. March and Herbert A. Simon, *Organizations* (New York: John Wiley and Sons, 1958); and Alvin W. Gouldner, *Patterns of Industrial Bureaucracy* (New York: Free Press, 1954).

27. Gouldner, *Patterns of Industrial Bureaucracy*. See also Bobbitt et al., *Organizational Behavior*, pp. 96–98.

28. Robert K. Merton, *Social Theory and Social Structure*.

29. Robert G. Corwin, "Bureaucracy in Education," *Education in Crisis* (New York: John Wiley, 1974), Ch. 1.

30. See David Easton, *A Systems Analysis of Political Life* (New York: John Wiley and Sons, 1965) and P.R. Lawrence and J.W. Lorsch, *Organizations and Environment* (Homewood, Ill.: Richard D. Irwin, 1961).

31. Callahan, *Education and the Cult of Efficiency.*

32. Michael D. Cohen and James G. March, *Leadership and Ambiguity* (New York: McGraw-Hill, 1974).

33. Richard Carlson, "Environmental Constraints and Organizational Consequences: The Public School and its Clients," in Daniel G. Griffiths, ed., *op. cit.*, pp. 262–276.

34. Karl E. Weick, "Educational Organizations as Loosely Coupled Systems," *Administrative Science Quarterly* 21 (March 1976): 1–19.

35. Weick, "Educational Organizations," p. 3.

CHAPTER 4

THE WORK OF SCHOOL ADMINISTRATORS

In previous chapters we looked at the nature of adminstration, the environment of schools, and the organizational characteristics of schools. We turn now to the work of school administrators. To begin, we describe the administrative positions found in most schools and school systems, and suggest the major functions for them. We then turn to the characteristics, the roles, and the stresses and rewards of administrative work.

ADMINISTRATIVE POSITIONS AND FUNCTIONS

Positions

Traditionally, in the military there are line officers and staff officers. While we do not equate school organizations with military organizations, the distinction between line and staff is a useful one and, with some adaptation, we use the term here. Line officers are those in charge of operating units of an organization, in this case a school district or a school. Thus, we would classify superintendents and principals as line officers. Staff officers, on the other hand, are those who assist line officers or provide some service to the line officers. An assistant superintendent or a director of research would be a staff officer.

There are in the United States about 16,000[1] school districts, and some 14,000 of these have an officer usually called the superintendent of schools. In a few states this officer may bear the title of supervising principal. In most cases the superintendent is appointed to the position by the district board of education. In some states, however, particularly in the Southeast where school districts often comprise an entire county, the superintendent may be elected by public ballot. Whether appointed or elected, the superintendent is ordinarily seen as the chief or top executive of the school district, and as such, a line officer.

There are in the country some 77,000 elementary schools, about 64,000 public and the remainder nonpublic. There are also about 29,000 secondary schools, 25,000 public and the others nonpublic.[2] Most of these schools have a principal. While in smaller schools the principal may also be a part-time teacher, in larger schools the principal is ordinarily a full-time administrator. In any case, the principal is the executive officer of the school, and thus a line officer.

In the larger school districts and in larger schools a wide variety of assistants to superintendents and principals are employed. For our purposes we shall classify them as staff officers. In addition, a great many directors, such as the director of federal projects or the director of special education, are employed. Again, we would classify them as staff officers. A precise count of staff officers in the schools of the country is not available, but estimates suggest that staff personnel may number 45,000 to 50,000. In all, some 150,000 school administrators work in the school districts of the nation. In addition, at least one-tenth that number work in the nonpublic schools of the country. There are, too, many other posts, in government and business particularly, where persons are called upon to direct or supervise educational programs. While our focus will be on the work of school superintendents and school principals—those we designated as line officers in the schools and school districts—much of what we have to say also applies to other administrative positions.

Functions   To reiterate the point we made in Chapter 1, the basic purpose of administration is to enhance teaching and learning. We also suggested in Chapter 1 six distinct functions that administrators should perform if they are to fulfill their purpose. Those functions, it will be recalled, had to do with school goals, program development, establishment and coordination of the organization, management of resources, representation to community groups, and the appraisal of both the processes and the outcomes of the organization. The work of superintendents and principals is to implement these functions.

The effort required to implement each of the six functions varies according to position. For instance, the superintendent has system-wide interests, while principals are mainly concerned with single schools. Superintendents also devote more time and energy to the procurement and management of resources than do principals. On the other hand, principals might spend more time and energy on program development than the superintendent. Other variables can also contribute to these differences. For instance, in some urban schools, neighborhood gangs call for principals to pay more attention to community groups than is required in communities where no such gangs exist.

In Chapter 1 we took exception to those who define the principal's role as merely the instructional leader. At the same time, we stress the importance of the function to the development and supervision of instructional programs. These programs are of two kinds: (1) those that concern direct and formal instruction, whether in reading, mathematics, or one of the other content areas; and (2) those that can be called aspects of the school regimen. In the latter type are the relationships between students and faculty; between the principal and students; between the school and parents and other adults in the community; the relationships among students, and the relationships among the faculty. In all of these relationships the principal is concerned with the values and attitudes that are exemplified—courtesy, openness, fairness. In short, is the school a decent place in which to live and learn?

To be more specific, Goodlad has recently lamented the fact that in many schools the only role models seem to be athletes.[3] Many schools seem to lack any intellectual climate, and even bright students find it does not pay to be too smart. We suspect that in a school where little or no value is placed on intellectual achievement no amount of formal instruction can overcome the pervading atmosphere. For our purposes the pervading atmosphere of a school is seen as part of the school regimen.

No other person can do as much as school principals to establish the quality of the school regimen. By the very nature of the job they have responsibility for the school. To exercise that responsibility they must be in communication with faculty, with students, with parents, and with other adults in the community. They need help from all of these groups, but it is principals who must give the leadership necessary to help them coalesce around some working principles. Implementation of common objectives can determine the regimen or atmosphere of the school as a social system. Let us move now from what administrators should do to a consideration of what they actually do.

CHARACTERISTICS OF ADMINISTRATIVE WORK

Describing what administrators really do is not as easy as it sounds. In the first place, there have been relatively few observation studies of administrators. Second, even if there were more studies, observation of the overt behavior of administrators is subject to a number of limitations. For one thing, it remains with the observer to say what the behaviors mean. Moreover, much behavior, particularly the conceptual and judgmental aspects, may not be revealed in overt actions. Thus, descriptions of administrative behavior are often based on self-reports or the perceptions of others who work with administrators. While all of these approaches have their limitations, we shall make use of them and convey the most valid picture possible of administrative work. Again, we shall deal with superintendents and principals since the best data we have focuses on these two positions.

As noted in Chapter 1, Mintzberg[4] provided a breakthrough in the study of administration by describing the work on the basis of direct observation. It should be noted that he used only five cases, one of which was a superintendent of schools. Mintzberg was clearly operating on the assumption that administrative work has much in common, regardless of setting. This is an assumption that has to be examined, and for that reason we will not rely solely upon Mintzberg in this discussion. His findings will be supplemented with other studies of superintendents and principals. Before leaving Mintzberg, however, let us note the characteristics he ascribed to administrative work. He concluded, among other things, that managerial work goes on at an unrelenting pace; that activity is brief and fragmentary; that live action is preferred over paperwork, and that much reliance is placed on verbal communication.[5] These conclusions are suggestive descriptions of the work of school administrators, and we shall return to them in later discussion.

Self-Reports   As a continuation of past efforts, the National Association of Elementary School Principals recently published *The Elementary School Principalship in 1978: A Research Study.*[6] The report contains much information about the principals' responsibilities and relatively less about what principals actually do. Indeed, one has to try to infer from the information given. In one part principals reported their serious problems, a compilation that is revealing. Dismissing incompetent staff headed the list and was considered serious by 54 percent of the principals. Next in order were managing student behavior (52.9 percent); declining enrollment (50.5 percent); staff reductions (44.7 percent); vandalism (43.8 percent); pupil absenteeism (43.2 percent); and pupil disregard for authority (41.9 percent).[7] While we have to assume that principals work on these serious problems, we question that principals spend much time on dismissing incompetent staff, for instance, since few principals dismiss staff.

In 1978, the National Association of Secondary School Principals completed a three-volume study of *The Senior High School Principalship.* We shall refer here specifically to volume 2, *The Effective Principal,* of that study.[8] From a total survey population of 1,600 principals, 60 "effective" ones were identified and interviewed by members of the research team. Among other things, principals were asked to indicate how they planned to spend their time and how they actually spent it over a two-week period. The data are shown in Table 4–1.

Note that the numbers represent rankings of time spent—that is, principals planned to spend most time in program development, but actually spent most time in personnel.

These rankings, useful as they are, have two limitations. First, as is true with all sets of categories, many tasks or activities can be masked under the major headings. In this case the problem has been mediated to some extent by the parenthetical explanations. The second limitation concerns rankings themselves: we do not know how much time is represented by each. For instance, we

Area of activity	Time planned (biweekly)	Time spent (biweekly)	TABLE 4–1 Principals' planned time and time spent
Program Development (curriculum, instructional leadership)	1	3	
Personnel (evaluation, advising, conferencing, recruiting)	2	1	
School Management (weekly calendar, office, budget, correspondence, memos, etc.)	3	2	
Student Activities (meetings, supervision, planning)	4	4	
District Office (meetings, task forces, reports, etc.)	5	5	
Community (PTA, advisory groups, parent conferences)	6	6	
Planning (annual, long-range)	7	7	
Professional Development (reading, conferences, etc.)	8	8	
Student Behavior (discipline, attendance, meetings)	9	9	

Source: R.A. Gorton and K.E. McIntyre, *The Effective Principal,* vol. 2, *The Senior High School Principalship* (Reston, Va.: National Association of Secondary School Principals, 1978). Used by permission of the NASSP.

cannot tell whether time spent on personnel activities was twenty hours or sixty hours for the two-week period. Even with these limitations, however, the table gives us some indication of what effective senior high school principals actually do.

In another recent study Ogawa[9] interviewed twenty superintendents regarding the tasks they perform. His conclusions:

The analysis of superintendents' descriptions of the day-to-day tasks they perform resulted in the identification of one major theme. Superintendents interact and communicate with staff members, members of boards of education, various elements in their communities, and state and federal agencies. This communication is largely characterized by: face-to-face contact, a two-way flow of information, and a tendency to communicate with socially and politically defined categories of participants (e.g., individuals who rank highest in organizational and political hierarchies, representatives of community and professional groups, parents).[10]

There can be no doubt that superintendents spend a great deal of their time and energy in interacting and communicating with other people, both in and out of the organization. This confirms Mintzberg's finding about the preference managers have for verbal communication. Communication, however, is a very broad concept and does not tell us specifically enough what it is that superintendents do.

Willower and Fraser conducted telephone interviews with fifty school superintendents in Pennsylvania, focusing on how they felt about their work. They summarized their findings as follows:

> The empirical picture that emerged from the interviews was of 50 individuals dealing with a range of problems, irked by the paper work demands of governmental agencies, feeling uneasy about not being closer to instruction and the classrooms but proud of their accomplishments in that realm, caught up in the specifics of their work and viewing it through particularistic lenses, and feeling the pressures of the job but ready to do it over again if they could. Finally, it seems to us that school superintendents are not quite as beleaguered as is sometimes claimed and when they are, they appear to have come to grips with it rather well, often with good humor.[11]

As intended, Willower and Fraser did ascertain how superintendents feel about their work. For our purposes, what superintendents actually do must be inferred from the data. It seems clear that superintendents process a good bit of paper work; that they give attention to ways of improving instruction; that they feel pressures from many groups; and that they are faced with many problems. Despite these job demands, most like their work.

Combined Self-Reports and Observations

In 1975 the Montgomery County (Maryland) Public Schools did a complex study of principals.[12] Three types of data were collected: (1) observations of the activities during the working day of a randon sample of 50 principals, (2) logs of school-related activities performed outside the regular school day by 179 principals, and (3) surveys filled out by 155 principals providing estimates of time spent on various duties. The categories used in the study are shown below:

> *Management*
> Executives (setting priorities, developing local school policies and communicating such policies to students, parents, and staff)
> Student body (interacting with students, maintaining attendance records, reviewing and approving referrals to Pupil Services, and contacting parents)
> Personnel (selecting staff, resolving staff problems, making assignments, and supervising)
> Facilities and Finances (establishing safety procedures, planning capital projects, preparing budgets, and approving school expenditures)

Instructional Leadership
Program development (implementing new programs, discussion of program needs with teachers and planning with faculty)
Program evaluation (directing administration of standardized tests and conducting Middle States evaluation for accreditation)
Staff evaluation (carrying out formal evaluation procedures)

Liaison with Schools, Central, and/or Area Offices

Public Relations: School, Community, and Local Agencies

Outside Special Professional Activities

Combination (activities which fall into more than one of the major categories above)

Personal[13]

Some of the more illuminating data from the study are shown in Table 4–2.

While in many areas the differences between the *estimated* percent of time devoted to a task and the *observed* and logged time given to a task are not great, two tendencies deserve our attention. Principals consistently estimated that they spent about twice as much time in instructional leadership as they were observed to spend. Principals consistently also *underestimated* by about 20 percent the amount of time they spent in management. The discrepancy between time estimated and time actually spent on instructional leadership probably stems, at least in part, from a widely accepted professional ethos that principals *ought* to spend their time in instructional leadership; thus, when principals estimated their time allocations, we suspect that they were influenced by this ethos. The differences between estimated and time actually spent on management may be due to a widely ignored fact of life in the profession; namely, that the principals must manage their schools. Particularly, with respect to time allocations for both instructional leadership and management, the Montgomery County data seem to convey the reality of principalship.

Observation Studies

We turn next to studies that are based specifically on the observed behavior of school administrators. In terms of the principalship, perhaps the most notable of these is the work of Wolcott.[14] Wolcott spent a year in one elementary school in the Northwest, where he observed the daily life of the principal, Ed Bell, and his many interactions with faculty, students, and others in his own school, as well as the interactions he had with other professionals in the school system and with parents and others in the community. Wolcott, a former teacher, conducted the study in an ethnographic framework. In addition to observing the life

TABLE 4-2
Principals' estimates of, and research findings on, principals' distribution of time to different areas of responsibility

Percent of time spent in each area of responsibilty

Area of responsibility	Elementary school principals		Middle/junior high school principals		Senior high school principals	
	Percent of time estimated by principals	Percent of time observed and logged	Percent of time estimated by principals	Percent of time observed and logged	Percent of time estimated by principals	Percent of time observed and logged
MANAGEMENT						
Executive	12	14	10	15	12	15
Student Personnel	15	17	16	21	12	20
Personnel	10	7	12	8	13	8
Facilities and Financial	6	6	6	4	8	4
Combination and Other	0	8	0	11	0	8
TOTAL	43	52	44	58	45	54

INSTRUCTIONAL LEADERSHIP

Program Development	14	6	11	7	14	5
Program Evaluation	6	3	6	0	6	1
Staff Evaluation	15	7	17	10	16	5
Other	0	3	0	1	0	1
TOTAL	35	20	34	17	36	12
LIAISON WITH SCHOOLS, AREA AND CENTRAL OFFICES	6	8	8	5	6	7
PUBLIC RELATIONS—SCHOOLS, COMMUNITY, GOV'T AGENCIES	12	12	10	12	8	17
OUTSIDE PROFESSIONAL ACTIVITIES	4	3	5	2	4	6
COMBINATION*	—	2	—	2	—	1
PERSONAL*	—	2	—	3	—	3

*These two categories were not included in data collection instruments for estimates or logs.

Source: Department of Research, *Report of Findings of a Study of the Principalship in Action in the Montgomery County Public Schools* (Rockville Md.: Montgomery County Public Schools, 1975).

of the school and particularly of the principal, Wolcott made use of many bulletins and other documents generated by and for the school, and he interviewed and received questionnaire responses from many of those who worked with the principal. Wolcott divided what the principal did into formal encounters and informal encounters. In terms of formal encounters, Ed Bell broke down an "average" school day as follows[15]:

Prearranged meetings and conferences	26%
Deliberate but not prearranged meetings and conferences	25%
Casual or chance encounters	15%
Telephoning	9%
Talking on intercom	1%
Alone in office	15%
Alone and en route	9%

These data take on more meaning when broken down another way[16]:

Time spent alone	25%
Time spent with others without verbal interaction	6%
Time spent listening to others	35%
Time spent talking to others (giving information, asking questions, giving directions)	36%

The data clearly indicate that the predominant activity of this school principal is his interaction with others. The nature of these interactions is shown more specifically in Table 4–3.

Note that more than 50 percent of the principal's time was spent in interacting with teachers and staff members in the school. About 20 percent of his time was spent interacting with students individually and in groups. The remaining 30 percent of his time, categorized as formal encounters, was allocated among many others, most notably parents, other principals, and central office personnel.

Wolcott suggests that Ed Bell's time was so filled with prearranged meetings and other formal encounters that the time available for informal encounters was limited.[17] Nonetheless, there were many unscheduled demands on his time. A number of these were organized under the headings of receiving requests and handling problems; orienting and greeting; and taking care of the building. One of Wolcott's comments throws further light on these matters:

A principal who cannot cope effectively with the range of strangely diversified demands described here would be ill-suited to the principalship. Some principals become meticulous about and obsessed with the details of running a school. Ed's response was to try to elude some details on the assumption that pressing problems would catch up with him eventually. As this and pre-

TABLE 4–3

Who the principal interacts with during an average school day, 8:00 A.M.–5:00 P.M., based on all instances of interactions recorded during a sample of 12 two-hour periods of observation during a two-week period

Category	Numbers of instances when interaction was recorded (6-second intervals)	Percent of total time spent interacting with each category
Teachers, individually	187	16.3
Teachers, collectively (Subtotal, all interactions with teachers, 22.1%)	67	5.8
Counsellor	146	12.7
Other professional staff	81	7.1
Secretary	49	4.3
Other non-professional staff (Subtotal, interactions with teachers plus all other staff, 50.4%)	48	4.2
Pupils, individually	160	14.0
Pupils, small groups	46	4.0
Pupils, entire class or school (Subtotal, all interactions with pupils, 19.3%)	15	1.3
Student teachers and cadet teachers	12	1.0
Other principals	89	7.8
Central Office (superintendent or assistant superintendent)	2	.2
Central Office personnel (other than superintendent or assistant superintendent)	70	6.1
Parents	97	8.5
Other adults in community	15	1.3
Others	63	5.5
TOTAL INSTANCES RECORDED	1147	100.1

Source: Harry F. Wolcott, *The Man in the Principal's Office: An Ethnography* (New York: Holt, Rinehart & Winston, 1973).

vious chapters have illustrated, many not-so-pressing problems caught up with him as well. Like his formally scheduled time, his unconstrained time at school was taken up almost totally by demands placed on him by others.[18]

As part of a larger study, Ellett and his associates[19] did a time-motion study of the six principals—three elementary school, two middle school, and one high school—in the Thomas County (Georgia) school system. Six observ-

TABLE 4–4
Total number of
minutes spent by
principals in each
functional area of
responsibility in one
week

| Functional area | PRINCIPALS | | | | | | Grand total |
	A	B	C	D	E	F	
Curriculum and Instruction	19	0	18	253	5	57	352
Staff Personnel	629	369.5	299	411.5	387.5	410.5	2507
Student Personnel	383.5	637	794	311	418	454.5	2998
Support Management	289.5	406	386.5	459	384	401	2326
School-Community Interface	330	109	237	345	61	110	1192
Fiscal Management	23	28.5	25.5	47	146	57	327
System-wide Policies and Operations	25.5	326	68	145	194	249	1007.5
Miscellaneous	424.5	420.5	40	301.5	318.5	245	1750
Unclassified	200	237.5	371	340	277	356	1781.5
TOTALS	2324	2534	2239	2613	2191	2340	14241.0

Source: Chad D. Ellett et al., "A Time Motion Study of Principal Performance," CCBC Notebook 1 (October 1974): 11.

ers, after training by the project staff, collected the data over a period of one week. Time distributions by functional areas of responsibility ascribed to each principal are shown in Table 4–4.

The data raise a number of questions. For instance, why do principals spend so little time in curriculum and instruction? Or, have activities depicting curriculum and instruction been defined too narrowly? Why is there so much variation among principals? No time on curriculum and instruction is ascribed to Principal B and 253 minutes on such activities are ascribed to Principal D. All principals seemed to spend much time on staff personnel, student personnel, and support management. It seems possible that many of those activities may have at least an indirect relationship to curriculum and instruction.

Martin and Willower[20] applied the structured observation technique developed by Mintzberg to the high school principalship. They observed five high school principals at work, each for a period of twenty-five days. Some analysis of the activities observed for all five principals, computed in minutes, is shown in Table 4–5.

Almost half of the principals' time was devoted to meetings, some scheduled and even more unscheduled. In terms of the purposes of these activities, over one-third of the time was devoted to maintenance tasks and about one-

TABLE 4–5
Analysis of task
performance by five
high school principals

Type of activity	Number of activities	Total time	Average duration*	Percentage of time
Unscheduled Meetings	1221	4122	3.4	27.5
Scheduled Meetings	117	2601	22.2	17.3
Desk Work	254	2394	9.4	16.0
Exchanges	1355	1355	1.0	9.0
Tours	88	1158	13.2	7.7
Phone Calls	393	868	2.2	5.8
Monitoring	82	828	10.1	5.5
Personal	133	767	5.8	5.1
Other	87	914	21.4	4.1

*Computed in minutes.

Source: Adapted from W. J. Martin and D. J. Willower, "The Managerial Behavior of High School Principals," *Education Administration Quarterly* 17 (Winter 1981): 72.

sixth to the academic program. Pupil control tasks demanded about one-quarter of the principals' time. The authors compared their findings with Mintzberg's characterization of administrative work as follows:

> The principals engaged in a large number of activities and they performed their work at a rapid pace. The types of tasks they performed were many and varied, and interruptions were frequent. Most of the principals' activities involved verbal communication, but unlike Mintzberg's managers, most of the principals' contacts occurred with organizational insiders. The principals demonstrated an affinity for the livelier action aspects of their role. Finally, they seemed to exercise a firmer command of their role performance than did the five managers Mintzberg observed.[21]

In another study, Pitner[22] observed the activities of three suburban superintendents, each for a period of five days. She also conducted interviews with the superintendents. She saw the superintendents essentially as managers of information, finding that they spent about 80 percent of their time in verbal contact with others. Five types of information were processed: technical information, legal rules and regulations, past activities of the district, the preferences of people in and outside the school system, and the probable reactions of different constituencies to decisions and conditions. The superintendents' activities proved to be largely desk work, phone calls, and scheduled and unscheduled meetings.

Feilders[23] examined in depth the activities of one urban superintendent, Robert Alioto of San Francisco. For three days each week over a ten-week period Feilders shadowed the superintendent. Attention was given to where he spent his time, with whom, at whose initiative, and at what time. The study focused not only on the superintendent's manifest behavior, but on his thoughts, feelings, and intentions. The most obvious features of the superintendent's job were that the work week was long; he spent most of his time in the office meeting with staff members for brief periods of time; he initiated less than half of his activities; face-to-face communication was the main medium of interaction; discussion usually centered on personnel issues; and the main purpose of his activities was to process information.

Implications   What do these studies show us? Can we now characterize administrative work more accurately than we could before? Three problems keep us from answering these questions as well as we would like to. First, each study employs its own .approach or framework; hence comparisons across studies are difficult. Pitner, for instance, interpreted her data largely in terms of information theory. Little wonder she found the superintendent to be a manager of information. Second, most of the studies of groups of principals dealt with how they ranked issues facing them, rather than what they did. Third, the observation studies, while more useful, were built around observations of one or a few administrators; hence one must be cautious about generalizing from them.

Keeping these limitations in mind, let us examine to what extent Mintzberg's characterization of administrative work is confirmed in the studies. As to unrelenting pace, there is little direct evidence. There are indications in the Ellett study that principals work long hours and have many demands on their time. Ogawa also found that superintendents worked long hours. Feilders found the superintendent he studied subject to many demands. Except for Martin and Willower, it may be that those who did the studies did not employ unrelenting pace as one of their concepts; hence they did not find it. Or, perhaps unrelenting pace is another way of saying that administration is arduous and seems to demand long hours. This the studies did find.

Mintzberg characterized administrative activity as brief and fragmentary. The studies offer some confirmation of this. Feilders, for instance, found that the superintendent's day tended to be filled with many brief conferences in his office. Wolcott also characterized the informal encounters of the principal, particularly, as representing a wide range of demands. Martin and Willower provide direct confirmation of this point. The Montgomery County study also lends credance to this notion, particularly with the discovery that the outside world makes many demands upon the principal's management of the school.

The preference for live action suggested by Mintzberg also gets some support from the school studies. Particularly in the Wolcott and the Martin and Willower studies does the extensive interaction of the principal with other people confirm this. The other school studies imply that administrators prefer live action but that concept does not appear to have been examined explicitly in those studies.

There is no question about the preference for verbal media, another Mintzberg characterization. Feilders speaks of the face-to-face communication employed by his superintendent. Pitner concludes that a large amount of the information given by the superintendent is in verbal form. Ogawa, Wolcott, and Martin and Willower also note the important place that verbal interaction has in the life of their administrators.

Another way of viewing an administrator's work is from the standpoint of role. A role can be defined as a set of behaviors associated with an office or position. Mintzberg[24] has suggested that administrators play ten different roles. He categorizes these under three major headings:

ROLES OF ADMINISTRATORS

> Interpersonal roles
>> Figurehead
>> Leader
>> Liaison
> Information roles
>> Monitor
>> Disseminator
>> Spokesman
> Decision roles
>> Entrepreneur (promotes change)
>> Disturbance handler
>> Resource allocator
>> Negotiator

Using Mintzberg's characterization for comparison, let us again examine self-report and observation studies of school administrators to determine what they say about roles. The Pharis and Zakariya[25] study of elementary school principals, discussed earlier in the chapter, permits some inferences. Recall that the respondents listed among their most serious problems dismissing incompetent staff, managing student behavior, staff reductions, and evaluating teachers. Assuming that principals work at these problems, we can see that in each case the principal is called upon to serve as a decision maker. Mintzberg also emphasizes the administrator's decision-making role, though without adequate coverage of the actual activities and processes involved.

Self-Reports

Again, in the data on effective secondary school principals in Table 4–1, we can draw some inferences about roles. For instance, listed under Program Development is instructional leadership. Under personnel, evaluation is listed, suggesting the principal as a decision maker. The activities listed in the Community heading suggest that the principal is frequently called upon to perform as information disseminator and spokesperson.

The categories developed in the Montgomery County study also imply something about the roles played by the principals. For instance, under Management, Executive, setting priorities is mentioned. This would seem to suggest an exercise of the decision-making role, particularly as a resource allocator. Another example of the resource allocator role is found in the task of approving school expenditures under Facilities and Finances. The decision-making role is also suggested under Management, Personnel, in the selection of staff and in their assignment. Resolving staff problems, another item under Management, Personnel, also seems to cast the principal into the decision-making role, in this case as a negotiator. Two of the major categories in the study, liaison with schools and public relations, imply that the principal plays the role of communicator as well as information giver (and receiver).

In the Ogawa study discussed above, the roles of the superintendents were given explicit attention. In his study, Ogawa has this to say:

> The subsequent analysis of superintendents' descriptions of their work responsibilities identified three general occupational roles, coordinator, mediator, and resource manager. As coordinators, superintendents work to adjust the various parts of their school systems and environments to produce harmonious action. While the mediative role calls for them to conciliate between the various elements of the school system and its environment to develop a consistent position or view among these varied elements. Finally, as resource managers, superintendents acquire the resources necessary to operate a school system, staff and money, and allocate these resources throughout their school systems.[26]

The roles of mediator and resource manager seem to fit nicely under Mintzberg's decision maker roles. The role of coordinator, while it does not fit as neatly, probably suggests the combination of communicator, information giver and decision maker roles. Again, we have the problem of different terminology used by the two students of administrative behavior, one using a more detailed breakdown than the other.

Observation Studies   We turn next to the observation studies of administrators to see what they may imply about roles. Pitner[27] did her study of superintendents within the framework of information theory, and she found the superintendent to be a manager of information. The information role is one of the major role categories projected by Mintzberg and to that extent Pitner confirms the Mintzberg formulation. We can only guess what Pitner might have found had she chosen to collect data on the interpersonal and decision-making roles of the superintendent. We have a clear example of how a framework both enhances and limits a study. The information theory framework permitted a more explicit analysis of the Pitner data but the focus on information tended to ignore other aspects of the superintendents' behavior.

The Feilders[28] study dealt less with the roles of the superintendent and more with the tasks that were actually performed. Feilders does suggest that the purpose of the superintendent's activities was to process information. Feilders goes on to say that the predominant role of the superintendent was that of spokesperson for the administration, again emphasizing the information role of the superintendent. The study has little to say about the interpersonal and decision-making roles of the superintendent.

Turning to the Wolcott[29] study we find some of the same limitations. Wolcott was intent on describing what the elementary principal did; he was not explicitly concerned with ascribing roles to the principal. However, from the Wolcott data we can deduce a number of roles played by the principal. For instance, in the great amount of time spent by the principal in interacting with faculty, staff, students, and parents, the principal must have been called upon to play (extensively) the interpersonal role. In like manner, these contacts suggest the importance of the information giving role. By implication we have evidence in Wolcott that the principal also plays the decision-making role.

Wolcott suggests that "school principals serve their institutions and their society as monitors for continuity."[30] To provide the stabilizing effect of continuity Wolcott thinks that principals frequently engage in the rhetoric of change more than in change itself. If this is so, and we suspect it is, the role clearly implies that many decisions must be made, some of which may be difficult to rationalize to others. Wolcott also contends that the latent function of many meetings is really that of validating existing status hierarchies in the school system.[31] This conclusion implies that meetings help establish the principal as one who has the right to make decisions. Thus, the Mintzberg formulation regarding the decision-making role has further support.

Martin and Willower had difficulty in ascertaining the extent to which the five high school principals in their study exhibited the role behaviors suggested by Mintzberg. They said: "The fact that Mintzberg's roles are less clear cut than his characterization of work makes the applications of the roles to the principalship a rather imprecise exercise. Moreover, the fact that principals were not chief administrators as were Mintzberg's managers further complicates matters."[32]

Implications

Overall, neither the self-report nor the observation studies of school administrators provide substantial evidence of the roles that Mintzberg ascribed to managers. In both types of studies the emphasis was more on what administrators did than on what these activities may have meant in terms of roles. Indeed, in the self-report studies we frequently had to infer from lists of problems what it was that administrators did. In two of the observation studies, the specific frameworks used limited the significance ascribed to observed behavior. In the third study the focus was so completely on describing what the principal did that less attention was given to the meaning of such activities. Perhaps, as Martin and Willower suggest, Mintzberg's role categories are too imprecise to permit a useful comparison of conclusions with those of others.

STRESSES AND STRAINS

The data presented above support the common observation that administration is a stressful occupation. Administrators are not only required to make decisions themselves; they are also in charge of the decision-making process. It is often more difficult to appropriately involve others in decision making than it is to make a unilateral decision. Either way, decisions are influenced by facts and in that sense are rational. However, decisions are also influenced by the values of the people and groups involved and may at times seem quite irrational. The values of those participating in the decision-making process are frequently affected by their own self-interests. Consciously or unconsciously, people perceive the organization from their own perspective. Thus, even when there is agreement on the facts pertinent to a decision, the meaning of those facts or the consequences of taking one course of action or another is open to interpretation. It is in this welter of human behavior that school administrators must make decisions and such a decision-making role is stressful. The processes and stresses of decision making are discussed further in Chapter 6.

Differential Expectations

The stressful nature of school administration becomes even more apparent when we note that administrators are nearly always in the "middle." Put otherwise, there are many expectations held for them. For instance, the board of education has one or more sets of expectations for superintendents; school principals have one or more sets of expectations for superintendents, teachers have one or more expectations for superintendents. Parents or groups of parents have expectations for superintendents as well. Community business leaders may have still another set of expectations for superintendents. It is clear that superintendents cannot completely fulfill the differential expectations of all these groups.

Likewise, school principals have at least four major reference groups: the teachers, the students, the parents, and the central office. Teachers expect the principal to be interested in what they do in their classroom instruction. Students, on the other hand, expect the principal to be interested in them as individuals and available to them if someone tries to abridge playground rights or cause other troubles. Custodians expect the principal to manage the school in such fashion that teachers and students are orderly and do not leave messes to be cleaned up. The supervisors from the central office expect the principal to conform with district policies in the organization of the instructional program and in other areas.

These differential expectations sometimes run counter to one another. Administrations must strive to reconcile them and in so doing bring their own expectations to bear on each situation. In the struggle to find a resolution to these differential expectations administrators may experience considerable stress.[33]

One of the more insightful treatments of the sources of conflict (and thus stress) in organizations has been presented by Getzels and his colleagues.[34] Noted in that study are conflicts between cultural values and institutional expectations, role expectations and personality dispositions, between roles and within roles, conflicts arising from personality discorders, and conflicts arising from the perceptions of role expectations.

Let us deal more explicitly with one of these: the possible conflict between professional expectations and personal dispositions. For the school administrator this may involve the choice between pursuing an advanced training program (professional expectation) and the desire to spend extended periods of time with the family during the summer (personal disposition). Perhaps even more common is the conflict between the long hours of the administrator's job and expectations of spouse and children that he or she be a participant in family activities.

Still another source of stress to the administrator is time management. Those who are new to administrative positions are quickly struck with how much others determine their agendas. Ed Bell, the principal in Wolcott's study, found himself acting in response to many persons and groups. The San Francisco superintendent described by Feilders spent most of his day in his office engaged in short conferences with a wide array of individuals. These observations of school administrators find confirmation in the work of Mintzberg, who ascribed to the managerial work a network of contacts between the organization and its environment. Mintzberg also calls specific attention to interpersonal and informational roles, both requiring considerable interaction with others. Clearly, any one who heads a school or a school district can expect many persons both in and out of the organization to request or demand some of his or her time.

Agenda Conflict

These time demands create stress for administrators in at least two respects. First, if every request for time is met, administrators may have no time left for anything else. Indeed, they may not even have time enough to become acquainted with the nature of the requests submitted. Even more serious, when others usurp all or most of administrators' time, they have no time to determine what their own agendas ought to be, or to initiate conferences with the appropriate persons concerning these agendas. The stress for administrators resides in the conflict between a wish to be open and available and the necessity to have some time to think and project courses of action.

Second, some petitioners are more articulate and persistent than others. Those who are more persistent will probably get on the administrator's calendar most often. Those who are more articulate may make more persuasive arguments for the positions they represent. Those who are both persistent and articulate could be in a position of exercising great influence over the administator. But there is not necessarily any relationship between a petitioners' persistence and persuasiveness and the merit of the position espoused. The stress for the administrator comes from the conflict between the strength of petitioners' arguments and the feeling that there are other aspects of the issues under consideration for which there has been no time for exploration. While there may be no way of eliminating the stress resulting from the conflict between a desire to be available and the need for time to think, every administrator must work out ways of exercising control over his or her time. We give more attention to this problem in Chapter 9.

A National Study   Concern with the stress of administration prompted Koff and his associates[35] to examine the matter empirically. They sent a pretested questionnaire to a national sample of 2,400 elementary and secondary school principals. On the basis of 1,291 responses they drew some interesting conclusions. Principals in the study thought that events associated with conflict between teachers and administrators—forced resignations, unsatisfactory performance of teachers, refusal to follow policies, and the like—were most stressful. This confirms for a larger population what Wolcott found for one principal. Threats to security and status, such as the unrelenting demands of the job, lack of time, and the threat of unexpected occurances, were also seen as stressful in the Koff study. The elementary school principals seemed to feel more stress than secondary principals. An explanation for this finding may be that elementary schools tend to be smaller than secondary schools and thus elementary principals must deal more directly with teachers and other personnel. In one area, student conflict, secondary principals reported more stress than did elementary principals, a finding that seems to confirm ordinary observation.

REWARDS   Why would anyone want to be a school administrator? Indeed, as we review the characteristics of administrative work, as we note the complex roles administrators are expected to play, and as we suggest the stresses often encountered, one might conclude that few people would wish to. But the facts are quite otherwise: many teachers and other school workers wish to be administrators. Some of these may not initially understand the requirements of the role and they may be unduly enamored with its attractions. There are nonetheless, for at least some people, certain rewards in administrative work.

A Challenge   To begin with, an administrative post nearly always offers challenges. One challenge is frequently that of purpose or direction. If the school or school district has been having trouble or merely marking time, a new administrator might be able to marshal support for a new direction or a more definitive purpose. To be sure, the new administrator may not fully understand why the organization seems to be faltering; that teachers no longer feel challenged, for instance, or that for years factors other than competence have influenced appointments, or the reluctance of the controlling board to approve and finance new programs. Even if the new administrator is aware of the problems, he or she may feel that they can at least be mediated and that the opportunity to work at such mediation is attractive.

A related challenge to a school administrator is one of motivating organizational members to accept and perform organizational tasks and allowing the fulfillment of personal needs at the same time. For instance, assigning a teacher to a school near his or her residence may be an important consideration. Reviewing alternative teaching assignments with a teacher before their final determination could also be important. The challenge to the new administrator is one of keeping each person in the organization a willing participant in its programs.

Another reward in administration has to do with such things as power, prestige, and influence. Power (or authority), as Getzels has noted, may be vested or entrusted. Vested power is power derived from the office. Principals and superintendents, for instance, have some power by virtue of the positions they hold. Entrusted power, on the other hand, must be earned. When administrators demonstrate knowledgeability, fairness, decision-making skill, and consideration for people additional power accrues to them. New administrators who try to rely entirely on vested power are probably in for some rude shocks. On the other hand, administrators who go to the other extreme and try to be just good old boys or girls—who ignore the power of office—may also be in line for some shocks.

Power, Influence, and Prestige

The power of the administrator is a much more complex phenomenon than many ascribe to it. Prospective administrators who seek power for power's sake or for their own personal gratification will probably encounter great difficulty in the administrative role. At the same time, we suggest that only those who are willing to exercise some power and who get satisfaction from doing so should accept administrative posts. The exercise of power, not for personal satisfaction but for organizational goals, can bring great rewards in administrative work.

Influence can be defined as the exercise of power, and many administrators are called upon by their positions to exercise influence. A superintendent, for instance, is generally expected to make recommendations to the board of education. A school principal is in a position to make recommendations to the faculty. If school boards or school faculties find these recommendations supportable and if they suggest action that might not be taken otherwise, their acceptance and implementation suggest that the administrator has been influential. The potential for this kind of influence is present in many administrative positions and this, too, can be a reward in administration.

The appropriate exercise of power ordinarily brings some prestige with it. Wolcott reported of Ed Bell, for instance, that "in the principalship he finds a way to achieve prestige, acceptance, and sufficient ego-gratification to see him through the myriad problems incumbent upon that office."[37]

Prestige is a psychological phenomenon; it exists only when people think it exists. Many people who accept administrative posts, however, think of the appointments as prestigious and many members of the organizations do also. Thus, those who aspire after the prestige can find it in administrative office.

Compensation   Still another reward in administration is financial compensation. In most school districts superintendents, principals, and other administrative officers are paid higher salaries than are teachers. In one city school district in a Rocky Mountain state, for instance, teachers' salaries in a recent year ranged from $11,720 to $24,205 per year. In that same district principals' salaries ranged from $21,353 to $34,156. The superintendent was paid $48,000 per year. It is well to note, however, that teachers had work obligations for nine months while administrators had work obligations for eleven or twelve months. Thus, if prorated, administrative salaries may not exceed teaching salaries on a monthly basis. For most administrators, however, the prospect of longer employment each year and compensation for the additional time is an attraction; whereas many teachers find it necessary to hold a second job, fewer administrators must do so.

Accomplishment   Still another source of satisfaction to administrators is the feeling that they can get things done. Administrators are generally people of action and they find satisfaction in coordinating the work of an organization in such a way that there is accomplishment. As noted earlier, Mintzberg found that administrators had a proclivity for action. He expressed this tendency in such characterizations as "work at an unrelenting pace"; "activity characterized by brevity, variety, and fragmentation"; and "preference for live action."[38] When Ogawa questioned superintendents about what provided them satisfaction they "identified tangible indicators of progress such as the construction of new buildings, the passage of a tax issue and the development of a new curriculum component."[39]

This is not to suggest that school administrators *always* enjoy a feeling of accomplishment. Indeed their influence is limited. Many times administrators find lack of readiness on the part of the staff, objection on the part of the electorate, or lack of money that prevent any action. All schools and school districts make many operating decisions, from the adoption of particular courses of study, the employment of staff, the alignment of attendance areas, and the reconditioning of buildings, to the allocation of resources through the budget process. At times these decisions are rather mundane and repetitive, but sometimes challenging new directions are involved.

In any case, superintendents, principals, and other administrative personnel are charged with making a decision-making process work. Many groups are involved, data must be collected and organized, some assessment of the values and dispositions of those affected must be made, long-range implications must be considered, recommendations must be formulated, and implementation plans must be developed. All of these activities can find fruition with the approval of a faculty, action by a board of education, or by vote of the electorate. With such approval the administrator can shift the focus from planning to implementation. For most administrators this process is rewarding.

Achievement of   Finally, administrators often find reward in fostering the achievement of others.
Others   Administrators, unless they are also part-time teachers, do not deal directly with

the formal instruction of students in the classroom. In the end, it is the students who achieve: who become better readers, who develop respect for American traditions, and who learn to examine evidence surrounding public issues. It is the students who achieve in the arts, in the sciences, in athletics, and in other activities. Administrators may have much to do, however, with the daily regimen which establishes the tone or atmosphere of the school. Administrators can also do much to see that competent teachers are available to students and that the school environment is one that encourages learning. Even though administrators contribute to student achievement in an indirect way, they can and should find satisfaction in this achievement because their contributions can be quite substantial.

Administrators can also find satisfaction in teachers' achievement. Again, most of the contributions administrators make toward teacher achievement are indirect. To be sure, some administrators help teachers with instructional procedures or classroom management. Most of the time, however, teachers are on their own. Moreover, teacher achievement, like student achievement, comes chiefly from internal motivation and not from external supervision.

A new teacher may be starry-eyed, not quite sure how to adapt content to the level of the young, and somewhat uncertain about student control. This same teacher, over a period of years, develops a sense of reality, learns what interests young minds, and recognizes that student control resides in the activities of the classroom. The teacher may have approached his or her first meeting with parents with great trepidation. In time, however, the teacher sees a meeting with parents as an opportunity for sharing the reasons behind many classroom procedures, and eliciting appropriate cooperation from parents in the development of their children. Developments such as these are achievements that can and should bring satisfaction to the school principal.

In addition, teachers are sometimes called upon to fill specialized roles. These may be temporary assignments such as a year's leave to help in the development of curriculum materials or long-term promotions to supervisory or administrative positions. In any case, the administrator—most often the principal—is in the position to recognize the qualities needed for the new role, and to recommend those best qualified. Recognition of potential and encouragement of greater service in the organization can and should bring satisfaction to the administrator.

SUMMARY

The chapter began with a survey of administrative positions found in schools and school districts. We noted that about 150,000 persons work in a wide range of administrative positions in the public and nonpublic schools of the nation, most of them in the public schools. For the remainder of the chapter we focused on principals and superintendents as the line officers in schools and school districts. We held that principals and superintendents should recognize that their chief reason for being is to enhance teaching and learning. The implementation of this broad objective can be achieved through direct instruction and through the daily regimen of the school. We noted the key role of the principal in creating a tone or atmosphere for the school.

With this background we then turned to a description of administrative work. Taking off from Mintzberg's work, we examined a number of studies dealing with both self-reports and observations to determine just what it is that administrators do. We had some difficulty in interpreting the school studies since many of them dealt with the problems encountered by administrators rather than descriptions of what administrators do. Even so, there seems to be considerable evidence that administrative work in schools can be characterized as follows: brief and fragmentary, reflecting a preference for live action, and relying heavily on verbal communication. These characteristics generally conform with the description set forth by Mintzberg.

Next we examined the same studies with respect to the roles that school administrators play. Here we had more difficulty in comparing their results with Mintzberg's formulations. While most of the school studies had not been designed to collect data about roles pursued, there was some evidence to indicate that school administrators perform the interpersonal, informational, and decision-making roles suggested by Mintzberg.

School administrators do work in stressful situations. Most stressful to principals is their relationships with teachers and the evaluation of teaching performance. Superintendents, while acknowledging stress from the pressure of many groups, seem to accept such stress as part of the job. Most superintendents, if they had it to do over, would choose superintendency again. These administrators gain substantial rewards from administrative work, including meeting challenges, prestige and influence, getting things done, higher salaries, and contributing to the achievement of students and teachers.

ENDNOTES

1. National Center for Educational Statistics, *The Condition of Education, 1979* (Washington, DC: U.S. Government Printing Office, 1979), p. 78.
2. Bureau of the Census, *Statistical Abstract of the United States* (Washington, D.C.: U.S. Government Printing Office, 1979), p. 134.
3. John I. Goodlad et al., "An Overview of 'A Study of Schooling'," *Phi Delta Kappan* 61 (November 1979): 174–178.
4. Henry Mintzberg, *The Nature of Managerial Work* (New York: Harper & Row, 1973).
5. Mintzberg, *Managerial Work*.
6. William L. Pharis and Sally Banks Zakariya, *The Elementary School Principalship in 1978: A Research Study* (Arlington, Va.: National Association of Elementary Principals, 1979).
7. Pharis and Zakariya, *Elementary School Principalship*.
8. Richard A. Gorton and Kenneth E. McIntyre, *The Senior High School Principalship*, vol. 2, *The Effective Principal* (Reston, Va.: National Association of Secondary School Principals, 1978).
9. Rodney T. Ogawa, "A Descriptive Investigation of the Occupational Ethos of School Superintendents" (Ph.D. dissertation, Ohio State University, 1979).
10. Ogawa, "A Descriptive Investigation."
11. Donald J. Willower and Hugh W. Fraser, "School Superintendents, Their Work," *Administrators Notebook 20* (1979–1980):4.

12. Department of Research, *Report of Findings of a Study of the Principalship in Action in the Montgomery County Public Schools* (Rockville, Md.: Montgomery County Public Schools, 1975).

13. Department of Research, *Report of Findings*.

14. Harry F. Wolcott, *The Man in the Principal's Office: An Ethnography* (New York: Holt, Rinehart & Winston, 1973).

15. Wolcott, *The Man*.

16. Wolcott, *The Man*.

17. Wolcott, *The Man*.

18. Wolcott, *The Man*.

19. Chad D. Ellett et al., "A Time Motion Study of Principal Performance," *CCBC Notebook* 1 (October 1974): 8–13.

20. William J. Martin and Donald J. Willower, "The Managerial Behavior of High School Principals," *Educational Administration Quarterly* 17(Winter 1981): 69–90.

21. Martin and Willower, "Managerial Behavior," p. 86.

22. Nancy J. Pitner, "Descriptive Study of the Everyday Activities of Suburban School Superintendents" (Ph.D. dissertation, Ohio State University, 1978).

23. John F. Feilders, "Action and Reaction: The Job of an Urban Superintendent" (Ph.D. dissertation, Stanford University, 1978).

24. Mintzberg, *Managerial Work*, Ch. 4.

25. Pharis and Zakariya, "Elementary School Principalship," p. 97.

26. Ogawa, "Descriptive Investigation," p. 185.

27. Pitner, "Descriptive Study."

28. Feilders, "Action and Reaction."

29. Wolcott, *The Man*.

30. Wolcott, *The Man*, p. 321.

31. Wolcott, *The Man*, p. 122.

32. Martin and Willower, "Managerial Behavior," p. 87.

33. It is interesting to note that Ed Bell (Wolcott, *The Man*, p. 273) found that the evaluation of teachers was the thing that most clearly set him apart from his teachers and challenged him with difficult decisions. Without the insistence of the central office, Ed probably would have foregone any formal evaluation of teachers.

34. J.W. Getzels et al., *Educational Administration as a Social Process* (New York: Harper & Row, 1968), Ch. 5.

35. Robert Koff et al., "Stress and the School Administration," *Administrator's Notebook* 28(1979–80): 9.

36. Getzels et al., *Educational Administration*, p. 135.

37. Wolcott, *The Man*, p. 65.

38. Mintzberg, *Managerial Work*, Ch. 3.

39. Ogawa, "Descriptive Investigation," p. 211.

CHAPTER 5

THE ADMINISTRATOR
AS A PERSON

In Chapter 1, we mentioned some ways in which the personal goals and attributes of administrators can distract them from their proper concerns for the school, for the classroom, and for teaching and learning. Obviously, educational administrators are human beings first and it would be foolish to assume that human attributes can or should be eliminated as important determinants of their behavior as administrators. These attributes, however, must be recognized, must be understood, and must be managed so that they contribute to administrators' and school success rather than failure. The recognition, understanding, and management of the human or personal aspects of the administrator are the subjects of this chapter.

The stock in trade of the administrator is human relationships—relationships with individuals and groups from all walks of life and of almost all age ranges; relationships in all kinds of settings from the social and informal to the business and highly formal; relationships in which the topics and the atmosphere are distinctly unpleasant. Consequently, administrators should have an understand-

**IMPACTS UPON
HUMAN BEHAVIOR**

93

ing of the psychological bases of human behavior and should be aware of factors that influence it. Every situation, every relationship involves conditions within a person and conditions in the person's environment that interact to influence one's behavior. This description of behavior is discussed by Allport as "the field theory of personality."[1] Just as a particle of matter behaves in keeping with both its own mass, density, and electrical charge, and the force fields through which it passes and with which it interacts, so human actions are determined by one's inner being and the enviromental setting at any given time.

It is important to note that this interaction is "open" or "transactional." Both the environment and the person are changed by and changing each other; neither is the same after the interaction. The transaction between an individual's inner and outer worlds is constantly changing both worlds.[2]

These concepts provide a framework for considering human behavior, but they do not provide absolute rules of behavior, as is true in some of the sciences. Neither the "field"—the environment and the situation—nor the "matter"—the administrator—can be controlled as is done in a particle accelerator in physics or in a clinical test in medicine. The importance of this concept in human behavior is that there is a relationship between a person and the world. The variables may be many and yet some ability to predict how an individual and various environments will interact is possible, and the ability to vary environment and to vary behavior based upon such predictions is also possible. In spite of the difficulty in predicting behavior, some efforts have been made to predict the degree to which individual characteristics lead to successful behavior in administrative roles.[3] Our view of the interaction of a person and an environment leads us not to rely too much on the so-called inventory approach to predicting effectiveness; nevertheless, inventories can be of assistance in understanding oneself.

One of the difficulties of teaching administration is the inability to prescribe behavior to suit various situations. Each of us reacts differently in different settings and to different conditions. While a stress situation generally produces similar physiological results in all of us, our behavioral responses to these physiological changes vary greatly. We react differently to stress caused by fear and to stress caused by workload. Some find the former stress exciting and it sharpens their mind, adds keeness to their actions; others are immobilized by fear and can neither think nor act in such a situation. As sad as it may be, school administrators in many schools today have to live in an atmosphere in which fear is present, and need therefore to understand how they behave in such a setting.

Thus our behaviors and the environments in which we behave are in constant interaction and our roles in this interaction are highly personalized. Can behavioral science pinpoint specific causes of specific behavior? In general terms that is possible, but not often in ways which are helpful to any specific individual. Rather, it is more appropriate to understand the kinds of things which do affect behavior and for each of us to be aware of how those things appear to affect us. Even this excercise is difficult, for what we imagine or perceive to be our environment or our situation may not be precisely what exists. One may think he or she is responding to how another person looks when in fact the response is to the person's voice which sounds the same as that of a disliked aunt. Neither the environment nor the response to it is simple and the administrator will find that the study of both is a lifelong professional requirement.

We will speak, then, of factors that in general affect human behavior. We will describe how these factors *may* affect people; we cannot describe how, if at all, they *will* affect any given person. We will discuss factors in the individual that can be changed if the personal half of the person-world transaction is not leading to effective administrator behavior. Throughout this book we describe the world in which the administrator works and the tasks and processes that the administrator undertakes and follows. This chapter focuses upon the inner world of the administrator from the standpoint of (1) perceptions of self, (2) perceptions of the environment, and (3) the ways in which these perceptions influence administrator behavior.

PERCEPTIONS OF SELF

In *My Fair Lady*, Henry Higgins wonders, "Why can't women be more like us?"—in which the "us" represents English gentlemen exactly like Henry Higgins. As we watch or listen to a performance of this song, few of us realize the extent to which Henry's question dominates our interactions with others. And few of us stop to wonder if the "us" we think we are is the "us" we really are. If we are to "see ourselves as others see us," we must first try to see ourselves as we really are.

In this section of this chapter we shall look at several aspects of one's self-perceptions. First, we will examine the reason that self-awareness is important for the administrator. Following that discussion we will look at the two basic factors of one's self—motivations and their origins and personal attributes.

Self-Awareness

There is a delicate balance between proper self-awareness on the one hand and egocentricity, narcissism, or self-consciousness on the other. Because the role requires that administrators work with and lead other people, it is important that they understand "where they come from" and who they are. In a very real sense, the person of administrators is the primary instrument through which their professional work is done. Because of this fact, each administrator must first understand that person. Through self-knowledge, administrators can insure that their reactions to situations and to other human beings are understood as personal reactions. For example, am I a person who adapts well to change—do I welcome change and am I comfortable with it? If I know the answer to this question, I can then understand how I react if change is suggested to me. If I am totally unaware of my personal response to change, I will then believe that I am responding to a change on the merits of the idea, when in fact my unknown personal ideas about change may be the determinants of my response.[4]

Administrators regularly have to overcome innate personal biases or predilections.[5] It is difficult to do so without awareness of these innate factors. This does not mean that as administrators develop self-awareness, they become increasingly detached from administrative decision making and response. We do not believe that administrators can or should purge themselves of their own human input to their tasks. We do believe, however, that administrators should insure that they are as aware as possible of that input. One of us, for example, has been aware for many years that he finds dismissing (firing) a colleague the most distasteful aspect of administration. He views it as a failure and he does not enjoy the strained human relationships the act creates. He tends, then, to seek and to follow every conceivable alternative to dismissal. By understanding himself, he does not act in ways contrary to his person, but neither does he construct an elaborate set of rationales to pretend that his pursuit of alternatives is based upon some grand administrative theory. Occasionally he pursues alternatives beyond the time when they make sense, but he knows what he is doing and why.

It is that kind of understanding of one's self that is important to administrators. It is aimed at understanding imperfection rather than at creating perfection; it is aimed at understanding how they are affected by others so that they can come to understand how they influence others; it is aimed at understanding the source of the sweaty palm or of the sense of comfort or of the feeling of distress; and it is aimed at learning where changes in the self should be sought so that leadership is enhanced rather than inhibited.

Motivations
Values and beliefs

Values and beliefs are important determinants of behavior.[6] Values are expectations of what ought to be; beliefs are expectations of what will be—expectations that a given course of action will lead to given results. The strong influence of beliefs upon action is stressed by Karl Weick, who suggests that "seeing is believing" can appropriately be reversed to read "believing is seeing."[7] "Spare the rod and spoil the child" is a statement of a belief; "turn the other cheek" is a statement of a value. These two statements illustrate the fact that values and beliefs often lead to conflicts as to how to achieve results. A key factor in the choice among alternative courses of action is the degree to which a specific action fits one's value system. It is not unusual for one to "believe" that a choice will achieve the given end most efficiently and yet to select another alternative because of concerns about the way the first choice fits one's value system.

One attribute common to most educational administrators is that they were motivated originally to enter the teaching profession. Thus educational administrators are teachers with a great deal of faith in the intellect, in learning, and in the schools. To some extent this teaching background differentiates educational administrators from other groups of executives and tends to create a group whose values and beliefs cause them to lean more toward organizations and administrative styles that stress people rather than structure, and those that honor both institutional goals and the goals of those who make up the institution. In years past, many have felt that an emphasis on the goals of those who make up an institution in addition to the institutional "bottom line" leads to inefficiencies in achieving institutional goals.[8] The school, even though it has an obvious hierarchy, has been seen along with other social agencies as permitting the concerns of teachers and of pupils to interfere with productivity. Recently, however, the success of foreign corporations in which concerns for the worker have been expressed in both structure and policy have led students of organizational research to rethink the appropriateness of stressing individuals and their goals as a part of institutional practice.[9] Perhaps, then, the attributes that motivate people toward teaching will receive new appreciation as attributes for administrators.

In addition to the values and beliefs that motivate people to become educators, each of us has a set of values and beliefs about human beings, about leadership, and about institutions. We need to be aware of our framework for viewing each of these areas. Most of us value human beings more than we believe in them. Our sense of what ought to be in human relationships is of a much higher order than is our belief in what will be. We need to be clear about what we value and what we believe about human beings so that our expectations are neither too low nor too high. If our belief structure is too much at variance with our values, we need to examine the difference and to attempt to determine its source. Unless we are motivated by a high degree of belief in human beings as well as strong positive values about them, educational administration will be extremely difficult.

When many of us think about leadership, the value we place on human beings is forgotten sometimes. We may value and believe in human beings, for example, but believe that the only way to get a group of them to get anything done is to command them to do so and to exact some form of retribution if they fail. We have discussed earlier the general leadership tasks of educational administrators and we shall discuss these in greater specificity in later chapters. These discussions often use words such as "influence," "persuade," "stimulate," and "ascertain." These are not "words of command," but are words appropriate to a special type of leadership that is designed to capitalize upon the abilities of many people.

Our beliefs about how able people are influenced, persuaded, or stimulated to work on behalf of organizational goals are crucial to our behavior as administrators. It is not important at this point to attempt to outline the "right" beliefs; indeed, there may not be any that are totally right for every situation. It is important, however, to be aware of our own beliefs about leadership.

Finally, each of us has a set of beliefs and values about the school as an institution and about schooling. These beliefs and values are also crucial to the behavior of educational administrators. Where does learning take place in a school? What should a good school look like and sound like in the middle of a school day? What is the teacher's responsibility as a role model and how is that responsibility best met? What are schools for, anyway? These are questions to which an administrator's values and beliefs help provide answers. The answers one gives to these questions color greatly the ways in which a person behaves as an administrator in a school.

By and large, one's values are firmly developed by the time one enters an administrative role. Thus values need to be recognized and to be understood as factors that influence behavior, but it is not likely that they can be changed to any major degree. To the extent that values create problems, administrators must simply understand that and go about their work. Beliefs, on the other hand, are shaped by experience and should be subject to evaluation and revision. Each of us needs regularly to consider whether our expectations of what will be are realistically based on our continuing and expanding experience.

Success and failure   A strong motivating and shaping force in our lives is our own measure of our personal success or failure.[10] Each of us in hundreds of undramatic but significant ways each year experiences what the American Broadcasting Corporation sports announcer describes each week as the "thrill of victory and the agony of defeat." In life outside of the sports arena, however, neither victory nor defeat is measured or announced with the clarity, definitiveness, and immediacy that marks the end of the race or game. In education in general and in administration in particular, the results of one's work are rarely readily apparent and are often so mixed that only time can reveal whether one has succeeded or failed in a specific undertaking. Thus in being aware of the impact of success and of failure upon our behavior it is necessary to consider how we define both, how dependent we are on rapid feedback of success or failure in a given undertaking, and how we respond to each.

Personal beliefs about success are important to the realistic development of our expectations and goals. For example:

> Ah, but a man's reach should exceed his grasp, Or what's a heaven for? (Robert Browning, *Andrea del Sarto*)

> Hitch your wagon to a star. (Ralph Waldo Emerson, *Civilization*)

> There is the greatest practical benefit in making a few failures early in life. (Thomas Henry Huxley, *On Medical Education*)

> It was better, he thought, to fail in attempting exquisite things than to succeed in the department of the utterly contemptible. (Arthur Machen, *The Hill of Dreams*)

> In public we say the race is to the strongest; in private we know that a lopsided man runs the fastest along the little side hills of success. (Frank M. Colby, *Constrained Attitudes*)

> If a man has a talent and cannot use it, he has failed. If he has a talent and uses only half of it, he has partly failed. If he has a talent and learns somehow to use the whole of it, he has gloriously succeeded, and won a satisfaction and a triumph few men know. (Thomas Wolfe, *The Web and the Rock*)[11]

Success and failure, then, depend upon our talents and upon our expectations for the development and use of those talents. The measurement of success or failure needs to be based upon *our own* talents, not those of other people. While it may be true that a one-armed person can play the piano or a wheelchair-bound person run a race, neither will do so as well as a talented pianist or runner without such physical handicaps.

In most areas of work and certainly in educational administration, our concept of success—the way in which we want to use our talents—should contain a major element of service to others, as opposed to a major element of personal accumulation of material or psychic income. The latter may be a result of success, but should not be the measure of it. But assuming that one has all of the right success objectives and is oriented toward service on behalf of people, of teaching and learning, and of the institutions of education, how can success be measured? Some will do so in terms of positions achieved—to have become a superintendent will permit greater service than remaining in a principalship, for example. Others will measure in terms of size of school or of school district—to be a principal in Urban High permits greater service than did a superintendency in Rural School District. And people in similar roles will judge their personal success or failure in different ways. Principal A may deem herself a success because the school she leads is quiet, efficient, and produces students who measure well above grade level on standardized tests; Principal B may judge himself a success because the school he leads appears to be a happy school in which students score extremely well in various measures of social adjustment and adaptation.

Regardless of how we measure success, that concept will influence our behavior. It will influence the choice of positions we accept, it will influence the tasks of a position that we choose to emphasize and in which we especially strive to excel, and it will influence the ways we relate to all of the people with whom we are in contact in the work setting. Striving for success and fearing failure may greatly enhance the quality of one's performance—or they may virtually immobilize an individual. All of us must both strive to understand our own concept of success and to insure that the concept is an appropriate one for a leader in a school or school district setting. To some extent our concept of success can be adjusted and changed to become a positive force in our professional life and so it should be examined regularly.

Deferred satisfactions are a hallmark of teaching and educational administration. If one requires instant gratification in order to function, one should enter neither profession. The work a curriculum supervisor does today to introduce new materials or methods into some schools will lead to known results only several years from now. By that time many other variables will have been introduced into the situation, and it will be almost impossible to know for sure that the work of the supervisor was critical in the lives of students.

It is not difficult to become attached to tasks that do provide instant success. These tasks rarely, however, are important to the major work of an administrator. Some administrators develop a "paper flow fetish." The speed with which paper flows across a desk or through a word-processing system can be measured and great speed can bring satisfaction—particularly if we do not pay too much attention to the quality of the thoughts expressed on the paper. Some administrators take great satisfaction in the daily completion of a crowded schedule. The number of events in a day, the number of people in and out of the office, the hours worked, become measures of success—again because they can be measured.

The higher the level attained in an administrative hierarchy, the more likely it is that personal success will be difficult to measure and deferred. If we are motivated only by rapid feedback concerning success (the "applause factor," which is said to be the motivator of the actor and actress), we will either find less fulfillment in such positions or will substitute quantity for quality in considering success. Either result tends to have negative influences upon administrator behavior and so the need to understand how one reacts to deferred results is important for the prospective administrator.

The final factor to be considered is how we respond or react to personal success or failure. It is inevitable that administrators will experience failures. Leadership involves risk and decision making in the absence of certainty. Some decisions will be poor ones and the visibility of administrators leads to a situation where not only the administrators are aware that something did not work out. While constant and major errors would not be tolerated, administrators who never make a mistake are administrators who are not leading.

Thus, the ability of administrators to react to an error of their own making is important and those who would be administrators need to be aware of how they react to failure. People who "play it safe" are not preparing themselves for leadership. Just as it is valuable for teachers to have taken course work that was difficult to master, so it is valuable for people who would be administrators to know how it feels inside to have tried something and failed. If failure leads to despondency, to self-doubt, to the inability to move ahead, the potential administrator has a problem. Similarly, if we cannot accept responsibility for mistakes—if failure is always someone else's fault—we are not well suited for leadership. The very best leader is one who will share the credit for success and shoulder the responsibility for failure.

Some people have trouble responding to success. Small success sometimes leads to large egos. Success occasionally leads to the development of unrealistic new aspirations. The extent of success (and of failure) is often overestimated, leading to an excess sense of euphoria (or of despair) and relaxation. With both success and failure the crucial factor is to be analytical. We really can learn from failure as well as from success, but such learning does not come automatically. The causes of success and failure are rarely readily apparent and are usually complex. As we react to success or failure, it is important to try to respond to what really happened rather than to what appeared to have happened. In this way, we can use success and failure—properly defined and properly analyzed—as positive forces for improving administrator behavior.

Obviously, our behavior is influenced by what we are, by what we believe we are, and by our concept of the control we have over both. "What we are" includes our character attributes and our physical attributes, while our concept of control relates to our feelings about our degree of freedom in the world.

Personal Attributes

Little need be said about the many ways in which our character attributes influence—indeed, shape—our behavior. Because so much of administration involves decision making—big decisions and little decisions—and because our own character attributes are a key variable as choices are made, character does influence administrator behavior in major ways.

Character

"Why can't he be open and above board with us?" ask one's colleagues.

"She never tells us the whole truth!" say others about their administrator.

"He always seems so nervous and fearful," say still others.

The practice of administration reveals our character to the world. "Slight flaws" in honesty or truthfulness or thoughtfulness or kindness are magnified in the minds of those with whom we work. Whether or not it is true, administrators appear to others to have more power, more material rewards, and more professional enjoyment than are given to non-administrators, and their behavior—particularly as it appears to reveal character—is subject to close scrutiny. It is a task of administrators, then, to insure that their character is above reproach, and to insure that their behavior reflects that level of character.

How we feel and how we look affect our behavior and the perceptions others have of our behavior; and as a consequence our overall administrator effectiveness. We cannot change either height or the vocal cords with which we have been blessed, but we can work to insure that the most is made of whatever we were given. We should remember that superficial physical attributes do make an impression upon others. Because most educational administrators have been teachers, the influence of voice tone, diction, dress, and physical appearance upon others has already been experienced. Unlike the classroom where teachers have long periods of time to establish student-teacher relationships based on more substantive considerations, administrators are often the victims or beneficiaries of first impressions gained by important people with whom we do not have opportunities to develop rapport over time. The speech to a service club or a statement before a legislative committee is heard in the context of how the speaker sounds and looks to the audience:

Physical attributes

"What did he say?"

"I don't know because I was so entranced by his funny beard . . . by his squeaky voice . . . by the way he wiggled his head when he started a new sentence."

A second important physical factor is general health and energy. Administration is hard work and is often conducted in stressful situations. It requires stamina and good health. Because of the many constituencies with which an administrator works, there are "fresh audiences" from morning to night to face the increasingly fatigued administrator. Enthusiasm is important because each meeting is important to the group who sought it, regardless of how it may rank on the administrator's priority list.

Prospective administrators, then, should work to insure that their physical attributes are developed and used in ways that enhance effectiveness. In addition, prospective administrators should be aware of the demands of administration upon their energy and should act in appropriate ways to maintain physical health and stamina for the tasks.

Concept of control   Each of us possesses physical attributes, skills, aptitudes, and abilities that prepare us for various professional positions. We may believe that how these "personal tools" are used and how our lives work out are results largely of our own efforts. Or, we may believe that individuals have virtually no control over their destiny and that it is largely forces external to the individual that determine how things work out.[12] The circumstances in which administrators find themselves are often not of their own making. The school board, for example, may deny a salary raise and thus provide the principal with a teaching staff that is unhappy and disgruntled. The demographics of a neighborhood may change or a court may order new attendance boundaries and a principal may end up with a student body with no common background or loyalties with which to create cohesiveness and productivity. The meeting to discuss a new program of sex education may occur the same evening that the national news media do an "exposé" on sex education. And so the list goes. Obviously, administrators cannot always control either their setting or their agendas.

But administrators should perceive the control they do have over how they will deal with the setting or the agendas. There are not preordained responses to complex stimuli—unlike Pavlov's dogs, we can do something other than salivate when hearing a bell. Administrators are not powerless pawns of circumstance unless they adopt that stance. In the latter case, the administrator has abdicated leadership and will probably not have long to worry about responses to leadership challenges.

Finally, administrators need to value themselves and to have self-confidence. Confidence implies that we understand the difficulties of a task, are aware of the variables beyond our control, and yet know that we have the resources to deal successfully with such a challenge. Obviously, we should not have blind confidence—we need to have the skills and understandings that make up the basic person in whom to have confidence. What we speak of here is confidence that the tasks can be done, confidence that we are equal to the tasks, confidence that we can overcome the mistakes we will surely make, confidence that we can play leadership roles in the enhancement of teaching and learning opportunities.

PERCEPTIONS OF THE ENVIRONMENT   Just as administrators have inner feelings, motivations, and personal attributes that influence their behavior, so do they have views about and perceptions of the environment in which they work. These views and perceptions also influence behavior and need to be understood. Here we shall examine perceptions of other people, of how best to motivate and work with other people, and of organizations and structures.

Assumptions we make about the motives and the abilities of other people play a key role in determining how we act toward others. Administrators need to be realistic—not everyone and perhaps no one is completely altruistic in motivation. A school board member may really be less interested in schools than in future political office; the teacher may really be interested in pay rather than in children. On the other hand, administrators do need to believe in people and to avoid constant cynicism and mistrust of people's motives. Those who have no faith in people will find it difficult if not impossible to lead, to inspire, to gain the confidence of people—all necessary tasks of educational administrators.

Perceptions of Others[13]

Administrators who believe that people—other than themselves, of course—are lazy and forgetful will often inundate their staff with memoranda reminding people of work to be done, of deadlines to be met, and of penalties to be assessed on those who fail to accomplish work or to meet deadlines. Observing an administrator over a fairly short period of time can show how that administrator feels about the motives of those with whom he or she works. If the perception is accurate, his or her behavior is probably appropriate for the situation; if inaccurate, the behavior may be a barrier to the effective completion of the colleagues' work. It is certainly true that to a great extent we receive from people what our behavior leads those people to assume is expected of them. In an organization made up primarily of professional people, administrators are well advised to start with the assumption that the group's motives are somewhat similar to theirs.

In addition to adapting behavior to the perceived motives of others, administrators also adapt behavior to fit their perceptions of the skills or abilities of those with whom they will work. There are many examples in which a staff is said to be a "poor" staff and yet a new administrator—unaware of the reputation of the staff or at least unwilling to accept the reputation as fact—achieves great results with the "poor" group. Administrators who believe that they are the most talented person in an organization will—in addition to the probability of being wrong—find delegation difficult and will generally not provide staff with sufficient opportunities to learn and grow.

In viewing either the motives or the abilities of others, administrators are cautioned to avoid snap judgments—to defer decisions about people until there has been an opportunity to observe their performance on different tasks and under different circumstances. Administrators need to remember that each of us has good days and bad days, that each of us does some things better than others, that each of us needs room to breathe and to work. Administrators need to remember that their behavior with those with whom they work signals how the administrators feel about their motives and abilities. The signals are given great importance—often more than is intended—and they need to be aware that they are giving them. In educational administration particularly, it is difficult to work effectively if a high level of faith in people is lacking. Our views about people, then, should be reviewed, and if one has little trust in people, professional opportunities in a field other than one that depends so heavily on human relationships should be considered.

Perceptions of How to Work with People

Each of us has our own idea of how best to motivate others—how best to lead. Usually this idea is based upon the procedures that best motivate us. There is a dangerous tendency in working with people to assume that everyone else does—or should—react to things exactly as we do. We recall an administrator who liked to work with background music playing and when he reached an appropriately high administrative level, he had music outlets installed everywhere—in elevators, restrooms, waiting rooms, hallways, and the like. He was amazed and somewhat angered to discover that a great majority of the people for whom he was providing music preferred silence.

Others of us want to be asked our opinions about everything and if we reach an administrative level, we find we take polls and surveys before taking almost any kind of action. Then we find, to our dismay, that those with whom we work wish we would get on with our work and leave them alone to do theirs.

In working with people, then, it is important to have some sound psychological underpinnings—to be aware of how people generally react to various stimuli and to be aware of research on such topics as motivation and efficiency.[14] In addition to this basic awareness, we must be alert to the people with whom we are working and become a student of their reactions to our administrative style and behavior. Administrators must work hard to avoid stereotyping people. It is easy to believe that this year's group of new teachers is just like last year's:

"Ms. White looks just like Ms. Green looked last year. There's a fellow who looks and sounds just like Sam Smith. Oh, oh—that guy looks like that troublemaker we had for a few weeks last year before I could transfer him out. . . ."

That process of thinking is dangerous for administrators with new generations of students, board members, parents, and community leaders. We must really perceive and constantly test perceptions of those with whom we work. We must insure that we are reacting to the real people surrounding us rather than to some mental images of who those people are.

Whether it be in the introduction and management of change, in the institution and enforcement of rules and regulations, or in the day-to-day supervision of an educational unit, administrators should strive to insure that their behavior does fit and does contribute to the progress of the people with whom they are working. What they believe, for example, about change is important; what they think the people with whom they work believe about change is important only to the extent that what they think is close to reality. Otherwise, they will adapt their behavior and strategies to the imaginary people and the real people will wonder what they are doing.

Administrators—particularly at higher levels—often see very few of the people in the organization and instead see units, reporting channels, position descriptions, and titles on organizational charts. It is important for administrators to be aware of what they see in an organization chart, how important the organization as a corporate person is to them, and what they see as the relationship between the organization and the people who make it up.[15]

Perception of Organizations and Structures

It is possible for administrators not to be affected by perceptions of people within an organization, for they can become so imbued with structure and with channels that they fail to recognize people. It is easy for an upper-level administrator, for example, to think, "We must cut one million dollars from our budget!" without ever pausing to realize that in an educational institution most of that cut will affect flesh-and-blood people. To some extent, some of the shuffling of teachers and pupils to meet desegregation goals has been done by people who work with statistics and geography and have no need to think of the real people who make up the statistics and populate the geography.

Administrators, then, should perceive of the organization as a human system and their behavior should reflect that perception. Administrators should take care, however, not to bestow magical and human qualities upon "the organization":

"We can't do that because the system won't permit it!"

"Your name is too long—our computer system only allows twenty-one units per name!"

"You can't beat the system!"

These and similar statements imply a character and a force in the organization that should not exist. Certainly administrators need to perceive of the organization as a facilitator of human effort, as a set of relationships that assist in the achievement of objectives. Administrative behavior needs to be based upon a view of the organization as "subject to change." If an organization is complete and final and not subject to exception, change, or interpretation, then there is no need for administration within that organization. Such a system can be run by clerks of good quality and there is no need for leadership.

But there is a need for leadership in schools and school systems and the organization of each is subject to change. Administrators need to see themselves as positive and free forces on behalf of the attainment of objectives, and the organization structure as a tool rather than vice versa.

We have in this chapter spoken of the administrator as a person. We have done so because it is important that all administrators be aware of the fact that their personal attributes and functioning as people influence their administrator behavior in significant ways. We have indicated that we should be aware of ourselves as people—our motivations and attributes—and that we should also be aware of how other people, the environment, and our perceptions of both affect us as people. We have described human behavior as dependent upon the inter-

SUMMARY

action of an individual with his or her environment, and we have discussed both in some detail. The educational administrator is, for better or worse, a functioning human being in a people-dominated business. The primary skill requirement for a person who is an educational administrator is the management of human interaction. It is for the success of this management effort that the administrator must heed the injunction, "Know thyself."

ENDNOTES

1. Gordon W. Allport, *Pattern and Growth in Personality* (New York: Holt, Rinehart, and Winston, 1961).

2. This concept is central in a number of discussions of administration. See particularly Jacob W. Getzels, James M. Lipham, and Roald F. Campbell, *Educational Administration as a Social Process* (New York: Harper and Row, 1968). See also a review of literature pertinent to this concept in Daniel E. Griffiths, Lawrence Iannaccone, and James Ramey, *Perception: Its Relation to Administration* (New York: University Council for Educational Administration, 1961), p. 11.

3. See for example Edwin E. Ghiselli, *Explorations in Managerial Talent* (Pacific Palisades, Cal.: Goodyear, 1971).

4. See Sheldon S. Zalkind and Timothy W. Costello, "Perception: Implications for Administration," *Administrative Science Quarterly* 7 (September 1962): 218–235.

5. Many of these biases or predilections are strongly influenced by social or cultural factors. See Stuart Oskamp, "Social Perception" in Lawrence S. Wrightsman, ed., *Social Psychology in the Seventies* (Monterey, Cal.: Brooks/Cole, 1972), pp. 431–458.

6. See Manley Howe Jones, *Executive Decision Making* (Homewood, Ill.: Richard D. Irwin, 1962), pp. 56–96.

7. Karl Weick, *The Social Psychology of Organizing*, 2d ed. (Reading, Mass.: Addison-Wesley, 1979), p. 135.

8. See, for example, R.L. Granger, *Educational Leadership: An Interdisciplinary Perspective* (San Francisco: Intext Educational Publishers, 1971), pp. 215–216.

9. W.G. Ouchi, "Markets, Bureaucracies, and Clans," *Administrative Science Quarterly* 25 (1980): 129–141.

10. For a classical discussion of this topic, see Kurt Lewin, "The Psychology of Success and Failure" in Harold J. Leavitt and Louis R. Pondy, eds., *Readings in Managerial Psychology* (Chicago: University of Chicago Press, 1964), pp. 25–31.

11. Quotations selected from John Bartlett, *Bartlett's Familiar Quotations*, from the headings, "Aspiration," "Success," "Failure."

12. For an application of these concepts to the principalship, see Seymour B. Sarason, *The Culture of the School and the Problem of Change* (Boston: Allyn and Bacon, 1971), pp. 133–149.

13. For a thorough discussion of the assumptions that people make about the nature of man and of the role these assumptions play in affecting behavior, see Wrightsman, *Social Psychology*, pp. 69–96.

14. Lloyd H. Strickland, "Surveillance and Trust," *Journal of Personality* 26 (June 1958): 200–215.

15. J.W. Meyer and B. Rowan, "Institutionalized Organizations: Formal Structure as Myth and Ceremony," *American Journal of Sociology* 83 (1977): 340–363.

CHAPTER 6

DECISION MAKING

Up to this point we have provided an overview of the settings and structures in which educational administrators work, of the tasks that confront them, and of the administrator as a person. We now examine the specific processes through which administrators work to accomplish their tasks, beginning with the decision-making process. As we discuss these processes, we shall refer regularly to the actual problem and task areas that confront administrators to insure that consideration of process is not done at the expense of administrative and of educational substance. The next six chapters are the heart of the volume and should be viewed and reviewed as a unit.

THE NATURE OF DECISION MAKING

Life is made up of a constant process of decision making. Whether it be the time at which the morning alarm is set; the way one will have the eggs done this morning; which morning news broadcast, if any, to watch or hear; or a choice of means to get to work, a human being is constantly involved in decision making. Most people pay little attention to the ways they make decisions. Much of the time they choose from habit. An informal (and totally unscientific) observational study of colleagues by one of us revealed, for example, that regardless of how long any individual reads the breakfast menu at a restaurant, the odds are that he or she will always order exactly the same items prepared exactly the same way.

Regardless of how well or thoughtfully or carefully a decision is made, the basic nature of a decision is that it is a choice of one from among two or more alternative ways to achieve an objective. Theorists of decision making, some of whom will be mentioned here, become concerned when the process is described so simply. They point out that objectives may not be clear or, in organizational decision making, may not be universally accepted. Others point out that there is neither ability nor time to consider, or even to become aware of, all of the alternatives available and that there are, therefore, a host of selectivity factors that limit choice. Still others point out that in and for organizations there are usually multiple decision makers involved, and that neither alternatives nor objectives are the same for any two decision makers in the group.

These and many other cautions about decision making are appropriate and correct. Despite the complexities and the lack of clarity and definition, a decision is essentially a choice of one way to move toward the achievement of what someone perceives to be an objective. Because all definitions of leadership involve the responsibility to assist a group in the determination and achievement of group objectives, it is clear that leadership and decision making are intertwined.

Basically, decision making can result from one of two approaches. The first is the scientific method, where we could study a number of alternative approaches and on the basis of that study predict the results of each approach with a high degree of probability of accuracy. We might simulate the adoption of various approaches through computer programs or mathematical formulas. We would choose an alternative—make a decision—based upon the known probable results of given options.

The other approach is commonly known as trial and error. Rather than dealing with accurately predicted results, we could simply try out an alternative and see what happens. If it achieves the objective, all well and good; if it does not work, we could try something else.

Obviously, as is true for most elements of the administrative process, a pure approach is rarely, if ever, available. The decision maker will in most cases need to follow procedures that have some aspects of the scientific method and some aspects of trial and error. In many cases, however, it will be important to insure that an approach to a decision is more heavily weighted toward one method than the other.

These approaches illustrate the fact that decisions involve costs of two kinds. There are the costs of defining and studying alternatives and there are the costs of the results of a choice. If, for example, we are deciding upon the amount of money to seek in a school tax-levy election, the cost of a poor choice can be high and a great deal of prior analysis of alternatives is justified. If, on the other hand, we are interested in finding ways to communicate about school needs and school accomplishments to the public, some amount of trial and error is justified.

Decision making, then, involves choice and it involves cost. While it can be a most complex process in an institutional setting, it is a simple process to describe. The difficulties are in the proper execution of the process, and it is to that area of concern that we will now move.

While categorization of human endeavors is difficult, it is worthwhile to review the nature of decisions that face educational administrators and to do so in terms of some broad categories. We have chosen to speak of these as substantive decisions related to the institution and its programs, strategy decisions, and substantive decisions related to administrator behavior.

Obviously, the greatest number of decisions an educational administrator is called upon to make are decisions related to the school or school district and to educational programs. These can be implementation decisions related to scheduling or policy decisions related to curriculum. They include staffing decisions, allocation decisions, expenditure decisions, facilities decisions, planning decisions, and the like. These decisions are in a real sense what educational administration is all about. It is the quality of the processes through which these kinds of decisions are made, implemented, and evaluated that will to a large extent determine the quality of the institution and the degree to which it and its people meet their goals. But both strategy and behavioral decisions are also important, so the administrator must strive for quality in each kind.

Once institutional decisions have been made, leadership involves helping to implement them. This undertaking requires strategies or tactics. The study of leadership strategy is an old one.[1] Administrators need to decide how they will move the group or institution from A to B, or how they personally will move behaviorally from A to B. Strategy decisions require an understanding of personal abilities and style; of the abilities and attitudes of those involved; of the environment (history, traditions, resources, and the like); and of the priorities and training considerations involved in the move.

The kinds of decisions required here include (but certainly are not limited to) decisions about who should be involved in what and when; what means of communication, if any, are to be used and to convey what messages; what "carrots" and what "sticks" are to be used; and to what extent the administrator should reveal a personal preference for the outcome.

Strategy decisions are clearly important because unless they are made well, substantive decisions cannot be converted into reality. It does no good to decide that one wishes to move to B (a substantive decision) if one cannot effectively decide how to do it. Potential administrators sometimes feel as if discussions of strategy or tactics are somehow immoral or unethical in either a democracy or an educational setting. Strategies are independent of moral and ethical considerations—most are neither moral nor immoral by definition. Some are moral; others are not. But no leader, whether in a dictatorship or a democracy,

THE BASIC NATURE OF DECISION MAKING IN EDUCATIONAL ADMINISTRATION

Institutional Decisions

Strategy Decisions

can be effective without a strategy, and decisions about strategy are a regular part of administrative decision making.

Administrator Behavior

Closely related to strategy are decisions about our behavior as administrators. We spoke at length in Chapter 5 about the degree to which the person and personality influence administrator behavior. As administrators, we are faced with career choices about which decisions must be made, and within a given plan or strategy we must make a variety of behavioral choices. In general, how can we communicate best with various groups of people? How much communication with specific groups will be undertaken? What tone will we take with various groups?

We simply cannot behave in a random way; new situations, particularly, require decisions about our personal response. To make such decisions, it is important—as we emphasized earlier—that we know ourselves and use that knowledge as the primary data for decision making.

THE NECESSARY ELEMENTS OF DECISION MAKING

This volume is concerned with the educational administrator and with schools and school districts; thus, decision making is discussed here as it relates to the responsibilities of educational leaders. Decision making for such leaders requires a sense of the purpose of the institution or organization; an understanding of the problem or situation about which a decision is needed; information sufficient to permit the design or understanding of available choices; and information to support the choice of a course of action. Each of these elements will be considered in some detail. In considering these matters, it is wise to keep in mind that

> One basic problem of the profession of management is making reasonable decisions in the face of uncertainty or incomplete knowledge as to the consequence of one's actions . . . . Meeting uncertainty is a pervasive problem which appears in many areas of human affairs . . . .[2]

Thus we will speak here with some degree of certainty, but we do so with a keen understanding of the pervasiveness of uncertainty in leadership.

Sense of Purpose

There is an interesting saying that "if you don't know where you want to go, any road will get you there." Making a decision implies that one knows where one wants to go. There is also a school of thought claiming that decisions may come first and situations that may be solved by such situations are then created. Cohen et al. speak of "choices looking for problems."[3] Peter Vaill, on the other hand, in his studies of what he describes as high-performing systems, finds that a concept and use of purpose are essential to administrator success.[4] We agree with Vaill's view.

In earlier chapters we discussed the purposes of educational administration and schools. While it is true that one can defer any decision almost indefinitely by deciding first to form a "task force to update the statement of purpose of the (school) (department) (district)," administrative decision making can be neither consistent nor effective in the absence of some working understanding of purpose. Here, purpose means something more specific than, say, "to promote excellence in learning." Such a statement is appropriate, but for decision making it needs further elaboration. For example, excellence in learning requires an excellent professional staff. What are the characteristics of such a staff in terms of competencies, breadth of knowledge and skill, age, or experience? What are the characteristics of our staff in those same terms? What are the variances? From a knowledge of the variances, we can develop a set of personnel objectives to guide decision making in ways that the "pursuit of excellence" cannot. These personnel objectives will also influence financial decisions, may influence decisions about the ways teaching assignments are made, will influence plans for other in-service development activities, and will be of assistance in many other ways. Other basic and specific objectives will assist similarly.

Sense of purpose also implies a sense of priority—a sense of timing. It is not possible to accomplish everything all at once so some understanding of priorities brings order to decision making. But there will be, from time to time, "targets of opportunity"—choices that may be available through some set of special (and probably non-recurring) set of circumstances. An understanding of both short- and long-term objectives is helpful in deciding whether to take advantage of the opportunity. A sense of priority, however, must not lock us into a set of timed steps whereby freedom of action is unnecessarily limited.

Existence of a Need for Decision

A careful observer of administrators will often discover that they make decisions about problems that do not really exist. In the previous chapter we mentioned that people often act on their perceptions or expectations without pausing to insure that there is a reality base to which their actions are related. In general (and the extent of the generality of this statement is a product of experience and the thoughtful evaluation of that experience), there is more potential trouble for an institution when administrators make too many decisions than when they make too few. Just as "churning a portfolio" is generally not wise in the stock market, so is constant identification of "major problems" not wise in the school.

Decision making in administration is a series of "big D" and "little d" processes. In making or approaching a major decision, we must make a host of subordinate ones. One key subordinate decision is deciding if it is necessary to decide—does a problem needing solution really exist? Is it an important problem demanding immediate decision? Is it a crucial barrier to the achievement of an institutional objective? As is true of most elements of the administrative process, there are neither universal rules nor criteria to guide action. When does a situation really demand a decision or a response? What is a "crucial barrier"? How does a problem "demand" action?

In the absence of an obvious crisis, administrators should take the time to examine these and similar questions before jumping into decision making. Doing nothing should be considered as a logical and realistic alternative, and the probable results of doing nothing should be given the same kind of consideration as other alternatives. Unless administrators are really willing to honor the alternative of not responding, they will be eliminating an alternative that in many cases has a high probability of being among the best.

Administrators are told that it is important to anticipate—to try to "stay ahead of the game." To some this advice means that at the first hint of trouble some action should be taken. If, for example, one citizen criticizes a textbook, a textbook review process is initiated; if one person criticizes a teacher, an evaluation committee is activated. Administrators need to be selective in identifying problems and in reacting to them. The decision that there is a need for a decision is an important first step in the decision-making process.

The second step is to insure that one understands the problem or situation. It is unproductive to work hard at a solution only to discover later that what has been "solved" was not really the problem. Assume, for example, that a school appears to have real difficulty recruiting able teachers. The administrator could go to work and expend great energy to secure the financial resources for increased salaries. But are salaries always the answer? Could it be teachers' living conditions that discourage recruiting? Or could it be the lack of support services—textbooks, reference materials, and the like? Or could it be a great deal of community interference in the work of the teachers?

Several approaches could be taken to gaining understanding. In this example, the personnel office could develop a plan of follow-up with individuals who are offered teaching positions and do not accept them. The follow-up could include telephone interviews or written questionnaires. Periodic surveys of the attitudes of the current teaching staff could be conducted, as could exit interviews with teachers leaving the system. The key is to gather facts rather than to act upon superficial or quick assumptions. It is also obvious that the more facts administrators gather on a regular and continuing basis, the fewer the times they must mount special efforts in the face of a needed decision.

Reviewing Alternatives   When the decision has been made that there is a problem; that it needs to be resolved or changed for objectives to be achieved (or achieved efficiently or in a timely manner or the like); and that it is adequately understood, the decision is ready for consideration. In theory (called by some the "calculative process"[5] and based upon the scientific method), the decision maker should now develop a list of all of the available alternatives. In actuality, the educational administrator must be content with much less than "all of the alternatives." According to Simon, the typical administrator enters the process with a sense of what will work and what will be satisfactory, and limits the design or consideration of alternatives to items that fall into these categories.[6] For most problems in a social setting such as a school, the number of possible solutions is astronomical (if not infinite) and some limits must be imposed upon the list. There are a number of limiting factors: cost, law, contracts, available time, history, and so on. Many times a solution is "getting rid of" a person—a teacher, a board member, a student, a local editor, or what have you. Such a solution is almost never available to educational administrators. Nor can they generally "buy their way out of" a problem—create a new facility, raise salaries, increase library holdings, and so forth.

While it is clear that we cannot deal with every possible solution, it is important that we be careful not to restrict our view of potential solutions too much. Some administrators act as if the only solutions to be considered are solutions they thought of themselves. Some people reject any solution that represents significant change. (It appears, for example, that school administrators have not been particularly imaginative in dealing with surplus plants in a period of declining enrollments. Boarding up buildings or selling them appear to be the solutions adopted, with little attention paid to potential income-producing alternatives.) Others immediately reject alternatives that appear to involve new costs. It is necessary to limit the number of alternatives seriously considered, but the means for the limiting should be legitimate ones.

The number of alternatives to consider relates to the degree to which trial and error can be tolerated. If we view a decision as our "one" chance to solve a problem then we would want to consider a more comprehensive set of alternatives than would be the case if the decision does not have this air of finality.

Another tendency in restricting the alternatives to consider is to categorize problems and to deal with every problem put in a given category the same way. Any student missing a class results in three hours in detention; any candidate for a teaching position who did graduate work at State University is better (or worse) than any other candidate; or any complaint from a parent should be discounted because of the parent's obvious self-interest. The initiation of change takes place less frequently as the tenure of administrators lengthens (discussed further in Chapter 11); to some extent, an important test of administrators' ability is their continuing willingness to seek new nuances in problems that look similar to other ones.

In addition to the limited number of totally discrete alternatives to be considered there will be variations on each alternative. For example, in seeking a tax levy, the administrators start with needs but can develop several levels of levy requirement depending on the number of needs. If the choice is among six, eight, or ten mills, there are different "need packages" that will add up to each level. Is an eight-mill package emphasizing teacher salaries a better choice than an eight-mill package emphasizing increased numbers of maintenance and academic support personnel? If a six-mill levy will allow financing of only non-teacher items, is it better to propose eight mills and work in some basic teacher concerns? Thus, one has alternatives within alternatives that need to be considered.

A basic point in the design of alternatives is to make use of all of the facts that can be made available. Intuition (hunch) and experience are both legitimate tools of the administrator, but facts are basic. In the tax-levy problem discussed above, the administrator is probably already aware of the economic facts of the school district. But what about employment trends, savings trends, income trends? What kinds of attitude or opinion studies are available to indicate what things are important to the people of the district? Are there any data available to reveal the level of satisfaction with the schools in the minds of the citizens? How does financial support of schools here compare with support in other school districts? Facts such as these can and should be made available as alternatives are designed.

Here again, judgment should be exercised. It is important to know how to use facts before spending the time or money to gather them. If a school district is in Oregon, does it matter what school expenditure levels are in the Midwest or in New York? Does the educational leader or the electorate in rural Illinois really find data related to the Chicago schools useful? The answer to questions like these is not an obvious yes or no; the point is that the questions are important and that "smothering" an issue with facts does not necessarily increase the ability to make decisions about it.

Once sufficient, relevant data are collected and analyzed, a set of alternative ways to deal with an understood problem is designed using the creative abilities of the administrator and colleagues. In many cases, the administrator must do this design task rapidly and decide almost instantly what to do. When the heating system goes out in a rural school and it is 20°F outside, the principal or superintendent cannot convene a task force or study group to design alternatives. If a plan for such an occurrence already exists it can be activated; if not, some facts will need to be reviewed, some consultations conducted, some alternative courses of action developed and considered, and a choice of action made. A tax levy, however, is different. Here, some group action to design alternatives is appropriate. Factual background material should be written up for the group and alternatives developed in written form for study. While time is of the essence in both cases, the former problem requires immediate decisions and the latter provides a longer time frame for deciding.

Selecting a Course of Action

All of the elements we have described to this point are in preparation for the selection of a course of action from among two or more alternatives. The selection can be made through a voting process; it can be made through a consensus process; or it can be made by a responsible administrator alone. The various types of decisions that can be made will be discussed in the next section of this chapter, but regardless of type, a decision is made by one of these processes. In each case, the choice of alternative should reflect a judgment about the best way to meet an organizational objective (or overcome a barrier to the meeting of an objective), where the meaning of "best" includes both organizational and personal considerations. The best way to do something is usually (and, certainly, whenever possible) a way with which the decision maker is comfortable.

"Everything being equal, I would prefer not to have to institute disciplinary procedures." When people say this, it takes a high degree of inequality among possible courses of action to cause them to decide that instituting disciplinary procedures is the correct or best solution. The point is that personal style, values, beliefs, skills, and the like influence each decision—particularly if the decision involves a personal follow-up act on the part of the decision maker.

The best solution, of course, also relates to probability of success. Part of assessing probability is to be aware of the outcomes of similar cases in which similar alternatives were selected. We must be cautious, however, in deciding that problems or situations are similar. As we mentioned earlier, no two situations are exactly the same—the time, the place, and the people are different and the differences may be crucial in determining whether a given course of action will be effective in one situation and ineffective in another.

The best solution must also depend on resources—people, facilities, and perhaps money. In choosing a course of action, the administrator must visualize the people who will be involved in making it work and the support that can be given them. For example, dealing with a language problem in a bilingual community could depend on unpaid tutors from the community. The degree to which such help will be forthcoming is a crucial factor in considering that solution.

Which alternative is best also relates to timing. One solution may require more time to solve the problem than will another. The decision maker needs to consider how crucial speed is. Perhaps a given solution is best suited to the resources available, but it is one that requires time and patience. If time is of the essence, another solution should be sought.

Timing also involves political or psychological factors. It may be that none of the solutions to a problem is appropriate to a given time. If the only real solution to teacher retention is increased salaries this solution—even if urgent—cannot be achieved immediately after the defeat of a tax-levy proposal. If a curriculum review process reveals that the institution of sex education programs at several grade levels is needed, that decision probably cannot be implemented if the school libraries are under attack for the content of books on the shelves. Timing, then, involves both the urgency of the problem and the appropriateness of the solution to a given time.

It should be noted that this discussion of decision making assumes rationality—rationality in the organization and in the people involved in or affected by the decision-making process. Burlingame has pointed out that the process as described above represents a simplification of decision making—one that is important and probably useful, but a simplification nonetheless.[7] In discussing the planning function, Clark provides an excellent overview of the failures caused by assuming that organizations operate as completely rational systems.[8] It is clear that in analyzing leadership to discuss its parts, a "flavor" of the whole is lost. We have discussed the effect of personal values, beliefs, and perceptions upon leadership behavior, touched on conflict and stress (discussed further in Chapter 10), and provided some insight into the complexities of leadership, organizations, and the environment. These and other factors diminish the ideal circumstances under which decisions can be reached. It is critical, however, that an essentially rational process of decision making be followed in order to minimize the intrusion of arbitrariness and irrationality. Our discussion, then, is simplified, but it does describe a process to be desired and sought even though in a complex organization it is probably never to be attained.[9]

KINDS OF DECISIONS   Alternative courses of action designed as ways to move toward (or to remove a barrier toward) an objective include several distinct kinds of choices. Each of these kinds will be reviewed briefly.

Status Quo   As we discussed earlier, one option open to an administrator is to decide to do nothing—to decide not to initiate action to intervene. This kind of decision is just as legitimate as are decisions to take aggressive action, provided that it is a conscious decision rather than the result of an inability to make one. A very simple example is the choice of a response to a negative editorial in a local newspaper. If the editorial is factually correct and merely represents a difference of interpretation between the editor and the school administrator, will a debate in the Letters to the Editor column be helpful? A number of questions can be raised to assist in deciding: How crucial to the schools and to community attitudes is the subject of the editorial? Is the local paper as influential as other media available in the community? Is the editor generally supportive or is this editorial typical of a negative view toward the schools? Generally, arguing with an editor through his or her own vehicle of communication is not productive; occasionally, it is necessary. But the choice not to do so is a real choice and must be considered.

Griffiths reports from his studies that much administrative behavior is not related to decision making—or at least to current decision making.[10] He found that habitual behavior, path of least resistance, or any number of other patterns explained administrative outputs as well as did formal decision making. The truth of this finding does not necessarily indicate the wisdom of such behavior. While complex decision-making processes cannot be used to deal with every concern, some thoughtful analysis of alternatives is appropriate for all but the most routine administrative tasks. Indeed, administrators who seem never to consider alternatives are either drifting along through major problem areas or restricting their activities to routine affairs. Neither course is a wise one.

One of us has described the status quo kind of decision as "dynamic inaction." The phrase is meant to convey the fact that inaction may be what is observed, but it is inaction that grows from action—an expenditure of energy and even forcefulness. This concept is more readily apparent in the business world than in the school building.

Morris poses a typical management example: "Suppose that a manager feels confident of obtaining a certain important contract if he offers to do the work called for at a price, R. He is uncertain, however, whether the contract will yield any profit at this price." Morris then provides a complex set of mathematical approaches to the solution of this problem, in which all of the variables are inserted into equations.[11] The result of the analysis is a probability factor from which the manager concludes either to make the offer or not to do so. Obviously, the latter decision is a real decision to do nothing and is the result of careful analysis of alternatives. Mathematics, unfortunately, is of little help in deciding whether or not to submit a letter to the editor.

Defer

It is entirely possible to decide not to do anything *at this time* even though it is clear that some action must be taken sooner or later. The status quo decision is a "final" decision (placed in quotation marks because nothing is ever really final in administration). To defer is to make no decision—yet. In the case of the editorial mentioned above, an administrator might decide to ignore it—a status quo decision—or decide that the editorial represents a problem about which something needs to be done, but not immediately, and that the "something" is not yet clear.

Deferring decisions cannot succeed well as a regular practice. The agenda of an administrator is a full one and current concerns keep crowding on the schedule. To the extent that administrators defer decisions and thus add to future agendas, they are diminishing their ability to deal with those future agendas. The decision to defer, then, should be used sparingly and only when the justification is clear.

New Course

When thinking of administrative decision making, the usual thought is of someone starting on a whole new direction. If reading scores in the elementary school are too low, for example, the response is frequently seen to be the initiation of an entire new program—with new textbooks, new teaching aids, workshops for teachers to introduce new teaching methodologies, new interactions with parents, and the like. Or, perhaps if all of those steps were taken a year or so ago and improvement is not deemed to be sufficient, then major changes might be made in the ways the new program is conducted—changes in class schedules to provide more time for the new program; increases in the intensity and alterations of the content of the teacher workshops; or the addition of more teaching aids.

Educational institutions of all kinds are relatively conservative institutions and they do not thrive on an atmosphere of constant radical change. Thus a decision to introduce a new course of action is one that requires a whole subset of decisions. How rapidly are the new programs to be introduced? What kinds of phasing-in steps are possible? Obviously, if a new instructional program is to be introduced, the first steps must involve working with the teachers who will be responsible for introducing it. This work might take a year or more, particularly if the program represents major change and requires new teacher skills. Because there are uncertainties in any new complex program, perhaps a pilot effort is called for. In that case, where should it be conducted, for how long, and with what kinds of evaluation?

The selection, then, of an alternative that calls for a new course of action is one that requires a number of decisions about process and timing. These matters represent facts that should be considered as a part of the basic decision-making process. For example, if the problem appears to have some urgency about it, the introduction of a whole new course of action may not be feasible due to time constraints. If, for some reason, reading scores need to be improved *now*, the solution may be intensive efforts to do better what is now being done, rather than the introduction of a complete new approach. The "clean slate" approach or "out with the old and in with the new" has a refreshing ring to it, but rarely represents a real possibility.

Response   The most common kind of decision to be made is the response to a situation or a problem: the student newspaper runs an article that is clearly offensive to most of the adult population of the school district; the tax levy is up for renewal in six months; the teachers' union wants to start bargaining and wants to know what the district is going to offer; the plumbing in the chemistry laboratory in the oldest high school in the city appears to have sprung a fatal leak; or the local parents' organization wants the superintendent to speak at a meeting irrevocably scheduled to conflict with a dinner in the state capital honoring the state superintendent of schools—a group and an individual whose support is crucial to the district.

These problems or situations require a response and each offers a variety of possible responses from which a choice needs to be made. By and large they offer an opportunity for neither no response nor deferral and they are not problems requiring new directions—at least not at the moment. The administrator must respond. He or she must do so with some understanding that none of the possible responses will satisfy everyone (in many cases, the administrator will not be fully satisfied with the response); that time will not permit complete exploration of all the alternatives; and that making some sort of response is the crucial task of a leader. While leadership is also responsible for anticipating and taking steps to avoid the occurrence of such problems, responding to problems as they arise is an essential process. Administrators hope that their responses will work to alleviate situations and thus to permit the schools and the people in them to meet their objectives. They hope as well that their responses will exhibit some consistency in philosophy and behavior. If the responses do not work or create confusion about the leadership, they can themselves become a problem to which solutions must be found.

As is generally true in matters involving people, theoretical purity is rarely (if ever) achieved. Thus the administrator cannot really look at problems or situations and decide that this one needs a new course of action, that one needs a response, and another one can be ignored. Most administrative problems are complex and consist of a number of interrelated parts. Solving one part can aggravate another, and the approach to one part may need to be radically different than the approach to another.

Complexity

The case of the student newspaper is a good example. It involves legal questions, curricular questions, teaching and advising questions, and public relations questions. The curricular, teaching, and advising questions are important, but probably can be deferred during the crisis; the legal questions are complex and often little understood, but must be factored in to all alternative decisions. The crucial first problem is one of public relations or understanding—a problem to which some immediate response is needed. Before the entire matter is resolved or ended some things will be ignored and some deferred. There will be some responses to concerns and there well may be some new courses of action with regard to journalism in the school. Thus in a case like this multiple decisions are required and they will probably include each of the kinds we have described. All but the simplest matters exhibit this sort of complexity.

As one considers decision making, it is important to understand that the administrator can rarely make a decision, heave a great sigh of relief, and say, "There, that's over and done with!" Decisions breed decisions and the success of the first decision will usually depend upon the wisdom of follow-up decisions. If the decision is to implement a new reading program, many subsequent decisions are required. For instance, who will provide direct leadership to the effort? What teachers will be involved? Who will select learning materials? How will pupils be assigned to various parts of the program? The list of follow-up decisions is long and each is important to the success of the first decision in meeting an institutional objective.

THE CYCLICAL NATURE OF DECISION MAKING

Decisions also lead to a need for evaluation, discussed in detail in Chapter 11. Here, it is important to remember that a decision is supposed to lead to results, and that the degree to which it does should be measured at an appropriate time. The results of this measurement will lead to the need for other decisions. If, for example, reading scores have improved greatly in grades 3 through 6 but fallen off at grades 7 through 9, what should be done? Some literature shows that a 6–2–4 organization shows better results in learning at grades 7 and 8 than does our 6–3–3 structure. Should changes be made? Are the materials being used in the reading program at grades 7 through 9 adequate? Are the teachers really working at teaching reading in the junior high school? And so on.

Decisions lead to decisions, which need evaluation, which leads to more decisions. The sigh of relief over the finality of a decision is not the typical result of the decision-making process.

SPECIAL PROBLEMS IN DECISION MAKING

What we have just reviewed is decision making without complications. We have described how it works in the atmosphere of the textbook rather than that of the principal's or superintendent's office. Let us look at a few of the factors that complicate real decision making.

Conflict and Stress

The school and school district are organizations where a number of professional people other than administrators expect to be involved in decision making. This involvement can enhance decision making in that it can bring more talent than a single individual possesses to the design of alternatives and to the anticipation of probable results. It can also, however, bring conflict and lack of clarity as to who is to decide what.

Various studies have shown that in the school setting there are numerous situations that complicate decision making[12]: agreement about ends but disagreement about means[13]; agreement about means but disagreement about ends[14,15]; and disagreement about both means and ends.[16,17] Our discussion of decision making above mainly applied where there was agreement on both means and ends—a fairly rare occurrence in practice.

Administrators are responsible for achieving the ends or aims of the school system. They are aware that there are many other objectives held by individuals and groups who influence the system, but it is very important that they try always to be faithful to the objectives of the system. It is generally less important that they be the ones to select the means through which the ends will be attained. By and large, administrative decisions should specify objectives and probably time lines, but to the extent possible there should be freedom for other professionals within the schools to determine means.

Nevertheless, administrative decision making will take place in an arena where disagreements about ends, means, or both will lead to stress and conflict. This fact needs to be recognized and is covered in detail in Chapter 10.

Participation

While it should be obvious from much of our discussion so far, we have not made the specific point that the administrator is rarely the only one involved in reaching a decision. Administrators are responsible for insuring that decisions are made and are generally responsible for the results of decisions, but many others are involved in the process. The administrator should be concerned with the selection of people to be involved, as well as the processes through which they will be involved. It is important that participants be well aware in advance of the degree to which they will actually participate in reaching a decision.

Most individuals would rather not be involved in a process at all if their involvement is primarily for "window dressing" purposes. Many people do not feel that their involvement is useful unless the result is a vote that determines the decision. Various decisions involve various kinds of participation. It is important that the details of each given process are clear and are observed faithfully.

Deadlines

While our discussion of the elements of decision making has implied that there are occasions when time is of the essence, that point should be emphasized. Deadlines can be either helpful or harmful to decision making. It is possible to become so enamored with the processes of creating alternative solutions to a problem and analyzing those solutions that the administrator never gets around to making decisions. Often, studying a problem is much more enjoyable than having to deal with a specific solution. Situation-imposed or self-imposed deadlines do cause people to stop playing with a problem and come to grips with it.

Election deadlines make it impossible to study the need for a tax levy without finally acting; many decisions must be completed each month (or more often, depending upon schedules) in time for the regularly scheduled meeting of the school board; teacher and staff contracts do expire on given dates and decisions about terms must be reached prior to those dates; often there are legal deadlines for tenure and continuing-contract decisions. These and many other deadlines are known in advance and help the administrator to schedule work as well as prodding individuals or groups toward a point of decision.

Harmful deadlines—or at least potentially harmful—are those that grow out of crises. The broken heating system or the student newspaper item bursts upon the scene and requires instant response. The administrator must often act in the absence of consultation, complete information, or adequate time to design and review alternatives. The dangers in this type of situation are obvious: acting on impulse, not fully anticipating the chain reaction set off by the initial decision (for example, in these days of two-parent employment, what happens when the children are sent home because of the broken heating plant and cannot get into their homes?), and responding in the absence of consensus. Obviously, times come in the lives of all administrators when crises must be dealt with rapidly, and they must simply do their best. But if they find that crisis decision making is a regular occurrence and that a state of crisis becomes the normal environment, it is time for a careful examination of their own leadership and the general effectiveness of the organization. We sometimes view the administrator as a person who leaps from major crisis to major crisis blithely solving problems while simultaneously carrying the weight of the world; such an administrator is not leading but following, in fact, and is neither a good nor a realistic model.

Information

Educational administration deals with human beings of a variety of ages in a complex institution where individual roles are regularly shifting. The variables involved in most decisions are both numerous and not easily controlled. While the business executive can use economic models to predict costs of production, profit margins, and the like, the predictions of learning outcomes, voter behavior, or teacher effectiveness are not exact. Thus the educational administrator is frequently working with incomplete information and with uncertainty. While administrators should attempt to seek as much relevant information as possible, time, cost, and other factors almost never permit the collection of all of the information they might wish for. They must learn from experience and observation what seems to be necessary in the way of information for various kinds of decisions and accept that some degree of uncertainty is inevitable.

In today's world of computers and word processing a different kind of information problem can arise in decision making. We can be inundated with data, charts, models, and simulations. We can receive so much information that we become immobilized. As administrators approach an important decision, it is important to spend some time determining what information might be helpful in reaching that decision and what information would be extraneous.

It is not uncommon today to see decision-makers literally buried under printouts. Every bit of information that might even remotely relate to the problem at hand is drawn from every possible data bank. Too often, this surplus hides the important information. It is the responsibility of administrators (not the directors of computer services) to determine what information will be helpful and what will not. They should not easily accept either the computer expert's assertion that "you can't organize data on a computer that way," or that "more is always better."

The determination of the correct amount of information that is needed and can be made available within time and cost requirements is an important aspect of decision making. Administrators will always deal with uncertainty, but today that uncertainty can arise from too much information as well as from too little.

Solution Commitments

In almost every case, a decision made by an educational administrator affects other people and is made in conjunction with other people. This fact obviously complicates decision making. One problem sometimes arising is that groups affected by (or involved in) making a decision can develop a commitment to a particular solution that does not appear to the administrator to be the best solution. Recall our discussion earlier of a reading achievement problem in a school. It is possible that the teachers involved might decide that students who do not achieve some minimum level of reading competency will not be promoted and that if they fail to be promoted twice, they should be assigned to a school other than the "regular" one until they catch up or are old enough to withdraw. This solution may simply not be possible because of political, financial, or philosophical concerns. Unless the teachers can be persuaded that their solution is impossible to adopt, any other solution will be handicapped because those who must make it work are opposed to it.

As one works with groups in reaching decisions, it is important to state early in the process what the boundary conditions seem to be. If reviewed early, some of those conditions might be changed and, in any event, the decision-making process will move ahead with a clear understanding of acceptable ranges for outcomes. It is also important to keep a decision-making process as fluid as time permits. While it might seem to be a good tactic to get a quick commitment to a specific alternative and devote attention to implementation concerns, it is not the wisest course. Good ideas are generated in an open consideration of alternatives, and commitment to a specific solution is best made after considerable discussion of the facts.

Administrator Problems

As we indicated in the previous chapter, administrators themselves are a factor in their ability to be effective in administrative work. Because of its centrality to administration, personal ability in decision making is particularly important. Administrators need two characteristics: (1) the ability to make decisions and (2) the ability to live with decisions once made. Potential administrators should attempt to place themselves in situations where practice in each area can be gained.

We have also mentioned that decision making in educational administration almost always involves uncertainty, often involves time pressures, and occasionally involves conflict. In some people, these factors lead to an inability to act, to "freezing up." Obviously, this reaction then leads to complete administrative ineffectiveness.

We have also mentioned that decision making is a cyclical process and that it never ends. Effective administrators are those who are able to move along through the cycles. They do not get "stuck" at some point rethinking, agonizing over, or otherwise consumed by a "made decision." They do the very best job they can with each required decision and then move on to the next task. This statement does not mean that evaluation of results is not necessary or that learning from decisions is not possible. Rather, it means that administrators cannot meet their next task if they are worrying about the last one. Intelligent review of the results of decisions is essential; self-doubts, anxiety, and uncertainty are not.

SUMMARY

Regardless of the framework used to examine leadership and administration in any field of endeavor, decision making is viewed as a central task. While some have argued that administration and decision making are synonymous, it seems clear that such is not really the case. Nonetheless, administrators cannot administer without making decisions—decisions for themselves and for their groups or institutions.

In this chapter we have discussed the nature of decision making, the nature of the decisions facing educational administrators, the elements of the decision-making process, the kinds of decisions that are made, the cyclical nature of the process, and special problems facing decision makers in the real world.

Making decisions and observing the results are both the burden and the opportunity of leadership. On the one hand, there is risk, uncertainty, possible conflict, and divided support; on the other, there is movement toward important objectives, occasional success, and the sense of doing important and meaningful things. This duality is the nature of leadership.

ENDNOTES

1. See, for example, Niccolo Machiavelli, *The Prince*, trans. Ricci (New York: Mentor Books, 1952). Original manuscript in Italian, 1532.

2. William T. Morris, *Management Science: A Bayesian Introduction* (Englewood Cliffs, N.J.: Prentice-Hall, 1968), p. 1.

3. Michael D. Cohen, James G. March, and John P. Olsen, "A Garbage Can Model of Organizational Choice," *Administrative Science Quarterly* 17 (March 1972): 2.

4. Peter B. Vaill, "Toward a Behavioral Description of High Performing Systems," in Michael Lombardo et al., eds., *Leadership, Where Else Can We Go?* (Durham, N.C.: Duke University Press, 1978), pp. 103–125.

5. Thomas J. Sergiovanni et al., *Educational Governance and Administration* (Englewood Cliffs, N.J.: Prentice-Hall, 1980) discuss the calculative process in pp. 354–361.

6. Herbert A. Simon, "Theories of Decision Making in Economics and Behavioral Science," *American Economic Review* 49 (June 1959): 253–283.

7. Martin Burlingame, "Some Neglected Dimensions in the Study of Educational Administration," *Education Administration Quarterly*, Winter, 1979, p. 2.

8. David L. Clark, "In Consideration of Goal-Free Planning: The Failure of Traditional Planning Systems in Education," in Clark, McKibbin, and Malkas, eds., *New Perspectives on Planning in Educational Organizations* (San Francisco: Far West Laboratory, 1980), pp. 1–16.

9. For an excellent discussion of the problems related to "irrationality," see Wayne K. Hoy and Cecil G. Miskel, *Educational Administration: Theory, Research, and Practice* (New York: Random House, 1978), pp. 212–216.

10. Daniel E. Griffiths and Frank W. Lutz, "Synthesis and Conclusions," in Daniel E. Griffiths, ed., *Developing Taxonomies of Organizational Behavior in Educational Administration* (Chicago: Rand McNally, 1969), Ch. 7.

11. Morris, *Management Science*, pp. 67–81.

12. James D. Thompson and Arthur Tuden, "Strategies in Decision Making," in Fremont J. Lyden, George A. Shipman, and Morton Kroll, eds., *Policies, Decisions, and Organizations* (New York: Appleton-Century, Crofts, 1969), pp. 310–330.

13. Keith Davis, "Evolving Models of Organizational Behavior," in Keith Davis, ed., *Organizational Behavior: A Book of Readings* (New York: McGraw-Hill, 1974), pp. 4–15.

14. Charles E. Lindblom, "The Science of Muddling Through," *Public Administration Review* 19–20 (Spring 1959): 79–88.

15. Graham T. Allison, *Essence of Decision: Explaining the Cuban Missile Crisis* (Boston: Little, Brown, 1971), pp. 144–184.

16. Cohen, March, and Olsen, "A Garbage Can Model," pp. 1–25.

17. For a detailed discussion of these three conflict settings see Sergiovanni et al., *Educational Governance*, pp. 361–367.

CHAPTER 7

LEADERSHIP

Leadership is probably the most talked-about managerial activity in any organization. Managers or administrators are expected to be effective in a range of areas including planning, decision making, communicating, controlling, and managing conflict. In the eyes of many, however, leadership is an all-encompassing term that refers to the full range of managerial responsibilities. Our view is more limited. We consider leadership to be a process through which an individual (the leader) secures the cooperation of others (followers) toward goal achievement in a particular setting. In this chapter, we will explore the concept of leadership, examine some theories and research that deal with the concept, and give particular attention to their implications for behavior in school settings.

Leadership is a subject of great human interest. National and regional magazines often include articles about the top leaders in a particular field, and newspapers regularly carry feature stories about local leaders. Changes in top leadership positions attract considerable media attention and stimulate much conversation. Perhaps the best example is the attention given to governmental elections, but similar attention is given to changes at the top of leading local businesses, athletic teams and other agencies. Regardless of the extent of public notice, a change in the top leadership of an employer, church, or school is certain to attract attention and provoke discussion among those who are affected.

LEADERSHIP AS THE SOLUTION TO ALL PROBLEMS

A primary reason that leadership changes attract such attention is that people attribute great power to leaders. Indeed, leadership is one of the most popular explanations for the success or failure of organizations. At a very general level, there is a school of thought that explains history in terms of actions by leaders and heroes.[1] In contemporary affairs, governments or companies that prosper are said to enjoy good leadership; in those that fail, the leaders are to blame. People advocate electing particular candidates to office because they will bring "new leadership" that many regard as a *prima facie* benefit. Four years later, it is likely that other groups will support different candidates and again promise new leadership. The same phenomenon is apparent in the sports world. It is not uncommon for a professional or college coach of football or basketball who wins a conference title or national championship one year, to the high acclaim of local fans, to be asked to resign by the same fans after an additional two or three seasons that are less successful.

Similar conditions exist in school affairs. The board of education in a school district troubled by low student achievement, lack of public support, inadequate funding, and negotiation problems with the teachers may conclude that their problems are attributable to poor leadership. Accordingly, they dismiss the superintendent and undertake a nation-wide search for a successor. When the new person arrives, he or she is naturally hailed as "the best person in the country to lead our school system." This genuinely enthusiastic build-up in combination with the popular belief that leadership can make a difference encourages community residents to believe that their school problems will soon be solved. If the problems continue or if others appear in their place, at least some school-district patrons will blame the new superintendent and call for his or her replacement.

School administrators, like others in top management positions, often see themselves as having the ability to redirect the organizations they head. They come to a new position expecting that their efforts will ameliorate the problems that confounded their predecessors. Bridges[2] asserts that this view is shaped for educational administrators by the literature and rhetoric surrounding their formal preparation programs. Preparation programs emphasize the problems that confront the field and the need for strong leaders to address them. As a result, says Bridges, school administrators develop a concept of themselves as leaders that is both heroic and unrealistic. They overestimate the impact they can have on the organization because they underestimate the complexity of the organization and its setting.

THE EXPECTATION-PERFORMANCE GAP

The gap between our expectations for leaders and their performance is the result of several factors. As already suggested, the problem may have more to do with unrealistic expectations than with inadequate performance. A related difficulty is that some observers mistake the aggregate behavior of individuals in formal leadership positions (e.g., a superintendent or a principal) for leadership that is a more limited concept. Consider, for example, an individual who is an effective leader in the sense of being able to secure cooperation toward organizational goals, but is a poor planner. If the organization moves improperly, it is attributable to poor planning rather than to bad leadership.

Efforts to assess the performance of individuals in leadership positions depend upon establishing criteria for success. In general terms, these criteria include achieving objectives and maintaining a cohesive work group.[3] Application of such criteria is relatively simple in highly structured and quantifiable situations. We can differentiate rather easily between successful and unsuccessful leadership of football coaches, campaign directors, and sales managers. It is much more difficult to reach agreement about the leadership ability of school principals or superintendents. This is partly because they exercise leadership in many areas simultaneously. For example, a small part of a high school principal's agenda in a given month may include encouraging curriculum reform in mathematics, organizing a citizens' advisory committee, and helping teachers, parents, and other administrators resolve various problems. It would not be unusual for these groups to vary within as well as among themselves regarding expectations for the principal as this agenda is carried out. The assessment of his or her performance as a leader will involve diverse constituencies employing different criteria in relation to multiple events.

Our definition of leadership involves four elements: (1) the leader, (2) the goal or objective, (3) the followers, and (4) the setting. Factors related to each of these elements can impede leadership performance when successful performance is defined as achievement of organizational goals and maintenance of the group.

Factors That Affect Leader Success

As already noted, it is common for those who wish to place blame for unsuccessful endeavors to focus upon the leader. In many instances, leaders are an important reason for failure. For example, they may not understand the objective or fail to communicate it properly to the group. Sometimes they fail to work hard enough at a given task. Other times they adopt an inappropriate strategy or allow themselves to be distracted by peripheral issues. In some cases, the leader's overall style or approach to dealing with problems may be so alien to the group that he or she cannot establish sufficient rapport to be successful. Thus, in some instances, the leader actually is responsible when goals are not achieved. At other times, however, the responsibility can be placed elsewhere.

The leader

A second set of factors that may explain unsuccessful events pertain to goals and objectives. For example, Smith and Keith[4] analyzed the effort to create a highly innovative elementary school. The purpose of this School for Tomorrow, as it was called, was to help students become "fully functioning mature human beings." The objectives of the school were—

Goals and objectives

1. to develop each child to the limits of his or her potential;
2. to help each child achieve complete living in all phases of life;
3. to assist each child in becoming the architect of his or her character;
4. to foster self-actualization and self-realization;
5. to develop the child intellectually, socially, emotionally, and physically.

The School for Tomorrow was established in a brand new, open-space school, headed by a capable administrator, and staffed by dedicated, competent teachers. The curriculum was based on continuous progress and provided for individualized attention and student initiative. The program began amid great enthusiasm by school officials, teachers, and parents. Three years later, the superintendent, principal, curriculum director, and all but two of the original teachers had left the positions they held when the school was opened. The program reverted to the traditional patterns, and walls were erected to create classrooms in the previously open-space building.

The reasons for the failure of this school are probably complex, but attention must be given to the possibility that the original goals were unrealistic. A companion problem may have been difficulty in translating the general objectives of the school into specific and manageable tasks that could be readily understood and carried out. This is a common leadership problem. The ambiguous nature of school goals and attendant difficulties, discussed in Chapter 3, present significant obstacles to school leadership.

Followers   An old political adage defines a leader as a person who learns which way a group is going and then gets out in front of it. This is a cynical and demeaning perspective but it makes the point that leadership cannot exist without followers. Gaining the commitment and cooperation of others is the central problem of leadership. At times, prospective followers lack the basic skills or understanding required for the group to succeed. They will often have different perspectives about how important it is for the group to succeed and how to go about it. In most instances, there will also be other demands that compete for their time and attention.

Let us assume that a principal wants school faculty members to visit the homes of their students in order to establish closer ties with the parents. Some faculty members may feel uncomfortable in scheduling visits because they have not been taught how to do so. Others may consider it a waste of time. Still others may see value in such visits but feel they lack time to conduct them because of other job or family demands. The local teachers' association may regard the proposal as an infringement of their contract and urge teachers not to support it.

This example indicates only a few of many reasons that faculty members may resist particular leadership initiatives of a principal. However, the effect of followers on leaders goes beyond the options of resistance or noncompliance. In many cases, it is the followers who select their own leader. Not surprisingly, groups in this situation tend to select leaders whose goals are similar to their own. Even when leaders obtain their position without being selected by their followers (as is generally the case with the appointment of school administrators), they usually are sensitive to the values and expectations of the followers. Thus, they may hesitate to even propose objectives or plans if they anticipate that the response of the followers will be negative.[5]

Setting

Contextual factors affecting school administration (discussed in Chapter 2) can dramatically affect the initiatives of leaders. For example, the enactment of Public Law 94–142 in 1975 provided both resources and an agenda to administrators who were seeking additional means to benefit the education of the handicapped. The same law established a set of requirements that assured that even administrators who had little prior interest in educating the handicapped would become heavily involved with this problem. During the next several years, school districts hired many new employees, created advisory committees, remodeled facilities, and established new programs, routines, and procedures to assure compliance with the law. There was a need for people who could provide leadership to this growth process.

By the early 1980s, substantial progress had been made under the provisions of Public Law 94–142. At this point, however, the context changed in a way that had dramatic effects on leadership opportunities. Wanting to reduce federal spending, the Reagan administration proposed large reductions in federal funds for educating the handicapped, along with a block-grant allocation procedure that would allow the funds to be spent for less restrictive purposes. This change in the setting, over which local administrators had no control, meant that their leadership efforts in the area of special education had to shift from developing programs to retrenching or attempting to salvage them.

A general change in society, too, can have indirect effects upon leadership efforts. For example, increased energy costs have reduced the willingness of some faculty and parents to provide transportation for field trips. Similarly, the increased presence of women in the work force has made it more difficult for principals to recruit volunteers to help in day school programs. Less pervasive but noticeable events can also be influential. Thus, the publicity given efforts to remove sex education from the curriculum in one community can be an obstacle to the introduction of a new program nearby.

The organization itself is part of the setting for leadership, and it provides a set of expectations for its members. These are sometimes formalized in contracts, policy manuals, and written statements of procedures. Other expectations are communicated less formally but are nonetheless real. Administrators and those who work with them understand these expectations and accept them as bases for their interactions. However, expectations can change in ways beyond the control of any particular administrator. For example, the board of education can agree to a new contract with the teachers' association that restricts the prerogatives of principals to hold faculty meetings or to assign extracurricular duties to teachers. A new superintendent might reorganize the system in such a way that more or less authority is placed at the building level. Changes such as these can influence the exercise of leadership at the level of an individual school.

The Limits of Slogans

Aspiring leaders do not lack sources of advice. For general suggestions they can rely upon newspapers and magazine accounts of leadership in government and other institutions. These articles often provide analysis as well as descriptions of leader performance from which readers can draw inferences for their own behavior. For example, accounts of the early months of the Reagan administration emphasized the president's desire for strong cabinet government and his propensity to delegate responsibility to others. Another example of leadership advice emanating from the general culture is the current emphasis on cost-effectiveness and accountability.[6] Another source is the professional literature, which consistently offers exhortations and admonitions to leaders. Finally, colleagues and friends can always be counted upon for suggestions. It is hard to imagine a teacher who, learning of his or her appointment as principal, does not receive lots of friendly advice from fellow teachers about remembering what it means to be a teacher.

The problem with this advice is that it tends to come in the form of slogans (or, at the local level, as partisan suggestions for solving particular problems). Examples of general slogans include, "Let everyone know who is in charge," "Communicate,"and "You can expect what you inspect." Examples of slogans that have been especially influential in educational administration are "Provide instructional leadership," and "Involve others in decision making." None of these slogans constitutes bad advice; however, none is applicable to every situation.

Difficulties emerge when administrators rely excessively upon such simplistic notions. For example, we know of situations where organizational progress was impeded by an administrator who insisted that he approve the smallest details of daily operation. We are also aware of schools where the administrator's emphasis on participative decision making is carried to such an extreme that teachers resent spending time on making decisions that they consider to be of little consequence.

The Limits of Theory and Research

Theory and research have not provided as much useful guidance to leaders as we might wish. Perhaps this is not surprising, given the difficulty of defining the concept and the complicated interactions among leaders, goals, followers, and settings. Most research about leadership has focused on the relationship between leaders and followers. For many years, inquiry concentrated on identifying personal traits associated with successful leadership. To the disappointment of many researchers and practitioners, this work did not lead to a comprehensive set of personality attributes that are characteristic of leaders in all settings. Had it been possible to identify such a profile, the tasks of identifying and training leaders would have been simplified greatly.

Later research addressed the behavior of leaders. Initially, the focus was upon identifying a single set of behaviors associated with effective leadership. Again, no generalizable theory about the "one best way" for leaders to behave emerged from these studies. Contemporary research about leadership proceeds from the assumption that different behaviors are appropriate in different settings. This research does not yield simple directions for potential leaders, but it does offer some insights about the ways in which followers may respond to different leader behaviors under various conditions. The challenge this line of research presents to leaders is to understand the concepts on which the theories are based, to learn how to operationalize these concepts in their own behavior, and to analyze situations to determine which leader behaviors are called for. The complexity of this challenge will be apparent from the discussion of these theories.

OPPORTUNITIES FOR LEADERSHIP IN SCHOOLS

The importance of effective leadership in schools has been widely noted. Clark, Lotto, and McCarthy reviewed 97 studies of successful urban elementary schools and interviewed "leading researchers and writers on urban education [about] factors associated with success in urban elementary schools." Leadership, which they defined as "group or designated leadership that integrates or influences effort toward commonly accepted goals," emerged as a "crucial factor in determining school success." They observed that effective leaders "framed goals and objectives, set standards of performance, created a productive working environment, and obtained needed support."[8]

Leadership is often provided by persons who occupy positions of formal authority in schools. We typically think of the individuals who hold such positions as having leadership responsibility. On the other hand, leadership is also present in informal settings where it is sometimes provided by individuals without formal rank or authority.

Leadership and the Power of Office

The practical question for a leader is how to get others in the organization to follow. As noted in Chapter 4, individuals who hold positions of authority in the organizational hierarchy have an advantage in this regard. People in the organization expect them to provide directions on behalf of the organization. Thus, teachers expect principals to provide room assignments, teaching schedules, authorization to purchase supplies, and to perform other functions. Similarly, principals expect superintendents to provide them directions about matters of system-wide importance. People often accept the directions of those in formal authority even when they disagree with them because of their loyalty to the organization and respect for the office.

Why do some administrators have more power than others? Part of the difference is explained by variations in organizational structure and culture. For example, we would expect more unquestioning allegiance to a marine captain than to the chairperson of a university history department. The captain has the advantage of a more rigid authority structure and a greater range of sanctions to use with his followers. However, we also know that some principals have greater influence with their staffs than others and that such variations often exist within a single school system. This indicates that, although the power of office provides opportunities for influence, leadership involves more than relying upon one's title as basis for expecting others to act.

The power of office is a form of what French and Raven refer to as legitimate power.[9] It is power that derives from the fact that organizational members acknowledge the right of the organization to provide them some direction. Other forms of power identified by French and Raven include reward power, coercive power, referent power, and expert power. Reward and coercion are readily understood as forms of power. Referent power is similar to charisma; it refers to the ability of a leader to encourage affiliation or involvement on the part of followers. Expert power refers to influence based upon knowledge.

Each of these forms of power has applications in school settings. Principals can reward teachers with praise, favorable reviews, and certain discretionary assignments. They can coerce them by witholding the same. Some principals have the ability to build a sense of belonging and commitment to themselves or to their school, which is a form of referent power. Administrators have expert power when they understand how to teach or how to deal with problems faced by teachers. An administrator who does not understand and employ these forms of power as well as the power of office will probably enjoy a very limited sphere of influence.

Leadership in Informal Settings

Leadership is often provided by individuals who have not been appointed to office or otherwise formally designated as leaders. Consider, for example, a group of four third-grade teachers assigned to the same building. Perhaps in the course of eating lunch together one day they learn that each of them feels a need for more supplementary science materials. One of the teachers may take the initiative to encourage the others to pool their efforts and develop additional materials which the group would share. This initiative could include arranging one or more work sessions to discuss the kinds of materials that are needed, developing a schedule of assignments, and encouraging everyone to complete the work in timely fashion. Schools and other organizations provide frequent opportunities for individuals to provide such leadership, and many individuals find it personally rewarding to do so.

Informal leadership is not always as supportive of organizational goals as the above example suggests. For example, the implementation of Public Law

94–142 has been made difficult in some schools by teachers who have kindled the fears of their colleagues about the difficulty of mainstreaming handicapped students. When such teachers are perceived as influential because of referent, expert or coercive power related to their status in the group, they can have countervailing effects on official policy and directions.

Schools and other organizations include an extensive network of informal groups.[10] Some of them are work-related and others are largely social, such as lunch groups, teachers who share the same free period, or coworkers who regularly play bridge or golf together. These groups are very important to organizations; they provide incentives for individuals to belong and contribute to the organization. For example, it is not unusual for teachers or administrators to refuse better-paying jobs in another district largely because they like the people in the present one. Informal groups also help members understand organizational expectations, establish norms to guide worker behavior, provide communication channels, and constitute an arena where workers can test new ideas or express opposition to the policies and practices of management before speaking directly to management.

The activities of informal groups provide opportunities for the exercise of leadership. Leadership in such settings is often a useful background to a career in administration. Because informal leaders achieve status without the power of office, they often have the ability to build group morale and cohesiveness or provide expertise that the group needs. These qualities are often noticed when the organization is looking for people to promote into administrative positions.

Administrators who recognize the importance of informal groups sometimes want to dominate them. This is usually neither possible nor desirable, for even the most loyal and cooperative organization members want opportunities to talk "off the record" or "out of school" with their fellow workers. Rather than insisting on membership in all such groups, the thoughtful administrator will recognize their potential for developing leadership skills in others and be mindful of opportunities for communicating with staff members through the informal network.

LEADERSHIP THEORY FOR SCHOOL SETTINGS[11]

Most educational administrators have been trained to view and implement leadership from two perspectives. The first is an authoritarian perspective in which the administrator is regarded as a managerial link in a closely defined chain of command. The second and more widely prescribed (if not practiced) perspective is a democratic one which stresses participative decision making. Neither is entirely adequate for the contemporary scene.

The authoritarian model is the leadership analogue to bureaucratic organizations. It is based upon clearly defined lines of authority, responsibility, and communication. Because it accounts for specialization of functions, roles, and regularity, it is predictable, accountable, and in some respects efficient. Schools are bureaucratic organizations in some but not all respects. Because of this and because the authoritarian model prevails in the broader society, it has strongly influenced the leadership behavior of school administrators.

Whereas the authoritarian model emphasizes decisiveness by administrators and deference by subordinates, the democratic model stresses participative decision making, informality, and colleagueship. The authoritarian model emphasizes single-minded devotion to task completion; advocates of democratic leadership aver that concern for task completion must be tempered by consideration for the feelings of those to be affected by decisions. It is argued that democratic leadership is particularly appropriate for schools because teachers are professionals whose expertise should be acknowledged in decision making.[12] Advocates of student and community involvement argue that they too should be involved in making decisions that affect them.

The forces discussed thus far make it difficult for school administrators to develop, carry out, and be comfortable with a consistent leadership style. On the one hand, they work in organizations that are generally regarded as rational bureaucracies. As a consequence, they do feel accountable for achieving certain goals and assuring that others comply with organizational policies and procedures. These feelings and concomitant time pressures encourage authoritarian behaviors. On the other hand, these same administrators have been socialized by their colleagues and trained by universities to have high regard for democratic leadership behavior.

As noted above, research and theory about leadership have offered little assistance to individuals faced with this dilemma. Until recently, the standard view was that leader activities are of essentially two kinds: those that initiate structure and those that show consideration.[13] Initiating structure refers to establishing goals, procedures, timetables, and other routines. Consideration involves demonstrating warmth toward and concern for the interests of subordinates. The concepts are sometimes referred to as task and human-relations orientations.

Most of the leadership preparation literature recognizes that both of these dimensions are important, and encourages leaders to manifest both qualities as much as possible. The difficulties with this are that (1) not all leaders are equally inclined to and adept at both kinds of behavior; and (2) both kinds of behavior are not equally important in all situations. For example, initiating structure (providing directions) is clearly more important than consideration (demonstrating warmth and concern) in settings of emergency crowd control. Likewise, subordinates have indicated that they do not always want to be involved in decisions that affect them. Thus the problem is to know which kinds of leader behavior to employ in particular situations.

One widely-noted theory suggests that each administrator has a basic leadership style that governs his or her behavior. Fiedler[14] developed a contingency theory of leadership effectiveness that uses an easily administered questionnaire to distinguish among administrators according to how they regard their "least-preferred coworker" (LPC). People who describe their LPC negatively tend to be more autocratic and task-oriented and less democratic and relationship-oriented than people with high LPC scores. Fiedler's theory is that people with high or low LPC scores have different leadership styles and that the effectiveness of these styles varies according to situational factors.

Favorable situations, according to Fiedler, are those where the task is clearly structured, relationships between the leader and the group are warm and friendly, and the leader has strong position power. Unfavorable situations are those where the task is unclear, relationships are poor, and the formal power of the leader is weak. Fiedler used these variables to develop a three-dimensional model that contains eight different combinations of the task, relationship, and position-power variables. A large number of studies have indicated that low LPC leaders are most effective in situations that are either very favorable or very unfavorable. High LPC leaders are most effective in situations defined as moderately favorable.

The clearest implication of the Fiedler theory is that administrators should endeavor to understand their own leadership style and seek work settings where it is most likely to be effective. Beyond this, however, we must note that substantial disagreement exists about exactly what it is that the LPC instrument measures and how accurately, whether leadership style changes over time by intention or otherwise, and whether a leader can or should be taught to modify situational factors so as to be more favorable to his or her particular style.[15]

Another recent approach to leadership theory is that of Vroom and Yetton, who developed a model to guide decision making.[16] Their taxonomy of decision-making modes (see Figure 7–1) ranges from unilateral decision making through consulting with others to achieve consensus, to delegating the problem and responsibility for its solution to others. In choosing one of these modes, the authors say that the leader should be guided by the particular characteristics of the problem or situation. Among the attributes to be considered are the extent to which the leader possesses sufficient information to make a good decision unilaterally, the extent to which subordinates have necessary information, the importance of subordinate commitment to effective implementation, the likelihood that an autocratic decision would be accepted, and the extent to which subordinates are likely to disagree about preferred solutions. Vroom and Yetton then suggest a set of questions by which a leader can choose a decision-making mode for a given problem, according to the particular attributes of the situation and whether the leader wants to maximize decision quality, subordinate acceptance, or time efficiency in the process. These questions are set forth in Table 7–1.

Bobbitt et al. refer to the Vroom and Yetton model as the "most precise theory of leadership published to date."[17] The advantage of the model is that it suggests specific decision-making behaviors for leaders in particular situations. It is a contingency theory inasmuch as it recognizes that the choice of a particular decision-making mode should be determined by the kind of decision outcomes the leader seeks in a situation with particular attributes. Use of the model, of

FIGURE 7–1
Degrees of group
participation in
decision making
according to Vroom
and Yetton

Degrees of participation		Key	Explanation
None			
	Alone	A I	Manager makes the decision alone.
		A II	Manager asks for information from subordinates but makes the decision alone. Subordinates may or may not be informed about what the problem is.
	Consultation	C I	Manager shares the problem with and asks for information and evaluations from them. Meetings take place as dyads, not as a group, and the manager then goes off and makes the decision.
		C II	Manager and subordinates meet as a group to discuss the problem, but the manager makes the decision.
	Group	G	Manager and subordinates meet as a group to discuss the problem, and the group as a whole makes the decision.
High			

Source: Reprinted by permission from *Organization Behavior*, Second Edition, by Don Hellriegel and John W. Slocum, Jr. Copyright © 1979 by West Publishing Company. All rights reserved. Based on V.H. Vroom and P.W. Yetton, *Leadership and Decision-Making* (Pittsburgh, Pa.: University of Pittsburgh Press, 1973).

course, depends upon the ability of the administrator to select the most appropriate decision-making mode and to exercise the self-control required to implement it.[18] While people have been taught to do this,[19] we must caution that the model is still being tested and the effects of its implementation are not yet clear.

Some of the precision in the Vroom and Yetton model is achieved by focusing upon the decision-making behavior of leaders. Another recent theory with somewhat broader application is the path-goal theory of leadership developed by Evans[20] and House.[21] While this theory also requires further empirical support, it has an internal common-sense base suggesting that it can be helpful to administrators in day-to-day situations.

The basic assumption of path-goal theory is that leader behavior has its most direct effect on the psychological states of subordinates. A major proposition of the theory is that the function of a leader is to work with subordinates in ways that lead to motivation to perform or satisfaction with the job. A second proposition is that the particular leader behaviors that will achieve this motivating function are determined by situational factors. The theory suggests that the leader can provide whatever is not already present in the environment to motivate subordinates in particular directions. In general terms, the function of a leader according to this theory is to help clarify goals and ease the path toward them so that others are motivated toward their achievement.

TABLE 7–1
Summary of Vroom and Yetton contingency model of group decision making

DIAGNOSTIC QUESTIONS

Types of problems	1 Is there a criterion which will show that one solution is better than another?	2 Do I have enough information?	3 Is the problem structured?	4 Do I need subordinate acceptance?	5 Will I get acceptance if I decide alone?	6 Do subordinates share the organizational goals?	7 Is conflict among subordinates likely?	Degree of group participation
1	No			No				A I
2	No			Yes	Yes			A I
3	No			Yes	No			G
4	Yes	Yes		No				A I
5	Yes	Yes		Yes	Yes			A I
6	Yes	Yes		Yes	No	Yes		G
7	Yes	Yes		Yes	No	No	Yes	C II
8	Yes	Yes		Yes	No	No	No	C I
9	Yes	No	Yes	Yes	Yes			A II
10	Yes	No	Yes	No	No			A II
11	Yes	No	No	Yes	Yes			C II
12	Yes	No	No	Yes	No	Yes		G
13	Yes	No	No	Yes	No	No		C II
14	Yes	No	No	No				C II

Blanks simply mean that the information is not relevant due to the response to some other question.

Source: Reprinted by permission from *Organization Behavior*, Second Edition, by Don Hellriegel and John W. Slocum, Jr. Copyright © 1979 by West Publishing Company. All rights reserved. Based on V. H. Vroom and P. W. Yetton, *Leadership and Decision Making* (Pittsburgh, Pa.: University of Pittsburgh Press, 1973).

House and Dessler suggest that there are six ways in which a leader can carry out these functions. They include:

1. Recognizing and/or arousing subordinates' needs for outcomes over which the leader has some control
2. Increasing personal payoffs to subordinates for work-goal attainment
3. Making the path to these payoffs easier to travel by coaching and direction
4. Helping subordinates clarify expectancies
5. Reducing frustrating barriers
6. Increasing the opportunities for personal satisfaction contingent upon effective performance.[22]

Note that a building principal has the resources to act in these ways in relation to teachers, students, and others. For example, the principal can recognize a teacher's need for recognition and provide it for goal-directed behaviors. The principal can provide personal payoffs such as a desired room, free period or the opportunity to share in certain decisions. Principals also play a coaching or directing role by supporting teachers and helping them to choose a course of action when they lack confidence or are faced with ambiguous situations. Principals also help teachers and others clarify expectations in such a way that they are more likely to be achieved; a recent study, for example, found that SAT scores were less inclined to drop in high schools where traditional expectations for academic achievement were maintained.[23] Opportunities for principals to remove frustrating barriers are widespread. They include such things as securing central office approval for teacher-initiated proposals, providing transportation for field trips, and buffering unreasonable parent demands and complaints. The principal can also enhance opportunities for personal satisfaction by structuring teacher assignments so that teachers receive intrinsic rewards from working with their classes.

The key to successful implementation of the above leadership functions is to understand the particular needs and interests of each individual in a given situation. In this regard, path-goal theory holds that it is important for leaders to understand both their subordinates and the environment in which they work. Important subordinate characteristics include (1) needs for affiliation and social approval, (2) need for achievement, (3) need for intrinsic rewards and (4) self-perceived ability to carry out tasks. Important environmental characteristics include (1) the nature of the task, (2) the formal authority system and (3) the primary work group. These factors can contribute to or impede the achievement of goals. For example, the informal relationships among teachers in a building may or may not be supportive of innovative teaching efforts.

An important tenet of path-goal theory is that where characteristics of subordinates and the environment are such that path-goal relationships are already clear, a leader's effort to clarify them further is not appreciated. In this context, we can understand not only why teachers resent close monitoring or "teacher proof" activities, but also "opportunities" to participate in making decisions that are self-evident. Conversely, the theory indicates that leader initiatives are most appreciated when they help followers deal with uncertainty or frustration.

The most pervasive implication of the theories discussed here for school administrators is that there is no single best way for leaders to behave. In particular, the theories cast doubt upon the strong and recurring advocacy of democratic administration. For example, path-goal theory provides an explanation for the finding of Kunz and Hoy that teachers prefer principals who score high on initiating structure and low on consideration to those who exhibit the reverse.[24] It may be that the teachers in the Kunz and Hoy sample perceived sufficient ambiguity or frustration in their environment that they preferred more structured leadership.

While each of the theories requires further verification, all point to the need for administrators to be aware of their own tendencies in leadership situations and to understand the range of behaviors open to them. Moreover, they must combine this self-assessment with a perceptiveness about the characteristics of subordinates and environmental factors. Finally, for those who possess such understanding and the determination to act upon it, these theories offer new insights about how to proceed.

TACTICAL CONSIDERATIONS FOR SCHOOL LEADERS

As discussed in Chapter 3, schools are complex organizations, resembling other formal organizations in many aspects but differing from them in others. The differences were highlighted by describing schools as professional bureaucracies, organized anarchies, domesticated organizations, and loosely coupled systems. These formulations suggest some important tactical considerations for the leader who would be guided by the theories discussed in the preceding section.[25]

Persist Toward Clear, Attainable Goals

Despite the general ambiguity of the goals and purposes of schooling (discussed in Chapter 3), it is possible to identify subgoals that are both clear and attainable. Examples at the district level include developing and implementing plans to assure that all special education students are properly evaluated and placed in least-restrictive learning environments; introducing a new program to provide enrichment opportunities for all gifted students in the district; obtaining community support for an increase in the educational tax rate; or closing a school to achieve budget savings. Subgoals at the building level might include beginning a parent volunteer tutoring program, increasing student use of the library, or raising school-wide averages on achievement tests. Many administrators develop a lengthy list of such goals to guide their activities each year.

It can be expected that not everyone will agree with the goals that are established. However, their articulation makes it possible for people who do support them to become active on behalf of the organization. Moreover, the extent of opposition can often be lessened through the process of establishing the goals.

The Vroom and Yetton model provides guidance in this regard. When opposition does exist, it is faced with the problem of defining an alternative that is more attractive than that proposed by the leader. Sometimes several alternatives are proposed. Many people often prefer the status quo to the stated goal. Because opposition may come from diverse quarters and emerge at different points in time, it is important that the leader be willing to persist in the pursuit of goals. Of course, it is possible to reach a point when the opposition is overwhelming, or an appropriate goal becomes inappropriate due to changes in the environment. At such times, leaders should reassess their commitment to a given organizational goal. Nonetheless, many goals can only be accomplished over time and the tenacity of the leaders who espouse them is crucial to their realization.

Followers who believe that goals are indeed attainable are more likely to be motivated to achieve them. Citizens who believe that a tax levy can be passed are more likely to make speeches and ring doorbells than those who feel such efforts are useless. Teachers who believe that children can learn will devote more effort to teaching than those who believe children are dumb or disinterested and attend school only because the law compels them to do so. Moreover, the achievement of goals often leads to satisfaction that in itself encourages individuals to pursue additional goals. Thus, it is important for school leaders to insure that goals are attainable as well as clear.

Use Multiple Paths   The loosely coupled nature of schools permits different units of the organization to adapt to environmental changes in different ways. Thus there may be broad differences in how elementary mathematics or science is taught among schools in the same districts. Teachers in the same building, too, may have very different approaches to student discipline or the teaching of particular subjects. The nature of the system makes it very difficult for leaders to impose controls that have universal impact.

This situation presents school leaders with both opportunities and problems. The opportunities include focusing their attention on particular organizational units that need occasional attention or have potential for special growth. For example, an elementary principal who wants to improve mathematics instruction in her school may determine that all but two teachers are doing well in this area. She can focus her attention on working with these two teachers and assume that the others will continue to do well. Similarly, a superintendent who wishes to develop a program in computer literacy could provide resources to begin the program on a pilot basis to a school where staff members have expressed interest in microcomputers. The difficulties of designing a new curriculum could be worked out in this school without affecting the program in others.

Problems associated with loosely coupled systems arise when administrators wish to implement goals that affect more than one organizational subsystem. It is rarely possible to issue a single directive or provide a common training program to achieve system-wide change. If the goal is to establish district-wide procedures for classifying handicapped children, or improving mathematics instruction in a single elementary school, it is likely that the individuals who must help implement the goal will approach it from different paths. Successful leaders recognize this and endeavor to ease these multiple paths. Again, it is appropriate to emphasize perseverance: successful leadership in a complex matter such as starting a new program or closing a school requires continuing efforts at clarifying expectations, providing rewards and supports, and reducing frustrating barriers.

Utilize Information Networks

The loosely coupled nature of schools and the multiple constituencies with which administrators deal place them in positions to link various subsystems and constituencies when they have common interests. As noted in Chapter 4, school administrators spend most of their work time communicating with different groups and individuals. Principals communicate with teachers, students, parents, custodians, suppliers, and other citizens. Superintendents communicate with members of their staff, state and federal officials, members of the board of education, and others. These efforts provide school leaders with the most comprehensive understanding of what various constituents want and will accept from the school. They also provide the leaders with opportunity to influence the thoughts of those with whom they interact.

Ogawa and Pitner[26] suggest that this interaction pattern enables superintendents to have important influence on their systems. They hear, interpret, and mediate the preferences expressed for the system by others. Their ability to process and communicate this information effectively is an important source of power, for it contributes to the "shared meanings" that guide the actions of the systems. Effective leaders, according to this perspective, use their place in the information network to determine issues and concerns that must be dealt with, and to shape the others' views in ways that are consistent with their own preferences.

Acknowledge the Importance of Counterinfluence

The traditional view of leadership holds that the leader exercises influence over followers. Hollander[27] refers to leadership as a transactional process, and asserts that for leaders to maintain influence over a group, they must allow the group to exercise some influence over them. Followers assess the effectiveness of leaders based on their responsiveness to the followers' needs. Thus, leaders should be mindful of the views and preferences of followers as they communicate with them, for their effectiveness in exercising influence will depend upon their status and legitimacy with the group.

This view has implications for leadership in school settings in at least two ways. As professional bureaucracies, school systems are populated by individuals who are relatively well educated, view themselves as experts in particular fields, and are likely to consult external sources (e.g., professional associations) for guidance about professional matters. It is likely that they know more about their field (e.g., teaching reading or counseling students) than does the principal, superintendent, or any other administrator. Administrators who wish to retain legitimacy with (and hence the ability to lead) such groups allow themselves to be influenced in matters where the group's expertise is greater. Indeed, their ultimate influence may be strengthened if they not only allow but encourage the group to provide its own leadership in such matters.

When matters of consequence to a group must be presented outside the group, members will often expect their formal leader to be their advocate. Here we see a second and more difficult aspect of transactional leadership. As already noted, school administrators occupy linking positions among many loosely coupled subsystems. Thus, for example, if a question arises about the number of English credits that should be required for high school graduation, the English department and school counselors might have different recommendations and expectations for the principal to forward to the central administration. In such situations, the ability of the administrator to hear both sides, decide fairly, and communicate the reasons for the final decision may affect his or her ability to retain legitimacy and leadership of one or more subgroups.

Consider the Public Interest

Most schools are public organizations, and most of those that are not are subject to public scrutiny. We live in a time of great concern for the public interest, however ill-defined that term may be. Much of this concern stems from revelations of corruption and rampant self-interest in government, business, and the professions. Schools have not been immune to such accusations. Events of this kind, combined with the apparent impersonality of large organizations and other factors, have led many individuals to become very cynical about organizational leadership. A not-uncommon charge is that leaders use or manipulate employees to their own disadvantage but to the benefit of the organization.

In our view, manipulation involves forcing individuals to act contrary to their own interests without their knowledge, and occurs infrequently in organizations. It is not to be confused with the exercise of influence, which is an inescapable circumstance of leadership. An extended treatment of ethics in government and leadership activity is complex and beyond the scope of this book. Nonetheless, we think it useful to note that Harlan Cleveland has suggested a single question for administrators to ask themselves about the ethics of any proposed action: "If this action is held up to public scrutiny, will I still feel that this is what I should have done, and how I should have done it?"[28]

Honest answers to this question force administrators to come to grips with their own values in leadership situations; they also sensitize them to the growing possibility that their actions will indeed become public.

SUMMARY

Leadership is a process through which an individual secures the cooperation of others toward the achievement of goals in a particular setting. It is common to overestimate the impact of leadership on a given situation; other factors that must be considered include the nature of the goal, the followers, and the setting.

Schools provide a variety of opportunities for individuals to exercise leadership, including many that occur in informal settings.

Early theory and research pertaining to leadership focused upon "one-best-way theories." More recently, contingency theories have been advanced by Fiedler, Vroom and Yetton, and House. These theories suggest directions for leader behavior in school settings based upon the leader's assessment of the settings. In drawing on these theories, school administrators are advised to persist toward clear attainable goals, use multiple paths and information networks, acknowledge the importance of counterinfluence, and consider the public interest.

ENDNOTES

1. For discussion of this view, see Sidney Hook, *The Hero in History* (Boston: Beacon Press, 1955).
2. Edwin M. Bridges, "The Nature of Leadership," in Luvern L. Cunningham, Walter G. Hack, and Raphael O. Nystrand, eds., *Educational Administration: The Developing Decades* (Berkeley, Cal.: McCutchan Publishing, 1977), pp. 202–230.
3. The dimensions of task accomplishment and group maintenance have firm basis in the literature. See, for example, D.C. Cartwright and A. Zander, *Group Dynamics: Research and Theory* (Evanston, Ill.: Row, Peterson, 1960) and Andrew W. Halpin, *Theory and Research in Administration* (New York: Macmillan, 1966), pp. 81–130.
4. Louis M. Smith and Pat M. Keith, *Anatomy of an Educational Innovation* (New York: John Wiley and Sons, 1971).
5. Jeffry Pfeffer, "The Ambiguity of Leadership," *Academy of Management Review* 211 (1977).
6. This theme has a long history in education as well as government. See Raymond E. Callahan, *Education and the Cult of Efficiency* (Chicago: University of Chicago Press, 1962).
7. The most comprehensive review of this research is Bernard M. Bass, *Stogdill's Handbook of Leadership* (New York: The Free Press, 1981).
8. David L. Clark, Linda S. Lotto, and Martha M. McCarthy, "Factors Associated with Success in Urban Elementary Schools," *Phi Delta Kappan* 61 (March 1980): 467–470.
9. John R.P. French, Jr. and Bertram Raven, "The Basis of Social Power" in Darwin Cartwright, ed., *Studies in Social Power* (Ann Arbor, Mich.: Institute for Social Research, 1959), pp. 150–167.
10. See Lawrence Iannaccone "An Approach to the Informal Organization of the School," in Daniel Griffiths, ed., *Sixty-third Yearbook of the National Society for the Study of Education*, part 2, *Behavior Science and Educational Administration* (Chicago: The Society), pp. 223–242.
11. An earlier version of this section was published in Raphael O. Nystrand, "Leadership Theories for Principals," *Theory Into Practice* 20 (Autumn 1981): 260–263.
12. For example, see Thomas J. Sergiovanni and Fred D. Carver, *The New School Executive* (New York: Dodd, Mead, 1974).
13. Andrew W. Halpin, "The Leader Behavior and Leadership Ideology of Educational Administrators and Aircraft Commanders," *Harvard Educational Review* 25 (Winter 1955): 18–32.
14. Fred Fiedler, *A Theory of Leadership Effectiveness* (New York: McGraw-Hill, 1967).
15. See Chester A. Schriesheim and Steven Kerr, "Theories and Measures of Leadership: A Critical Appraisal of Current and Future Directions," in James G. Hunt and Lars L. Larson, eds., *Leadership: The Cutting Edge* (Carbondale: Southern Illinois University Press, 1977). See also the rejoinder by Fiedler and Schriesheim and Kerr's response in the same volume.
16. Victor H. Vroom and Philip W. Yetton, *Leadership and Decision-Making* (Pittsburgh, Pa. University of Pittsburgh Press, 1973).
17. H. Randolph Bobbitt, Jr. et al., *Organizational Behavior: Understanding and Prediction* 2d ed. (Englewood Cliffs, N.J.: Prentice-Hall, 1978), p. 272.
18. Schreisheim and Kerr, "Theories and Measures," p. 40.

19. Schreisheim and Kerr, "Theories and Measures."
20. Martin G. Evans, "The Effects of Supervisory Behavior on the Path-Goal Relationship," *Organizational Behavior and Human Performance* 56 (1970): 277–298.
21. The discussion here is based primarily upon Robert J. House and G. Dessler, "The Path-Goal Theory of Leadership: Some Post Hoc and A Priori Tests," in James G. Hunt and Lars L. Larson, eds., *Contingency Approaches to Leadership* (Carbondale: Southern Illinois University Press, 1974).
22. House and Dessler, "Path-Goal Theory," p. 30.
23. National Association of Secondary School Principals, *Guidelines for Improving SAT Scores* (Reston, Va.: The Association, 1978).
24. Daniel W. Kunz and Wayne K. Hoy, "Leadership Style of Principals and Professional Zone of Acceptance of Teachers," *Educational Administration Quarterly* 12 (Fall 1976): 49–64.
25. The ideas of Cohen and March regarding leadership in an organized anarchy are especially applicable. Some of them are reflected in the discussion following. See Michael D. Cohen and James G. March, *Leadership and Ambiguity: The American College President* (New York: McGraw-Hill, 1974), pp. 195–229.
26. Rodney T. Ogawa and Nancy J. Pitner "Organizational Leadership: The Case of the School Superintendent, or Up the Creek with a Paddle," *Educational Administration Quarterly* 17 (Spring 1981): 45–65.
27. Edwin P. Hollander, *Leadership Dynamics: A Practical Guide to Effective Relationships* (New York: Macmillan, 1978).
28. Harlan Cleveland, *The Future Executive* (New York: Harper and Row, 1972), p. 104.

CHAPTER 8

COMMUNICATION

In Chapter 4 we described the work of school administrators. Throughout that chapter, as various studies of administration and administrators were cited, the term "communication" occurred. We indicated that the term is a very broad one and covers many activites. This chapter will cover the meaning and the processes of communication, and the ways in which communication is an essential aspect of the educational administrator's tasks.

Because "communication" represents a set of concepts more than specific acts, it is important to begin this discussion with a description of what we mean by the terms "communication" and "communication processes," and a discussion of the criteria used to determine their effectiveness.

DEFINITIONS AND CRITERIA

During the 1960s and '70s, educational administrators—particularly in the secondary schools, colleges, and universities—were often subjected to demands from various groups for "increased communication," and were often accused of being totally without communication with "those who really mattered." Most administrators were perplexed by these charges because they knew they were spending an undue amount of time talking with people, listening to people, reading tracts, statements, demands, letters, and newspaper editorials, and generally engaging in what they supposed to be communication.

Communication

One explanation is that people have a tendency to complain about communication when results are not what they hope to achieve. If, after much talk, someone goes ahead and does something with which we disagree, we have the tendency to believe (or state) that there has been "no communication." Indeed, there are definitions that require the desired response by the listener for communication to have taken place. Merrihue, for example, insists that communication does not occur unless it causes a "desired response behavior from the receiver."[1] Obviously, the purpose of communication is to create some response,[2] but the absence of a particular response does not seem to us to indicate the absence of communication. Davis's definition posits *understanding* as a component of communication,[3] but does not necessarily require any action response.

As we shall use the term, *communication* is the transfer of information or of messages from a source to a receiver. It has little or nothing to do with the use to which a receiver puts the information or messages received, although that factor is a measure of the effectiveness of communication. It can, however, involve rapid changes of status from source to receiver: in what is often described as a "give and take" discussion between two individuals, each is alternately a source and a receiver.

One dictionary puts it nicely: "*Communicate* . . . means to pass something along. *Communicate* suggests . . . that it become the common property of giver and receiver."[4] The term *common property* implies that communication requires both the transmission and receipt of a message or unit of information. Without both, the commonality is lacking. For instance, if a principal asks a teacher to meet her at seven o'clock, there is no real communication unless both know where to meet and whether the meeting is for breakfast or for dinner. When transmitting by radio, one must often deal with "noise" or static. The request to meet at seven represents noise much more than it does communication.

For our purposes, then, communication requires a source, a receiver, and transmitted information or messages that become the common property of both.

Communication Processes

Perhaps no endeavor has received more attention, effort, and creativity than has the communication of humans with each other. From drawing on cave walls to burying time capsules on the moon, people strive to share their thoughts, their fears, their history with others. A primary distinction of the human species is the development of language—both sounds that can be spoken and heard and understood, and symbols that can be recorded and read and understood. Language, spoken and written, is the basic tool of communication and without it most communication as we know it would be impossible. It should be easy to understand why concerns for language (including mathematical notations, which are themselves a form of language) are at the heart of our concern about schools. Reading, 'riting, and 'rithmetic—the three R's—are nothing less than the basic tools of communication, the means through which messages become our common property. Language can be transmitted verbally, in writing, and, increasingly, electronically on computers. The last methodology is important, but it is the first two that are most pertinent to this discussion.

The use of the spoken word in a face-to-face setting is perhaps the most effective communication process available. It permits the exchange to take place rapidly; it allows the use of "body language" and expressions whereby the receiver can gauge meanings from nonverbal cues (e.g., smiles or frowns) as well as from words. Most educational administrators learn early in their careers, however, that what sounds humorous and appropriate in conversation can become devastating when printed in or out of context in the morning paper. As is discussed later in this chapter, there are opportunities for distortions and misunderstandings in verbal communication just as there are in other forms. A number of studies, for example, show strong positive correlations between the accuracy of an information exchange and the quality of the interpersonal relationships of those involved in the exchange.[5] Other studies confirm that the acceptance of information, regardless of its accuracy, varies directly with the organizational status of the source.[6] As effective as it can be, verbal or oral communication is by no means an error-free form of sending and receiving information.

Oral communication

Administrators are involved in a great variety of verbal communication settings, a few of which will be discussed later in this chapter. In each setting, verbal communication involves the elements of spoken language, the quality of voice and voice projection, expressions (facial, gestures, and the like) that accompany the words, and a set of perceptions held by the receiver.

From formal, printed annual reports to handwritten memoranda to colleagues, educational administrators are constantly engaged in written communication. As is true of oral communication, written messages involve more than just the language. The way a written message is prepared is crucial. Most educators probably experience the embarrassment of sending a letter to a parent or some constituent in which a word is misspelled. Unfortunately, in many cases the spelling error, rather than the substance of the letter, becomes the message. In the same way, the form of a written communication becomes part of the transmission. If a letter is sent, is it neatly typed with good style and form? If a brochure is produced, is it well organized, with a type face that is easily read? What sorts of tables, charts, pictures, or diagrams accompany the written words and with what effect? Written communication, then, is a total package and both words and the form of the package influence the transmission of the information or message.

Written communication

Obviously, administrators communicate through processes that involve several techniques simultaneously. Presentations to a board or a committee often involve the recorded spoken word, visual techniques ranging from slide projections to videotapes, charts and graphs displayed on easels, and perhaps even a musical background to stir the emotions. An administrator can point out a prob-

Combination processes

lem by using a picture—of an unsafe boiler, say—but the crucial part of the message almost always involves words. In this case the message would be answers to the questions: For how long has this been going on? How unsafe is the boiler? What do you want us to do about it? Sometimes words are accompanied by sounds or gestures to capture the attention of the listeners or to enhance the impact of the message. Sounds, gestures, and other nonverbal displays, however, can also be used to mask the lack of a real message.

Effectiveness of Communication

As is true of all measurement, we must know the purpose of something to discover its effectiveness. Some communication seeks direct, overt action on the part of the receiver. When a drill sergeant barks out, "Halt," the expectation is that the receivers will halt. If they do not, however, where is the ineffectiveness? Clearly, the word is one known to the receivers and it is a word to which the expected response is known. If only half the platoon halts, was the communication ineffective, or was it the response that was lacking in quality? Or, to give a more relevant example, what if a teacher barks out to the class, "Learn!" What if the superintendent barks out to the taxpayers, "Increase the millage!"

The point of these examples is that the appropriateness or suitability of the content of a message is a critical factor in the effectiveness of its communication. The message must have real meaning and credibility for the receiver; must be transmitted clearly and in terms that are understood the same way by both source and receiver; and should not be accompanied by "noise" or other messages that conflict with the intended transmission. Communication—depending upon its purpose—can lead to (1) overt action, (2) deliberative processes on the part of the receiver, (3) a response (the receiver becomes the source), or (4) simply an increase in the knowledge of the receiver.

Communication has byproducts. For example, a principal may direct a teacher to monitor the lunchroom, and the teacher may do so. But if the teacher resents the direction and forms a union as a result of it, was the communication effective?

We consider communication to be effective when (1) its purpose is known, (2) its purpose is accomplished, and (3) its purpose is accomplished without creating negative byproducts.

COMMUNICATION CHANNELS

Without taking the analogy too far, it is fair to say that communication flows, that it does so through channels, and that it stays within channels (does not overflow the banks) if the channels are well defined, well established, and adequate to carry the volume. Organization charts depict one set of channels within an institution through which communication flows, as well as authority, decision-making processes, and interrelationships among positions. But the formal organization does not show all of the communication channels available to the administrator. We now examine several different kinds.

Organizational structures provide formal channels of communication within an institution. They provide a means of facilitating so-called official communication: messages and information essential to the workings of the institution. The structure is an official network—it provides places for the origination of various kinds of communications; relay points through which messages and information are spread to the organization; and often monitoring facilities to determine if messages or information have been received and understood. The maintenance, operation, and evaluation of this network are key responsibilities of the administrator. Gathering accurate and sufficient information at the right place and at the right time is a constant requirement of leadership and a primary function of the organizational structure. In this sense, then, the organization chart is a diagram of the formal, internal communications network of an institution.

Organizational Structures

It is important to differentiate between the organization and the people who populate the various boxes on an organization chart. A failure of organizational communication flow can be a failure of the organizational arrangements or a failure of the people within those arrangements. Campbell presents an extensive overview of the ways people in an organization can impede information flow[7]: people may purposefully distort messages for their own purposes, fail to transmit parts of messages they do not understand, or pay more attention to the "noise" surrounding a message than to the message itself. On the other hand, Lortie points out that there may be organizational inhibitions to communication in schools as well, due to the typical separation of teachers from each other and from administrators in their daily work.[8] As an administrator examines his or her organization and its effect on communication, both the organization and the people need consideration.

The formal communication structure is important and must be used. It is inefficient and confusing to have official messages and information circulating throughout an organization in a random manner. Some people would probably receive duplicate or triplicate copies while others "never get the word." But the formal network does not provide administrators with all of the information they need.

Organizational Contacts

"How do the fourth-grade teachers feel about the new reading series?" "Do the custodians believe that the new inexpensive building-maintenance products are doing the job?" "What do the high school students think about lengthening class periods and eliminating study halls?" The answers to this type of question provide administrators with important information. Is the only way that the superintendent can discover answers to these questions to "go through channels"? Should the reading-series question go from the superintendent to an assistant superintendent to elementary school principals and to fourth-grade teachers with the answer working its way back through the same channel? Our view is that administrators must foster contacts within the organization to gather information informally. Decision-making processes need to follow channels, but administrators need to develop "feelings" channels so that they are aware of concerns and of attitudes—how things look "in the front lines."[9]

In the reading-series case, for example, a superintendent might lunch informally with teachers, visit schools during class breaks, or through other means talk with teachers and learn that there is unrest about the new series. This information needs to be put into the formal channels for review and study and, perhaps, for decision. The superintendent at lunch should not say, "We'll change that series!" but he or she can say, "I am glad to know about your concerns and will have the assistant superintendent look into this right away."

Within the organization, then, the administrator needs both formal communications channels for the official work of the organization, and informal channels through which feelings, attitudes, and concerns can be transmitted and received. The administrator must be sure to use each for its intended purposes, but both are important to administrator and organizational effectiveness.

External Channels— Formal

The administrator is almost always a part of one or more formal communications channels outside the organizational structure. Professional organizations often provide such channels. Legislative networks, professional seminars or journals, and conferences are also formal means of professional communication. Community organizations such as service clubs or chambers of commerce can provide still other formal means of communication. Administrators are often "joiners" and the reason for this is to provide themselves with formal communication opportunities and channels outside of the school organization.

External Channels— Informal

Both a burden and an opportunity to educational administrators is the extent to which they are recognized in their community, and the amount of communication that comes from this recognition. Principals often find themselves receiving or sending messages related to their work in the supermarket check-out line, hair salon, golf course, and elsewhere. As within the organization, administrators must use these informal contacts to gain or give information, but not to supplant the formal mechanisms used for decision making and "official business." Astute administrators find the informal channels crucial in their work; without them they are not sure what needs to be sent through the formal channels, or whether information sent through those channels is reaching the intended receivers in the form it was sent.

Networks

Information science today speaks much more of networks than of channels. The concept of channels tends to portray a rather restricted series of information-flow paths, whereas the network concept attempts to analyze in greater detail the complete flow of messages through formal and informal, and internal and external means.

For example, assume that a formal message goes "through channels" advising that due to budgetary restrictions a textbook-use charge will be imposed during the coming school year. This message might be sent only through internal channels so as to avoid premature disclosure of this plan to the public. However, there could be links from teachers to students to parents, or from typists who are parents to their husbands—from internal sources to external sources, creating a communications network. Administrators need to be aware of probable communications links so that they do not imagine that there will not be disclosure of information when the opposite is true. Most of the time messages about significant internal affairs might just as well be prepared for external distribution because the network will distribute them in any case.

While the concept of channels is a useful and important one, the expanded network concept is more realistic and more useful. Both should be understood and used by administrators in their communications efforts.

Whatever the channels or networks, the form of the message or information to be transmitted is a critical decision. Many forms are available. The key set of choices that must be made in choosing a specific form and technique depend on the purpose of the communication. (Note that "purpose" is the primary constant in administrative leadership.[10]) Let us look briefly at several of the forms and techniques to illustrate the factors that should be taken into account in choosing one form over another.

COMMUNICATION TECHNIQUES

Written forms of communication today include notes, letters, memoranda, newsletters and other publications, telegrams and, increasingly, printouts from a computer or word processing system. Educational administrators use everything from scribbled notes to a colleague to formal, comprehensive, printed reports. To decide what form of written communication is most suitable and effective they should review the following:

Written Communication

1. The message or information to be transmitted
2. The audience (receiver) for the message or information
3. The degree to which a permanent record of the transmission is required by the source and/or the receiver
4. The complexity of the message or information
5. The purpose of the transmission

Let us assume that a principal knows that a teacher is trying a new method of teaching about values and that the principal sees an article in a professional journal about the method. The message in this case is: "Take a look at this article." The audience is one person—the teacher. No record of the transmission is necessary; the message is simple; and the purpose is to be helpful to a colleague.

On the other hand, if the principal wants to undertake an evaluation of the methodology and can allocate some funds for it, then the message is: "It seems important to evaluate this methodology and I can provide funds to assist you in doing so." The audience is still one person—the teacher—but a record of the transmission is important for the teacher, the principal, and perhaps for district budget and curriculum people. The message in this case would be somewhat complex because it would need to establish basic ground rules for the evaluation, describe budgetary considerations, and suggest a time frame. The purpose here is to make a proposal and to elicit a response. The former message can and should be a simple note; the latter requires a letter or memorandum, some duplicate copies, and some degree of formality.

In general, the larger and more diverse the intended audience, the greater the necessity for formality in communication. If the members of the audience for a written communication know the source well, they will "read into" the written message their personal knowledge of the person sending the message. This personal knowledge adds to the communication and makes it more meaningful—sometimes even more than is intended. On the other hand, if the members of the intended audience do not know the source well or at all, the entire message will be interpreted from the written word. In this case, the audience will be less tolerant of error, less willing to work hard to discover the message within the communication, and generally less interested in the message. A close and trusted friend who recommends an automobile wax does not have to "pretty up" the message with color pictures and handsome cars and car owners as does the unknown advertising agency. Likewise, the principal communicating with his or her staff should not have to add the embellishments that might be necessary in communicating with the neighborhood taxpayers' federation.

The issue of maintaining a record of communication may seem somewhat minor but is important in terms of both substance and cost. Some administrators keep files of everything; others keep virtually nothing. Because records of communication also become records of history, and because the communicator should not be the one to have sole discretion in determining what records will remain for history, some organizational policy and procedures related to records should be established. There is some wisdom in the idea that if it is not worth keeping in the archives, it may not be worth preparing in formal written form. Each method, however, is basically a means of transmitting a message or information and the choice of method depends upon the requirements of the five test areas mentioned above.

Verbal Communication

Verbal or oral communication has the advantages of information exchange and quick response. In addition, it provides the extra communication medium of facial expression, tone of voice, and the like. When interaction and response are essential to the purposes of communication, the written techniques are much less satisfactory than are meetings, conferences, or even conference phone calls. Oral communication can also produce a record—either a voice tape or, increasingly, video-tape—which can be maintained in tape form or transferred to written records.

Much of the communication of an administrator (both sending and receiving) is related to the assessment of attitudes, feelings, or progress within a school or school district. This assessment is simply not possible by written communication alone. The administrator who depends solely upon attitude surveys or questionnaires to assess these things will not be successful in the assessment. Face-to-face communication, discussion, even argument, are necessary. If people complain about administrators being "behind closed doors," it is not only because they want to know what the administrator is thinking and doing; they also want the administrator to know what they are thinking and doing, and the administrator must be in touch with them to learn these things. Too often administrators "open the door" so that people can watch them work or listen to them, but by and large that is not what people want.

A disadvantage of oral communication is that thoughts and ideas do not usually come forth in as organized and comprehensive a way as they do in writing. It can be a humbling experience for administrators to read a transcript of their participation in an interview or a conference. Particularly if they are attempting to present a complex idea where completeness, consistency, and clarity are important and where it is valuable for the receiver to be able to ponder and review before responding, written communication is preferable.

Administrators find themselves speaking often to meetings of colleagues, service clubs, parents, and many other groups. This form of communication is generally not as effective as its prevalence might indicate, but it is an important aspect of administrative life and should be used as effectively as possible. The speech can be a productive vehicle to transmit one or two—rarely more—major ideas, or to raise (but not to solve) one or two major issues. It can also provide the possibility of response, althought it should be kept in mind that a quick and loud response from the audience is not necessarily representative of the majority.

The administrator in education is, by necessity, a verbal person. Oral communication is an important tool, then, and a skill that needs use and practice to be maintained.[11]

New Technology

Recent years have seen amazing growth in the technology of communication. The written word can be transmitted over telephone lines to be reproduced in written form on paper or computer display screens. Easy, self-dialed telephone conference calls are now possible. Microfilm and microfiche records can store in square inches of space what used to require cubic yards. Satellite transmission of words and pictures makes instant communication possible over thousands of miles. A world that has seen live pictures from the moon and planets is a world in which communication technology is highly advanced.

The educational administrator, however, is primarily concerned with communication that is local, personal, and comparatively simple. It is to insure the transmission and receipt of messages and information among those working on behalf of a school or school district, and on behalf of teaching and learning. Much of what can be done today would amaze the school principals of the 1930s, but the basic communication needs and purposes of those principals have little changed since then.

COMMUNICATION PROBLEMS

The basic purposes and processes of communication are relatively simple; however, there are a number of potential problems in this area and administrators need to be aware of them.[12]

One of the great communications devices in the schools is the report card. Resplendent with letter grades, number grades, check marks, and comments, the report card might appear to be a marvel of communication; but it is in fact perhaps the best example in the schools of communication difficulties. The report card can involve problems of accuracy, perceptions, authority, communication flow, volume, content, and timing. These problems are well known to educators, but a brief review is in order to illustrate communication problems.

The report card is supposed to be a report from the school to the students and to their parents or guardians on the progress of the student in meeting curricular and other achievement objectives during a period of time. Its accuracy, however, depends entirely upon the specificity with which achievement objectives are known as well as the accuracy with which progress toward those objectives can be measured. Each receiver of the communication has his or her own perceptions of its meaning. And because the report card is issued by the teacher in an official way on an official form it carries a sense of authority that gives an appearance of exactness and finality. In addition, despite various efforts to report pupil progress through conferences and encourage parent or student comments in response to report cards, the report of pupil progress is usually a one-way communication. And finally, as regards volume, content, and timing, the report card often provides too little information too late to be of much assistance in the teaching-learning process.

Let us look at each of these problems in more detail.

Accuracy

Most people are familiar with the game where a message is whispered from person to person around a circle. The message that comes back to the originator is usually markedly different from what was transmitted. One key aspect of communication is receiving, and unless the recipient is paying attention—is tuned in—receipt of the message will not be accurate. Accuracy cannot be achieved without first getting the attention of the receiver.

An increasingly significant barrier to accuracy in communication in the United States is language itself. Professional "mumbo jumbo" or "gobbledy gook" is certainly a barrier, but there is another barrier receiving more attention, perhaps, than ever before. Few administrators are multilingual and yet principals or superintendents in many schools and school districts have parents and patrons who are most comfortable communicating in a language other than English. Unless one understands the language in which a message is being transmitted, the message will of course be incomprehensible.

Apart from these barriers, accuracy is a primary problem when the person sending a message or providing information does not do so clearly, completely, and correctly. Lack of accuracy can result from any of several causes. It may simply be carelessness; it may be that the communicator has been given inaccurate information to transmit; it may be an intent to deceive; or it may be some combination of these.

Obviously, the more important the message, the greater the need for accuracy. Someone hurrying to catch a train who asks the time has a much greater need for accuracy than one spending an afternoon reading who asks out of curiosity. The greater the need for accuracy, the stronger the reason to have communication in writing and from a source known to the receiver. The telephone message from a young voice announcing that school will be closed because of snow is not the best way to be certain about school closings.

Accuracy is particularly important for a school administrator, who must communicate a great deal. Just as in the fable about the man who cried wolf, if the school administrator has a history of inaccurate communication, the messages will increasingly be ignored and the administrator's effectiveness will be diminished.

A crucial element in communication is the perceptions the receiver has about the source.[13] We just pointed out that a source not known for accuracy loses the attention of the receivers. Of equal importance are the perceptions various individuals or groups have of specific words or phrases.[14] Some phrases create such strong reactions—so much "noise" in the communications system—that real communication becomes impossible. "Sex education" is an example of such a phrase. The mere use of the term leads to perceptions that can literally close off communication. Other examples are "back to basics," "discipline," or "evolution." Communicators need to be aware of phrases that are perceived as "red flags" by large groups of receivers.

Both source and content, then, lead to perceptions that may inhibit receipt of the desired message or information. Receivers also have perceptions about the importance of various messages and sources.[15] Often school people do not perceive messages of community dissatisfaction to be important until after the failure of a tax levy. Some sources attempt to create a sense of importance by sending messages loudly (like television commercials) or with stamped symbols proclaiming urgency. These actions may be perceived by the receivers as saying more about the source than about the message.

A mechanical receiver receives what is sent to it without interpretation, emotion, or confusion. The human receiver, however, receives and perceives, and the final thing received is a combination of the message sent and perceptions the message and the sender created. As a result, sources often become stereotyped: "That principal is always blowing off steam," or "This superintendent sees a crisis behind every bush." Messages can become the victims of the stereotype. Administrators need to be aware that their behavior by itself is constantly communicating to people, and is creating an environment that will have a strong influence on the ways their intentional communication is received and acted upon.

Perceptions

Authority   The authority represented by a source has a special impact upon receivers.[16] A casual comment by a superintendent (e.g., "I certainly enjoyed those beets today at lunch.") can lead to incredible results (e.g., "Oh yes, beets are his favorite vegetable—really the only vegetable he enjoys. We serve them every day on the school lunch menu."). People who should question a message for clarification or validity, often do not do so if the message originates with someone of either expertise or position authority. Secretaries or staff members who are impolite and high-handed with those "lower" in the organization chart often reveal only charm to those "above."

Those who leave the teaching ranks to become administrators in the same school discover changes in their communications links. It is important to remember that a promotion can create increased opportunities for communication, but it can also create problems. In spite of our democratic society and the special democratic nature of educational organizations, administrators are no longer "just one of the boys" or "just one of the girls" among the teachers. What used to be gossip and good camaraderie among peers disappears because it may seem to be "carrying tales to the boss." People are more tentative, less direct with one who plays a key role in determining their salaries or assignments than with a teaching colleague. Administrative decisions often seem to favor one group or individual and some resentment creeps into the environment. Administrators need to be aware of these special problems in relating to their colleagues.

Flow   Most organizations are designed to facilitate communication flow "downward" or "through" the organization. Directions, policies, guidelines, requests, rules, procedures, and the like all flow easily and readily from the central office to the schools and classrooms. Communication flow in a school district is primarily self-contained. Most of the flow is internal to the school district, with only periodic flows to and from the external world.

Because the purpose of leadership is to assist a group in achieving organizational objectives (*group* here including the teachers, parents, staff, local citizens, and the like, of a school district), administrators must do more than send out messages to the internal portion of the group. Too often, administrative conferences on communication emphasize "how we can get out message to them." Of equal importance is "how can we receive their messages to us." "Two-way flow of communication" is a phrase used so much that it has become trite, but the concept is one that is crucial to effective leadership. The administrator needs to know "what is going on" and the administrator needs the ideas and the intelligence of all those involved in and with the schools. If the flow of communications in a school district is all one way and all internal, there are serious barriers to communication and effective leadership.

Another problem of communication flow is distance. Communication with those who share an office suite is much easier than it is with those who are in separate buildings. The usual geographical dispersion of a school district can create communication problems that should not be overlooked.[17]

Throughout this volume we have said that administrators must be alert to the situations in which they find themselves, be able to anticipate the appropriateness and effectiveness of an administrative act, and be adaptable. There are no hard-and-fast rules of behavior that permit administrators to look up the correct response to a given situation. This is particularly true of communication. Communication which is done in a formal way or official capacity needs to fit the occasion and be appropriate to the purpose. The length of the message, its form, and the specific content need to be determined within a clear understanding of the situation.

Volume, Content, and Timing

Most administrators, for example, have had the experience of being asked to give a presentation on an academic subject before a citizens' group. After preparing such a presentation, many administrators have also had the experience of arriving at the meeting to discover that instead of the expected fifty citizens in attendance only the committee and two others have arrived, for a total audience of five. The five are as deserving of the message or information as would be the fifty, but the form of the communication probably needs rapid, extemporaneous, and radical change.

It is probably a safe generalization to say that most administrators communicate too little with the public with which they should be in touch; it is perhaps also safe to generalize that when administrators do communicate, they include too much—too much real content and too much "noise"—in their communications. The fact that a subject (e.g., schools, learning, youth, academic achievement) is important does not necessarily require lengthy communication to illustrate its importance. The Bible, the Koran, the Declaration of Independence, the Gettysburg Address, and Franklin Roosevelt's First Inaugural Address all illustrate that significant and complex ideas, emotions, and suggestions can be expressed with brevity and clarity.

In addition to being expressed with appropriate brevity, the content of a communication should be meaningful, contribute to the attainment of its purpose, and timely. Whether a communication is designed to seek action or to inform, it almost always exists within a time frame. For example, the message to a board about preventive maintenance is more appropriate in advance of the leaking roof than after; a discussion with teachers about a school district's financial problems is called for when they are discovered rather than after others have considered and decided upon alternative solutions; and information about how to use a new text series should be available prior to its use by teachers and students.

Thus volume, content, and timing are important elements in communication. If adapted to the purpose and to the environment, they are factors that can enhance communication; if not, they can lead to major problems.

**ASSESSING
COMMUNICATION
EFFECTIVENESS**

There are several ways in which communication can be evaluated. First, there is the theoretical or content-analysis approach wherein the form and substance of the message are analyzed to determine if the communication was in fact what the source intended it to be.

Second, there is the direct pragmatic evaluation. The source had a purpose in communicating. Was that purpose met? Did the communication work?

Then there is the humanistic approach wherein the communication is assessed on the basis of not only whether it worked but also the feelings generated by the communication—feelings about the communicator and the organization of which both the source and receivers are part.

Finally, there is the cost-effectiveness approach, wherein the costs of various communications techniques are considered together with the projected results of each technique. For example, if a mimeographed bulletin costing ten cents a copy works well, would a printed bulletin costing fifty cents a copy work five times as well?

As is true of all evaluation, assessment of communication is not possible unless the purpose of the communication is known. Each of the approaches mentioned above can be of value to administrators when reviewing their own communication and the communication substance, channels, and procedures within the school or school district. Obviously, technique without substance is a hollow accomplishment. Many communications programs, however, are judged by their variety and attractiveness, and by the number of different methods and media used. Administrators are cautioned to be skeptical about the flashy multimedia presentation giving the impression of a real communication program where none in fact occurs.

SUMMARY

At the outset of this chapter, we said that the purpose of communication is to create a situation where a message or information becomes the common property of both a source (sender) and a receiver. As a result of this act action may take place, understanding may be enhanced, confusion may be removed, a sense of colleagueship may be developed, or none of these may occur. The response of the receiver may be to the technique rather than to the message; the response may be completely different from what was intended; or the response today may actually be to yesterday's message. Simple cause and effect are difficult to determine. Some terms have personal meaning to individuals, which can differ greatly from their common meanings. Also at the outset of this chapter, we posed three basic measures that should be used to evaluate the effectiveness of communication. To repeat:

1. The purpose of the communication is known.
2. The purpose is accomplished.
3. The purpose is accomplished without creating negative byproducts.

We live in a world where our senses are bombarded with communication. In such a world, educational administrators must operate their own communication systems on behalf of their leadership functions in the school. Through both formal and informal means, administrators need to send and receive messages and information within and without the organization. The flow of communication "up and down" and "in and out" is an administrative responsibility of critical importance. There are a great (and increasing) variety of techniques to facilitate communication, and administrators need to be aware of the variety but not overwhelmed by it.

A number of problems can interrupt or interfere with communication. These include problems of accuracy, perceptions, authority, flow, volume, content, and timing. Because so many elements can influence communication, it is difficult to evaluate the effectiveness of given techniques or particular transmissions. Because of its importance in administration, however, that evaluative effort must be made.

ENDNOTES

1. Willard V. Merrihue, *Managing by Communication* (New York: McGraw-Hill, 1960), p. 16.
2. Some define communication as the S part of a stimulus-response transaction. See Carl Hovland, "Yale Studies of Communication and Persuasion," in W.W. Charters, Jr. and N.J. Gage, eds., *Readings in the Social Psychology of Education* (Boston: Allyn and Bacon, 1963), p. 239.
3. Keith Davis, *Human Relations at Work* (New York: McGraw-Hill, 1967), pp. 316–320.
4. Clarence L. Barnhart, ed., *The World Book Dictionary* vol. 1 (New York: Doubleday, 1963), p. 402.
5. See, for example, O'Reilly and Roberts, "Information Filtration in Organizations: Three Experiments," *Organizational Behavior and Human Performance* 2 (1974): 253–365.
6. E. Paul Torrance, "Some Consequences of Power Differences on Decision Making in Permanant and Temporary Three-Man Groups," in A. Paul Hare et al., eds., *Small Groups: Studies in Social Interaction* (New York: Knopf, 1955), pp. 482–492.
7. D.T. Campbell, "Systematic Error on the Part of Human Links in Communication Systems," *Information and Control* 1 (1958): 334–369.
8. Dan C. Lortie, "The Teacher and Team Teaching: Suggestions for Long Range Research" in Judson T. Shaplin and Henry F. Olds, Jr., eds., *Team Teaching* (New York: Harper and Row, 1964), pp. 270–305.
9. See Amitai Etzioni, *A Comparative Analysis of Complex Organization* (New York: Free Press, 1964), pp. 137–141; or William G. Scott, *Human Relations in Management* (Homewood, Ill.: Irwin, 1962), pp. 185–191.
10. We hold to this centrality of "purpose" even though a school of thought holds that the "goal paradigm" is "intellectually exhausted." See P. Georgiore, "The Goal Paradigm and Notes Toward a Counter Paradigm," *Administrative Science Quarterly* 18 (1973): 291–310.
11. John K. Hemphill, "Personal Variables and Administrative Styles" in Daniel E. Griffiths, ed., *Behavioral Science and Educational Administration*, Sixty-third Yearbook of the National Society for the Study of Education, Part II (Chicago: The Society, 1964), p. 195.
12. Donald A. Erickson and K. George Pederson, "Major Communications Problems in the Schools," *Administrator's Notebook* 7 (March 1966): 1–4.
13. For a particularly good discussion of the effect of perception upon communication see Jacob W. Getzels et al., *Educational Administration as a Social Process* (New York: Harper and Row, 1968), pp. 297–315.

14. See Wayne K. Hoy and Cecil G. Miskel, *Educational Administration: Theory, Research, and Practice* (New York: Random House, 1978), pp. 241–244.

15. Richard Prince, "Individual Values and Administrator Effectiveness," *Administrator's Notebook* 4 (December 1957): 1–4.

16. Peter M. Blau and W. Richard Scott, *Formal Organizations: A Comparative Approach* (San Francisco: Chandler Publishing, 1962), pp. 128–131.

17. Herbert A. Simon, "The Architecture of Complexity," *Proceedings of the American Philosophical Society* 106 (1962): 467–482.

CHAPTER 9

SECURING AND ALLOCATING RESOURCES

Schools, like other organizations, require resources for their operation. In this chapter we shall deal with money, personnel, administrative time, and citizen support, looking at how these resources are secured and then allocated. Decisions are required in the securing of resources and perhaps even more in the allocation of resources. The decision making process was dealt with in Chapter 6 and will not be repeated here. We will note that while both principals and superintendents are involved in securing and allocating resources, there is some differentiation in the tasks they perform in this arena.

Because schools and school districts exist for teaching and learning, programs and supporting services having to do with teaching and learning need to be planned to determine the resources needed. More information on this planning, particularly with regard to money requirements, can be found in discussions of school budgeting.[1] But the determination of program requirements is basic not only to money needs, but for personnel and time needs as well. The formulation

ESTABLISHING PROGRAM REQUIREMENTS

of program requirements is not a simple process; it begins with community aspirations, particularly as they are translated into school purposes. In this process both professional and political elements are involved.

Community Aspirations

Any treatment of community aspirations and traditions is rather tricky. As noted in Chapter 2, there is the issue of whether schools are controlled at the local, state, or national level. Substantial control of schools at both national and state levels suggests to some that local or community control of education is a bygone and futile dream. We are not that pessimistic. Indeed, any function as important as education will inevitably require attention at all three levels of government, and thus all three levels will exercise some control over schools and school districts. Significant as are controls exercised at state and national levels, some important decisions should be and are made at the local level. In fact, education may be best governed when each of the three levels of government is vigorous in its consideration of educational problems and issues. We think state education agencies behave better when school districts respond forthrightly to proposed state educational policies. Likewise, we think the national education agencies behave better when state school agencies respond forthrightly and knowledgeably to proposed national policy directions and to the consequences of implementing national programs. In our view, no level of educational government should dominate any other level; there should be considerable give-and-take among levels.

School districts have only those powers delegated to them, or reasonably inferred by such delegation, by the respective state legislatures. These powers ordinarily include the establishment of schools, some jurisdiction over instructional programs, the setting of attendance policies, the employment of teachers and other personnel, the supervision of personnel, the adoption of the budget including a recommended tax rate, and the management of school funds. To be sure, some of these functions are to be performed within guidelines set by state school codes, and some districts (about 15 percent) are dependent financially on local municipal corporations for their funds, but overall local school districts still have considerable voice in the control of schools. And school boards, as they exercise their jurisdiction over schools in their districts, are much influenced by the aspirations and traditions of the communities they represent.

We recognize that there is not unanimity on this point, however. Zeigler and Jennings[2] conclude from their study that school boards do not govern, but merely legitimate the policy recommendations of school superintendents. McCarty and Ramsey found that school boards vary considerably, dependent largely on the type of community in which they are located.[3] For instance, factional communities tend to have factional school boards and inert communities tend to have sanctioning school boards. In one type of community boards exercise considerable voice in school governance whereas in other communities boards may be dominated by their superintendents. Boyd, however, comes to the following conclusion:

I have argued that if schools are not merely the "mirror images" of the communities they serve, neither are they almost completely insulated bastions dominated by unresponsive and self-serving professional educators. Instead, I have proposed that while educators tend to dominate local educational policy making, they usually operate within significant, and generally neglected or underestimated, constraints imposed by the *local* community and school board—not to mention those imposed by state and national forces. These constraints (or, put another way, the influence of the community and the board) are likely to vary primarily with the type of school district and the type of policy issue that is faced. The local citizenry and the board will tend to have more influence in *external, redistributive,* and *strategic* policy decisions, and in *smaller* and more *homogeneous* communities where the professionals tend to anticipate or reflect (especially in middle and upper middle class communities) community demands. The professionals, on the other hand, will tend to have more influence in *heterogeneous* communities. Because of the nature of the distribution in this country of the population and of school districts, this analysis suggests that in the vast majority of school districts, which serve a large majority of Americans, majority interests usually will be served.[4]

We agree with Boyd that in many communities citizen views reflecting their community aspirations and traditions are powerful determinants of school board policy on strategic or major policy questions.

The process by which community aspirations and traditions are translated by school boards and administrators to programs may not work perfectly but some things seem clear. In most cases, board members are elected by the citizens of the community and thus they tend to reflect community values. Most boards, too, are affected by citizen response to school programs and procedures, whether given through formal channels or conveyed informally. Frequently boards must appeal to citizens to vote for a bond issue or to continue or increase a tax levy. Finally, if citizens become dissatisfied with the performance of school board members, they can deny them another term and, in some states, recall them from office. While many boards, as Zeigler and Jennings contend, are dominated by their superintendents, there are numerous examples of boards that have responded to citizen demands. Some of these demands have involved the removal of particular text books and the elimination of programs such as sex education. On the more positive side, some citizen groups have insisted that the boards expend more money in order to provide a better program. In any case, boards and school administrators cannot for long ignore the aspirations and traditions of the community as they attempt to establish program requirements.

Purposes of the School

In examining statements of purpose for schools or talking to people about what schools ought to be about, one is struck by several impressions. Purposes seem to be numerous, ambiguous, and in many instances unrealistic. Schools are supposed to teach literacy, develop critical thinking, promote world understanding, sponsor creativity, train in work skills, cure poverty, dispel prejudice, promote upright behavior, and even more. These are commendable goals and there are always groups of citizens who are strong advocates for one or more of these purposes. Indeed, the multiplicity of purposes is another indication of citizen influence on school boards and school officials.

If we go beyond formal and informal statements of what schools should do and actually examine what schools are about, still other purposes emerge. In terms of how teachers and students spend their time, the formal curriculum often takes a back seat to the activity programs of the school. There are not only music classes but numerous performing choruses, bands, and orchestras. There are not only drama and speech classes but many performing groups in all forms of speech and drama. There are not only physical education classes but highly organized teams engaged in competitive athletics at district, regional, state, and even national levels. Teams are fielded in football, basketball, track, and frequently in tennis, wrestling, soccer, and other sports as well. Moreover, most of these teams seem to need cheering sections, hence still other students become involved as team supporters. High school students, particularly, often become so engaged in the performing arts and in competitive athletics that they have little time or energy for the regular school subjects.

Nor is the extensive activity program of many schools a phenomenon involving students alone. The competitive nature of these activities appeals to many of the parents of the students and they also become strong supporters and advocates for particular activities. Most high schools have had the support of the band mothers or fathers. Many of those high schools have also been faced by demands from the band mothers or fathers that more be done for the band—that new uniforms be purchased, that more time be allowed for practice, and that the band be just as good as the one in the next county. Similarly, most high schools have experienced what it means to have a football boosters club. Frequently such groups include townspeople who may or may not be the parents of students on the team, but who do demand that the school secure a coach who can produce winning teams. For many of these townspeople a state championship becomes the ultimate objective.

Without denying that many of these activities are important and, indeed, that significant learning may accrue to students who pursue them, the fact remains that for many students and adults who are caught up in these activities, the major purposes of the school are blunted or ignored. Examining the frenetic activity routine of many students, one can hardly escape the impression that the intellectual purpose of the school has given way to some kind of public performance. For those few who ultimately become professionals in one of the arts or sports these experiences may stand them in good stead. For others who learn to appreciate one of the arts or physical skill the experience may be useful. But for many the overemphasis on activities means an underemphasis on intellectual experiences which ostensibly the school should provide.

School people and lay citizens should consider the idea that schools have both primary and shared purposes. This idea proved useful to a task force in

Utah, made up of professionals and lay citizens, that was asked to formulate a statement of the school's purposes and nature.[5] It was suggested that the primary purposes include literacy, knowledge of our Western heritage, and critical thinking; in short, intellectual development. Purposes to be shared with parents and other agencies in society included physical, social, emotional, and moral development of individuals and training in work skills.

Obviously, the differentiation between primary and shared purposes is not an easy task. For instance, some see training in work skills or vocational education as a primary purpose of the school. Others agree with the task force noted above that for most high school students specific training in work skills is a shared purpose, with specific vocational education being done at the post–high school level, possibly in a community college or within industry itself. Regardless of where the specific work training is provided, it seems clear that students should become literate in reading, writing, and arithmetic, and acquire some knowledge of our economic system before turning to specific vocational training.

Moreover, accepting the position that for most students work skills training be a shared purpose does not rule out the desirability of the school program including work experience for all students. However, this work experience might best be seen as a part of general education and not specific training in vocational skills. Futhermore, if for most high schools vocational education is a shared and not a primary purpose, it should be recognized that for some students and possibly for some high schools vocational training should be a primary one.

Just as deciding the appropriate emphasis given to vocational education requires careful consideration by every school and school district, so do the emphases accorded the physical, social, emotional, and moral development of the individual. Each of these areas is important to the induction of youth into his or her own culture. But the school alone cannot take full responsibility for appropriate learning in these areas. In terms of moral development, for instance, the school is confronted with several problems. What is considered moral in one community or group may not be seen as moral in another. Moreover, direct instruction in the school in moral values may be of little avail if different moral values guide the actions of the home and the marketplace. While we strongly urge that schools in their own regimens exemplify a moral environment including such things as respect for each individual and an attitude of trust toward students and faculty members, in the end such teaching is relatively ineffective unless it is reinforced by parents, churches, and community practices generally.

We offer no prescription as to what the primary and the shared purposes of the school and school district should be. We do suggest, however, that communities involve both school people and lay people in the consideration of purposes; and that the outcome of these considerations should become another guide for establishing the school program requirements.

District and School Perspectives   Still another consideration in establishing program requirements is the recognition that perspectives at the school district level could vary from those at the individual school level. In small school districts with but a few elementary schools and one high school this differentiation is probably less marked. However, in larger districts we think viewing program requirements from both levels is of the utmost importance. We suspect that most large districts strive for some uniformity of programs in the several schools of the district, but we think such a policy should be open to examination. Some program requirements might appropriately be uniform over the entire district, while others might best be tailored to individual schools.

We follow the position of Goodlad and others[6] that the optimal unit for school improvement is the single school. Here, a principal, a group of teachers, parents immediately concerned, and students with specific capabilities and interests can work together to determine both the formal instructional program of the school and the daily relationships among students, teachers, and parents. Whereas programs of school districts must be somewhat general in nature, the program of a single school can be quite specific. To reiterate the example above, vocational education might be seen as a shared purpose at the district level, but a primary purpose at a specific school. As another example, programs for unwed mothers might at the district level be seen as a shared purpose of the school, and be conducted over most of the district by some other community agency. However, if there are some individual schools where there are no other suitable community agencies to conduct such programs then the school should take on the function.

To the extent that program decisions are left to individual schools, the roles of administrative officers are modified and expanded. When individual schools are given relative autonomy, principals must accept more responsibility not only in dealing with teachers and students but in dealing with school patrons as well. With more responsibility delegated to principals, the roles of officials in the central office also change. In this case there is less need for checking to see that district-wide programs and procedures are met, and more need for understanding the requests of individual schools with more effort given to facilitating those requests. In a number of large city school districts, considerable progress has been made toward the differentiation of schools within the district, particularly with the establishment of alternative schools. Some alternative schools, for example, emphasize an open, informal atmosphere while others focus on more formal, academic programs.

Finally, as we note in Chapter 11, community aspirations and traditions may change over time. For example, a homogeneous rural community may quite suddenly become a burgeoning suburban community. In all probability the newcomers will not be satisfied with a school program that seemed quite acceptable to the old residents. A circumstance such as this may well require a review of school purposes and perhaps also a consideration of how much autonomy ought to be granted to individual schools. Thus, establishing program requirements for schools and school districts is an ongoing process.

Establishing program requirements is largely a philosophical process; it deals with values, with what ought to be done.[7] But the implementation of a program is in large part a financial process. Necessary expenditures must be determined, available revenues must be considered, a budget wherein revenues and expenditures are balanced must be developed, school board and community approval for the budget must be secured, and finally, funds must be allocated internally to schools and to specific programs within the district. It is to these matters that we now turn.

Obviously, school programs cost money. Teachers and other personnel are needed to direct the programs, supplies and equipment are required for the instructional process, a place for instruction is required, services such as heat and light are necessary, and some supervision of programs is necessary. Without attempting to duplicate detailed treatments of budgeting and financial management found elsewhere,[8] we will give some attention to each of these expenditure areas.

Arriving at the estimated cost of the personnel needed for any program is not a simple task. For instance, decisions regarding student load become a major factor in determining the number of teachers needed. Should high school teachers in a departmental program meet 100 or 150 students per day? Should elementary teachers in a self-contained classroom arrangement have 25 or 35 students assigned to each room? There is also the issue of pay scales. Are first year teachers to receive $12,000 or $18,000 per year? Should maximum salaries go to $24,000 or $36,000 per year? Questions such as these are frequently settled by district policy. Often, however, district policy is affected by negotiations between the teachers' organization and the school district. Only as the bargaining issues are settled can teacher load and pay scale questions be reduced to district policies that permit teaching costs to be ascertained.

Since schools are labor-intensive organizations, most of the proposed expenditures in any school budget (often as much as 80 percent) are allocated to personnel costs. But other expenditure requirements cannot be ignored. Supplies and equipment are needed for most instructional programs. For the school shop, home economics, and some of the sciences, supply and equipment requirements may be relatively high. Such requirements for English and history may be relatively low but even here, textbooks, reference books, paper, pencils, maps, and many other items are needed. Frequently, to arrive at proposed financial costs questions of both quantity and quality must be answered. For example, are children in primary-grade reading classes to be surrounded by an abundant or a meager amount of reading material? For music classes, is the district to supply the musical instruments or are parents expected to supply them? In terms of reference material, is there to be a well-stocked library and audiovisual center, readily available to students, or must students get along with limited reference materials kept in some of the classrooms? Here again, district policy on supply and equipment provisions are necessary before costs can be determined.

SECURING AND ALLOCATING FINANCIAL RESOURCES

Necessary Expenditures

Quantity and quality decisions also come into play with respect to school plant demands. Is the building itself to be of cheap construction and require high maintenance costs, or of more substantial construction that requires relatively low maintenance costs? Do pupil stations fill the room or is there space for student interest centers and some group activity? Are rooms provided with acoustic treatment to promote quiet, or are they left with bare walls that echo the noise? Are seats fastened to the floor or is there capability for more flexible seating arrangements? Each of these issues has its cost components.

There are also services required for each room or instructional facility. These usually include heat, light, electric outlets, cleaning, and maintenance and repair. There may also be a need for water and gas outlets and air conditioning. The extent and quality of these services obviously affect projected expenditures. Each of these services also requires personnel either to supply the service (as in the case of custodial care) or to keep the services in good repair (as in the case of heat and light). Thus the service requirements raise the question of whether the school district is to maintain its own crews of repair and maintenance workers or contract for the services. Most school districts settle for some combination of the two but decisions regarding these matters and their cost implications must constantly be made.

Finally, projected expenditures for each program must include some allowance for the supervision of that program. Without going into detail about supervision, it seems clear that some attention must be given to student outcomes, to teacher performance, and to the use made of supplies and equipment. Much of this supervision might be supplied by school principals but some of it will require specialized personnel. For instance, the development of an appropriate testing program for students may be enhanced by enlisting the help of a testing expert. The analysis of test data may require the help of a specialist as well. Should the district employ its own specialists or can consultants be secured from a nearby university or consulting firm as needed?

We have discussed briefly many of the areas that should be considered in converting a desired set of program requirements to a projected list of expenditures. At this point we should note that one of the most significant considerations is the nature of the program itself. For instance, high schools may wish to establish a particular emphasis, such as science and mathematics, the arts, or vocational education. Frequently this means that general programs of instruction are offered in addition to specialized ones. Whatever the specialization, there are, of course, ramifications for personnel and each of the other expenditure areas discussed above.

Available Resources

To this point we have discussed how to establish a desired program and to convert that program into a projected set of expenditures. But these exercises are futile unless money can be found to meet the expenditures. Thus, we now turn to a consideration of available resources. Most school districts receive money from local taxes, state funds, federal subsidies, and private contributions. As noted in Chapter 2, states vary widely in their financial arrangements for the support of schools and we cannot explore those variations fully, but we shall give some attention to each of the sources.

As regards local taxes, most state school codes provide that local boards of education may set or recommend to the appropriate taxing unit a tax levy (within certain limits) for school support. In addition, many states permit boards of education to call elections at which electors may decide whether the local tax for schools can be increased. In some states school budgets must be approved by some other governmental agency, but essentially local boards in most states have the authority to raise money for the operation of schools. An important step, then, in determining available revenues is that of seeing what money can be raised locally by board action, by the vote of the electorate, or both.

An additional step in determining possible revenues is calculation of that available from state funds. These may be of two kinds: general support and categorical support. General support is often distributed by some kind of equalization formula that attempts to provide more to poor and less to wealthy districts.[9] Categorical support is provided for particular programs. For instance, many states provide categorical support for the transportation of students; it may also be obtained for special programs such as those for handicapped students and certain experimental projects. Categorical aid may be seductive in the sense that local matching or supplemental funds are often required. Categorical aid can also be used to start programs that must subsequently depend upon local funding. Thus, these implications need consideration prior to the acceptance of categorical aid. After prospective local and state revenues have been combined, however, the bulk of the revenue available to school districts will have been determined.

Federal subsidies provide another source of school revenue, but on average these revenues are not more than about seven percent of school costs. For some districts they may be as high as twenty percent; for others, as low as five percent. Nearly all federal money is categorical aid, and in nearly all cases assumes that local funds will be used to help support the programs. Thus, the matching requirements of categorical aid must be taken into account. But if such aid contributes to the program requirements initially established by the district, it should be accepted and counted as another source of revenue.

Some districts have made good use of private contributions as still another source of school revenue. Private giving has been used more extensively by nonpublic schools and colleges and universities but in many places donors may be found who wish to contribute to particular projects or programs in public schools. Public school administrators often find it advisable to cultivate this potential source of revenue since private donors may be quite willing to contribute to student fellowships of one kind or another, the extension of library holdings, the erection of a building for special purposes, salary supplements for meritorious teachers, and many other programs. In any case, the possibility of private contributions should not be overlooked.

In the happiest of worlds an inventory of available revenues is adequate to cover the projected expenditures. In most school districts, however, the projected expenditures initially exceed the available revenues; hence program requirements must once again be scrutinized and those of lowest priority eliminated. This process of balancing revenues and expenditures leads us to a further consideration of the budget process.

The Budget Process

As suggested above, a school budget should have three components: a description of the school program, a projection of needed expenditures, and an exhibit of estimated revenues sufficient to cover the projected expenditures. As presented here this sounds like a very rational sequence of procedures. Actually, the process is not always rational and the sequence is not always neat and ordered. At times, budget-makers begin with available revenues instead of the desired program. In any case, experienced budget-makers keep in mind the relationships among the components of programs, expenditures, and revenues as they move from one component to another. The annual budget, if well done, is probably the most important policy document enacted each year by the local board of education.

But budget making is more than a yearly exercise. Along with the short-term annual budget there is a need for long-term planning. For example, school districts have to consider the long-term consequences of bond issues for capital outlays. Frequently, bond issues must be repaid over a period of ten to twenty years. Thus, these obligations must be built into a whole series of annual budgets. Not quite so clear is the long-term obligation of a new salary schedule for teachers. A schedule that appears fundable this year and next may in five or ten years impose obligations on the school district that are not fundable. Not only do the long-term consequences of the spending program need consideration, but the long-term prospects on the revenue side also require examination. In the last few decades, for instance, some city school districts have lost a large proportion of their assessed valuation due to the movement of industry and business from the central city to the surrounding suburbs. Some of these cities find the gap between needed revenues and available resources continually increasing.

In recent years there has been much talk about program budgeting. This concept was first applied to the military in the 1960s and was given impetus by President Johnson in 1965 when he directed that all federal departments adopt "an integrated planning, programming, budgeting system."[10] Such a system was supposed to deal more specifically with outputs, to employ a longer time span in budget planning, and to utilize a cost-utility analysis to relate inputs to outputs. While increased emphasis on outputs and long-term budget planning seem to have been useful responses to the program budgeting movement, the input-output analysis does not appear to have gone far. It is now recognized that both the inputs and outputs of schools are difficult to define and measure. In time, more progress in such analyses will probably be made.

If budget planning has been a continuing process and if information pertaining to such planning has been shared with school board members, obtaining school board approval for the proposed budget is ordinarily not too difficult. As Boyd suggests, however, budget approval is clearly an "external, redistributive, and strategic" policy decision, an arena in which school boards exercise considerable influence. Moreover, if the school board is deeply divided or factional, to use the McCarty and Ramsey terminology, such approval will be more difficult to secure and will probably command, at best, a split vote within the board.

In some states annual budgets must be presented to a public meeting for approval. In other states, when anticipated revenues exceed those that can be authorized by the board, the extra millage must be approved by the voters in a special election. In either case, a majority of the citizens must be convinced that the proposed program has merit, that it will be effectively carried out, and that the cost is not excessive. In view of the growing skepticism about schools (discussed in Chapter 2), these convictions are not always easy to sustain.

Winning elections is obviously a political activity.[11] School managers, the board, and the superintendent, are engaged in a process of convincing the electors of the district that they should behave in a particular way. To be successful in such a campaign the school managers must have some understanding of their community—its values and aspirations, the political influentials in the community, and patterns of voter behavior shown in prior elections. Practical steps in the election campaign frequently include the following: (1) careful description of the program for which money is sought; (2) clear indication of what the tax implications are; (3) establishment of a campaign organization (often including professionals and leading lay citizens); (4) securing revenue for the campaign expenses (and in some states tax money cannot be used for this purpose); (5) development of appropriate campaign literature; and (6) making decisions about communication techniques such as television, the press, and door-to-door soliciting.

Following any election there should be an analysis of election results. If the measure did not pass, the analysis may suggest what needs to be done should the request, perhaps with some modification, be submitted again. If the measure passed but was closely contested, the analysis (a breakdown by voter districts, for instance) may reveal much about the values and aspirations of voters in particular categories. This information is useful for subsequent elections and perhaps also for the implementation of programs already approved. If the measure passed by a large majority, school managers may assume that they and the voters agree on their aspirations for the school.

Regardless of election outcomes, when school managers have done their best to influence voters to approve certain programs and have been rebuffed, school managers should accept election results with good grace. Voters may not share some of the aspirations of the professionals, and in our scheme of things voters have the last say. Professionals can either decide to try again after more education of the public, or they can move on to another school district where the citizens may be more in harmony with their professional objectives. We think it appropriate for professionals to encourage lay people to change their educational aspirations but in the end we think citizens should determine school policy.

Internal Allocation   Following budget adoption there is always the process of implementation, managing the money, and accounting for its use. We will not deal with money management in detail,[12] but we do want to say a word about the allocation of financial resources to individual schools.

This concern ties in with our conviction that in most school districts, individual schools should be gradually given more autonomy in their operation than they have had in the past. In our view, autonomy means that school principals have considerable voice in curriculum decisions and personnel decisions as well as budget decisions. In the preparation of the budget, attention should be given to the allocation of resources for each school. If that is not done or not made explicit enough at the time of budget preparation, such decisions need to be made after budget adoption. In either case, school principals should be given responsibility for managing some part of the money provided in the budget.

One way this could be done is by giving the instructional supply and equipment budget to the school as a "block grant," representing a stipulated sum of money rather than a list of standardized items. With such an allocation the principal and his or her staff, perhaps also with input from parents and students, could determine how best to spend the money. If science needed a particular boost, more supplies and equipment for the area might be provided. If remedial reading needed more emphasis, more materials supporting that objective might be obtained. If art had been neglected, additional attention might be given to that need. If, indeed, there was not enough money to meet all of the pressing needs, that too could be discovered and a case for a larger allocation made the next time around.

When principals and teachers come to feel some confidence in their control over the instructional supply budget, they might then be ready to take responsibility for the personnel part of the budget. Again, a lump sum, derived from the personnel policies of the district, might be allocated to a single school. With this money in hand principals might decide to continue traditional staffing patterns, or they might decide to try some innovations. For example, teachers might agree to increased class size providing they have a paraprofessional to assist them with certain classroom duties. This or other alternative modes of staffing might become a means of improving teaching practice over the district.

We recognize that at present the role of most principals in internal budget allocation is a relatively minor one, but we think that role is being expanded in many school districts. While we advocate allocating resources to individual schools and expect principals to take responsibility for their expenditure, we suspect that most of the accounting of funds expended will remain a central office function. Principals are not ordinarily trained as accountants, and even if they were they should be spending their time in other ways. Accounting is obviously a specialized occupation and should be done by those who have the disposition and the training to do it. As decentralization of budget implementation grows in any district, it might be desirable to move some members of the accounting staff to individual schools in place of having them all stationed in the central office.

Important as is money as a resource for school operation, there are other resources that should not be overlooked. These include personnel, administrative time, and citizen support, each of which will be dealt with here.

SECURING AND ALLOCATING OTHER RESOURCES

As noted above, the operation of schools is a labor-intensive task. While a wide range of workers is required for school operation, teachers constitute the largest segment of employees, and our discussion will focus on them. Castetter has suggested that the personnel function in administration is designed to plan for, direct, and motivate human resources, and includes a wide range of subprocesses such as recruitment, selection, induction, appraisal, compensation, and bargaining.[13] We cannot deal with all of these elements here, but we will give some attention to selection and assignment, in keeping with our concern about securing and allocating resources.

Personnel

In many ways, selection is the most critical aspect of personnel administration. Staff improvement programs may be useful, but they cannot compensate for the selection of mediocre teachers in the first place. Selection is not a precise science, but by being thoughtful and careful, the "batting average" of those who do the selecting can be improved. To begin with, a job definition should be developed for each position. Sometimes these job descriptions are prepared by the district office but they can probably be developed most effectively by the principals of the schools where the vacancies are to be filled. Principals frequently confer with the director of personnel or a comparable official in the central office, but essentially each job description should be drawn to fit a particular school or situation. We take this position for two reasons: (1) such an approach actively involves the principal in the personnel function, and (2) the principal ordinarily is best prepared to indicate not only what qualifications are being sought but also how the prospective teacher will complement the present staff and be able to work with parents in the community.

As a second step in selection, wherever possible a pool of candidates should be provided. These candidates may come from within or without the school system. The pool of candidates might include those on file in the central office as well as those who respond to the central office notice of vacancy. In addition, principals should actively recruit candidates who may be suitable for and interested in the available positions. In this recruitment process principals can often secure useful nominations from teachers already on the staff. Sometimes teachers recommend prospective colleagues more for reasons of personal friendship than professional competence, but that motivation can usually be determined. In any case, selection should be a wide ranging, active process aimed at securing the best possible candidate for each vacancy.

This brings us to the third step in selection—the application of a set of criteria to the qualifications of each candidate. If the job description has been well done, some of the criteria will already be determined. Application of other criteria, such as level of intelligence, emotional stability, interpersonal skills, and industry, may also be desirable. Appraisal of such characteristics usually requires that operational terms be developed for each. For instance, level of intelligence can often be inferred from college marks in such courses as English composition and mathematics. With operational definitions for each criterion, it then becomes necessary to examine many kinds of evidence. Such evidence may include a college placement document, letters of recommendation from those who have worked with the candidate, telephone calls to supplement or clarify the letters of recommendation, and structured personal interviews. While evidence from any one of these sources may not be very reliable, evidence from several sources tends to increase the reliability, particularly if it is examined by more than one person. This selection group might include the principal, someone from the central office, and two or three teachers in the school. The use of this procedure should effectively permit the selection of the best two or three candidates for any position.

The fourth step is then convincing one of the top candidates to accept the position. Here again the strategic role of the single school—the faculty and principal—comes into play. While most candidates cannot ignore proffered salary and fringe benefits, it is frequently the nature of the position and the characteristics of prospective colleagues that become crucial attractions. When a candidate knows which school is involved, who the principal will be, and has interacted with at least some of the teachers on the staff, he or she is in a much better position to evaluate the offer. Some large school districts may find this an elaborate selection procedure, but other districts follow essentially the steps indicated. Such a procedure emphasizes the importance of the selection process to all concerned.

If selection has followed a process similar to the one described above, the assignment function is relatively simple. New teachers are selected for particular positions in particular schools; hence it can be assumed that they will be assigned to those positions. To be sure, initial assignments do not last forever. Teachers of long tenure may wish a change in assignment at some point, or it may become apparent to the principal that certain teachers and positions could be more effectively matched. Or decreased student enrollment may require consolidation or change in some positions and thus make new assignments necessary. In these instances at least two criteria should be applied. Every attempt should be made to assign teachers to positions where they are most likely to be effective. At the same time, consideration should be given to the preferences of the teachers concerned. In schools where student enrollment has decreased sharply and teaching staffs are reduced, teachers may be asked to accept assignments for which they are not prepared. Under these circumstances, teachers' organizations may insist that seniority become the sole criterion for the retention of teachers. We think both practices are indefensible. While teachers should be accorded reasonable job protection, in the end, professional competence and not personal convenience must be the major criterion in teacher assignment, as in teacher employment.

Few would deny that time is a major resource for the administrator. Some find that they simply need more of it; thus the principal who teaches part time might give up his teaching duties to become a full-time administrator, or the principal in a large school might find it necessary to employ an assistant principal. Our chief concern here, however, is not with how more time for administration can be secured; rather it is with how an administrator allocates the time he or she has. In Chapter 4 we dealt at some length with how administrators actually spend their time, studies that are instructive and say much about the nature of administrative work. Even so, the studies say nothing about how administrators *ought* to spend their time. We thus turn to ways in which administrators might allocate their time most effectively.

Administrative Time

As the first step, we suggest that administrators make the most realistic assessment possible of the demands of their positions. High school principals might examine the findings of the Martin-Willower study[14] in which observations of how five high school principals spent their time is reported. It may be surprising for administrators to discover that these five principals spent 36.5 percent of their time on organizational maintenance tasks and only 17.4 percent of their time on tasks related to the academic program.[15] Principals might also find it useful to keep a log for a week or two of how they divide their own work day. Those who do so probably discover to their dismay that it is teachers and students that largely determine their agendas.

But a realistic assessment of the job demands does not mean that these demands are inexorable. At least some demands are more important or more immediate than others. This leads us to suggest, as a second step, that the administrator set some priorities. Some maintenance tasks might be delegated to others, or some of them might be deferred. Without established priorities, principals and other administrators tend to respond to every demand, regardless of its nature or by whom it is being pressed, as though each is of equal importance. Open as administrators must be to the demands of others, some differentiation among those demands can be and ought to be made.

A third step in the process of time allocation involves the delegation of some tasks to others. Most administrators have secretaries, and these people can and should take over many of the routine tasks associated with the administrator's office. Obviously, secretaries should answer the telephone, but they can also perform other tasks such as conveying information on the time and place of meetings, the distribution of materials to teachers, students, and parents, and assisting with the implementation of the varied programs found in any school. Naturally, secretaries who are given enlarged roles as staff assistants should also receive suitable titles and compensation.

Administrators can also delegate tasks to many others in the organization. Principals, for example, can delegate most of the supervision of extracurricular activities to staff members. Many high schools have a director of athletics who can assume supervision of athletic events. In most high schools there are also directors of drama, speech, music, and other activities, and these directors can assume responsibility for the supervision of their respective activities.

A word about delegation: Important as it is in most organizations, its implementation is rather tricky. To again use the case of the high school principal, delegation to the athletic director the supervision of athletic activities means that the principal actually turns the whole job over to the staff member in question. The principal holds the director responsible for the delegated task and backs him or her up in its execution. Only if the principal becomes convinced that the staff member has performed ineffectively should the delegation be withdrawn. It is the power to delegate, to exercise oversight, and to withdraw the delegation that makes it clear that the principal is ultimately responsible for the task. Thus, delegation requires the reasonable exercise of ultimate and immediate authority and a compatible working relationship between a superordinate and a subordinate in the organization.

Finally, we suggest that administrators retain some control over their time. For example, some administrators have found that in order to have time to themselves for necessary activities such as reading and thinking they go to their offices as early as 7 A.M. Likewise, it is understood that between 7 and 8:30 A.M., barring genuine emergencies, there are to be no interruptions and no conferences. Some superintendents, who think school visitation is important, have set aside the period of 10:30 A.M. to 12 noon for that purpose. Again, barring emergencies, this is time to be protected from any appointments or other interruptions. Many administrators who do not permit an unscheduled visitor to interrupt their scheduled activities do permit the telephone to interrupt them. A set time for telephone conversations is also desirable. In maintaining control over their time administrators can also make clear that there are major segments of the day or the week when those who wish a conference may have one.

We think it important for administrators to give attention to the allocation of their time, but we must emphasize that such control will be achieved against the odds. At times emergencies will take over. The demands of persons in and out of the organization will always compete with the need of administrators to shape at least part of their calendars for their own priorities. With effort, however, the competing forces can be kept in balance.

Citizen Support   In Chapter 2 we stated that citizens are now more skeptical about school effectiveness than they once were. There are a number of reasons for this attitude, including the fact that the schools, in their emphasis on teaching critical thinking, have probably helped create their own best critics. In any case, citizens generally are now more informed about, and frequently more demanding of, their public institutions. We would not have it otherwise. But the fact remains that schools must command citizen support or they "go out of business." Money, personnel, and administrative time, important as they are, are useless unless citizens want to have public schools and have the will to support them in their mission. In this section we deal more with how to secure citizen support.

To some educators, citizen participation is the royal road to citizen support. In a recent bibliography over 800 titles dealing with citizen participation were listed. Many slogans such as "shared governance" have been coined by those who embrace the new gospel. We have no objection to citizen participation; indeed, we advocate it.[17] But it is important for the appropriate place of citizen participation to be delineated. Moreover, it should be emphasized that citizen participation is no panacea to citizen apathy or controversy. When citizens find out more about a particular school or district, they get a better sense of its weaknesses as well as its strengths. If perceived weaknesses override perceived strengths, citizen participation can, at least in the short run, lead to citizen non-support.

There are three kinds of citizen participation: governmental, school-initiated, and community-initiated. As mentioned above, most school districts of this country elect their school board members by popular ballot. In about 15 percent of the school districts, board members are appointed (most often by the mayor of the city in which the school district is located), but even in these cases they are not insulated from citizen preferences. Most state codes also provide that increased tax levies for operation and bonding for capital outlays must be submitted to the electors of a school district. Moreover, every state legislature, made up of persons selected by citizens, is the plenary body for education just as it is for other state functions. These formal governmental arrangements, providing for direct or representative citizen voice, are the most significant forms of citizen participation in school affairs. Other forms of citizen participation cannot and should not subvert these governmental arrangements. Active citizens and citizen organizations can do much to see that these arrangements work as they were designed to do.

To supplement the governmental arrangements, citizen advisory bodies at the district or school level can be created. In some cases these advisory groups act on a continuing basis. More frequently, they are established on a temporary basis and charged with a specific task. For example, a school district may establish a committee advisory to the board and superintendent and ask it to examine the long-term housing needs of the district. Such a task force ordinarily gives some attention to the school program that needs to be housed, the organizational arrangements for the schools, and alternative uses of the present buildings as well as to the financial implications of one or more plans. With input from the advisory committee the board of education may adopt a long-term housing program. The plan may require new buildings or the closing of some buildings and the remodeling of others. The board can obviously use the committee report, and perhaps committee members as well, to help promote whatever steps are necessary in implementing the long-term plan.

The use of school-initiated citizen advisory committees at the school level is less common. However, if single schools are given additional autonomy the need for such groups will probably increase. Indeed, in some states the legislature has mandated school-level advisory committees. In all probability school-based committees will become more common in the future.

The composition of citizen advisory committees at both district and school levels should be a matter of concern to administrators. On one hand, it can seem desirable to select citizens who have expertise and prestige; an elite group. On the other hand, it can seem desirable to select citizens who fairly represent the numerous groups found in most school districts. As a practical matter, some compromise between these two alternatives should probably be struck. Expert opinion, however well founded, must be understood and acceptable to many non-experts if it is to be useful to the school or district. Representativeness also has its limits. To strive for representation of every group in the community may make the committee large and cumbersome, or may equate views of minor groups with those of major ones. In the end, advisory bodies should be so composed that they give promise of helping produce and implement useful recommendations rather than serving as debating societies.

In addition to governmental and school-initiated citizen participation, most school districts have community-initiated or individually initiated participation. The most common of these is the Parent Teacher Association. Particularly in the past, some PTA's were dominated by school administrators, but that situation seems to be changing. PTA's now often take vigorous stands on proposed or existing school policies and school officials are called upon to respond to such positions.

The media—newspapers, radio, and television—also frequently cover school issues. Coverage is often the reporting of newsworthy events such as the outcome of student competition in athletics and other activities. But radio and television, particularly, also provide forums for the discussion of academic and social issues. Frequently, such forums seek as participants those who hold diverse views on the issue at hand, and newspapers, especially, editorialize about school questions. Whether through regular news coverage, organized forums, or editorials, the media exert influence on the opinions of many citizens. In most school districts citizen participation in any form is thus affected.

In most school districts there is still another kind of citizen participation. Citizens of like mind form interest groups and promote their positions.[18] These groups may form around instructional materials, racial discrimination, handicapped students, tax levies, and many other issues. We see these groups as legitimate and useful to school governance. They articulate positions that have often been neglected and thus force all citizens to take a look at such issues. These groups may have strident voices, so citizens and school people alike must take care not to mistake noise for consensus. At the same time, appropriate processes for hearing such groups and giving their positions due attention should be devised by school officials and other citizens' organizations.

We think citizen participation in all of its forms is appropriate and can often be useful. We think, however, that such participation, even though influential, is and should be advisory and should not replace the official provisions for governance. School codes in each of the states have made it clear how schools are to be governed. Thus final decisions about school matters should be left in the hands of those who have legal authority to exercise such governance. Moreover, we think that citizen input to the governance process should as far as possible be confined to policy questions and not operating procedures. It may be appropriate, for example, for a citizen group to raise questions about the reading achievement of students and even to recommend that more emphasis be placed on it, but we do not think it appropriate for any citizen group to prescribe the nature of an improved reading program. The details of reading instruction are professional matters and should be kept in the hands of those who have acquired expertise in the area. In short, citizens may appropriately deal with the what, professionals with the how of education.

Active participation in policy and program formulation can be critical, but there are other important ways to help secure citizen support. One is for school people to "shoot straight" with citizens. Information about the school—its purposes, procedures, and results—should be readily available and, indeed, regularly distributed. Second, there is no substitute for a good instructional program. Public relations gimmicks cannot hide a shoddy program of instruction. Third, the school should be a decent place for people to be. Students and teachers can spend as many as 1,000 hours per year in the school; thus the quality of living or the daily regimen should reflect an attitude of caring, an intellectual climate, high expectations, and a balance between freedom and conformity. Conditions such as these do much to differentiate between effective and ineffective schools.[19] Finally, schools must make their precepts and practices comprehensible to parents and other patrons. It is not wise for schools to advocate fashionable practices as though they had been demonstrated scientifically, or to invoke obtuse language to describe everyday concepts.

Just as the single school is the most effective unit for school operation and improvement, we think the single school is the most effective unit to invoke citizen support. It is at the school level that programs are actually implemented. Central-office or district-level activities are instrumental, designed to foster the instructional programs at each of the schools. The single school has the clearest and most direct opportunity to generate support for the schools, particularly from parents. Indeed, for many parents the value of the school is defined by the responses of their own children to school programs. When those responses are positive (or at least understood), parents are inclined to be school supporters. And support at the school level frequently carries over to support at the district level as well.

SUMMARY   Money, personnel, administrative time, and citizen support are crucial resources in the operation of schools and school districts. Basic to securing or allocating any of these resources is the necessity of establishing a school program. Establishing program requirements should be based on an examination of community aspirations and traditions and a consideration of school purposes. Despite state and national influences much discretion remains with local school districts, which could and should be delegated to individual schools.

Securing and allocating financial resources are important functions of administrators. Central to the process is the development of the school budget in which program requirements are converted to proposed expenditures, and revenues necessary to cover expenditures are set forth. Often in balancing revenues and expenditures, priorities must be placed on needs, and all available revenues, even private contributions, must be taken into account. Once established, the budget must receive board and community approval and the internal allocation of budget provisions within each school must be determined.

Administrators are also responsible for the securing and allocation of nonfinancial resources—personnel, administrative time, and citizen support. The selection and assignment of personnel is particularly important. To effectively allocate their time, administrators must balance a realistic appraisal of job demands with a determination to keep some control over their calendars. Citizen support is crucial to schools, and appropriate citizen participation in decision making can be useful in securing it but does not guarantee it. The best way to secure citizen support is for schools to maintain a strong instructional program and provide a healthy and supportive daily regimen in which students and teachers may thrive.

ENDNOTES

1. Roe L. Johns and Edgar L. Morphet, *The Economics and Financing of Education* (Englewood Cliffs, N.J.: Prentice-Hall, 1975) Ch. 15.
2. L.H. Zeigler, M.K. Jennings, *Governing American Schools* (North Scituate, Mass.: Duxbury Press, 1974).
3. Donald J. McCarty and Charles E. Ramsey, *The School Managers* (Westport, Conn.: Glenwood Publishing, 1971).
4. Wm. L. Boyd, "The Public, the Professionals, and Educational Policy Making: Who Governs?" *Teachers College Record* 77 (May 1976): 572–573.
5. Report of Task Force #3 to the Utah Statewide Planning Commission on Education, "The Purpose and Nature of the Public Schools." Utah State Board of Education, Salt Lake City, 1981.
6. For instance, see John L. Goodlad, *The Dynamics of Educational Change* (New York: McGraw-Hill, 1975), particularly Ch. 7.
7. For a discussion of values in administration, see Christopher Hodgkinson, *Towards a Philosophy of Administration* (New York: St. Martin's Press, 1978), Ch. 7.
8. For instance, see Johns and Morphet, *Economics and Financing.*
9. For more information, see Johns and Morphet, *Economics and Financing* and other treatments of school finance.
10. See Stephen J. Knezevich, *Program Budgeting* (Berkeley, Cal.: McCutchan Publishing, 1973), p. 1.
11. For instance, see Michael Y. Nunnery and Ralph B. Kimbrough, *Politics, Power, Polls, and School Elections* (Berkeley, Cal.: McCutchan Publishing, 1971).

12. For instance, see I. Carl Candoli et al., *School Business Administration* 2d ed. (Boston: Allyn and Bacon, 1978).

13. Wm. B. Castetter, *The Personnel Function in Educational Administration* 3d ed. (New York: Macmillan, 1981), Ch. 1.

14. Wm. J. Martin and Donald J. Willower, "The Managerial Behavior of High School Principals," *Educational Administration Quarterly* 17(Winter 1981): 69–90.

15. Martin and Willower, "Managerial Behavior," p. 77.

16. Don Davies and Ross Zirchbov, *Citizen Participation in Education* 2d ed. (Boston: Institute for Responsive Education, 1978).

17. See Roald F. Campbell and John A. Ramseyer, *The Dynamics of School-Community Relationships* (Boston: Allyn and Bacon, 1955); John E. Corbally, Jr., "A Study of Critical Elements of School Board-Community Relations," doctoral dissertation, University of California, Berkeley, 1955; and Luvern L. Cunningham and Raphael O. Nystrand, *Citizen Participation in School Affairs* (Washington, D.C.: The Urban Coalition, 1969).

18. See Roald F. Campbell et al., *The Organization and Control of American Schools* 4th ed. (Columbus, Ohio: Charles E. Merrill, 1980), Chs. 13 and 14.

19. For instance, see Michael Rutter et al., *Fifteen Thousand Hours: Secondary Schools and Their Effects on Children* (Cambridge, Mass.: Harvard University Press, 1979); and Wilbur Brookover et al., *Creating Effective Schools* (Holmes Beach, Fla.: Learning Publications, 1982).

CHAPTER 10

MANAGING CONFLICT

In Chapter 1 we noted that the basic purpose of educational administration is to enhance teaching and learning and that to do this an administrator must carry out several functions. Securing the cooperation of others is an essential part of such work. However, cooperation is not always forthcoming. The contemporary administrator is confronted with conflict of various kinds and multiple origins. Our discussion in this chapter focuses upon the nature of conflict and ways of dealing with it in school settings.

The rhetoric of education emphasizes nurturance and cooperation. Teaching is a "helping profession" in which all concerned presumably share the goal of doing what's best for children. An important historical reason for organizing local school systems under the jurisdiction of local boards of education rather than general purpose government was to minimize the partisan conflict associated with general government. Most people associated with schools—board members, administrators, teachers, and others—profess discomfort with conflict and strive to avoid it. However, conflict is clearly a fact of life in schools. Its presence has become more noticeable in recent years as a result of widely publicized clashes over such matters as desegregation, student rights, textbook selections, sex education, and teacher benefits and prerogatives. Many smaller conflicts are just as real and have been present in schools for many years.

CONFLICT IN SCHOOL SETTINGS

Definitions   Conflict is a word that in the vocabulary of most people refers to some kind of incompatibility and has a negative connotation. Most of us think of conflict as being unpleasant and resulting in consequences that are detrimental to some if not to all of the participants. In contrast, we usually think of competition as a healthy process. Parents encourage their children to compete for awards and recognition in school. Schools as well as other organizations sponsor contests in a wide range of fields including athletics, music, photography, debate, art, and many others. Competition is a fundamental value of our economic system, and our society tends to reward those who are the best (i.e., those who compete most successfully) in every sector.

An important difference in the popular view of conflict and competition is that the latter is legitimized by a set of rules which are known and agreed upon by the participants. Thus entrants in a golf tournament agree that the contest will be played over a given number of holes on a particular course and will be governed by a certain set of rules. Entrants accept the fact that most of them will not win, and most are willing to recognize the accomplishment of whoever does, provided they play within the rules. In contrast, the rules are less clear and the range of outcomes less satisfying for two teachers engaged in a dispute over which of them should be able to teach the only advanced-placement English course in their school.

The literature of the social and behavioral sciences tends to regard conflict in neutral terms, recognizing that it can be positive or negative in its effects. No single definition has achieved universal acceptance largely because the concept has been studied from a variety of perspectives (e.g., cognition, structural, cultural). Our preference is to treat the concept in fairly general terms consistent with Deutsch's view that "conflict exists whenever *incompatible* activities occur."[1] An advantage of this definition is that it permits consideration of conflict within as well as between individuals and organizations.

Types of Conflict   Getzels defines personality as the dynamic organization within the individual of
Intrapersonal conflict   those need dispositions that govern his unique reactions to the environment.[2] The central analytic elements of personality are the need dispositions that we can define with Parsons and Shils as "individual tendencies to orient and act with respect to objects in certain manners and to expect certain consequences from these actions."[3] An essential relevant concept is selective perception: people see what their backgrounds permit them to see. That is to say, individuals with the same formal responsibility in an organization may perceive these responsibilities very differently because of differences in their personalities.

Individuals may sometimes perceive the environment in ways that bring two or more of their need dispositions into conflict. Consider, for example, a beginning high school teacher who has high needs for both achievement and affiliation. It is very possible that the juxtaposition of these needs will create some stress for the teacher as he or she makes decisions about student assignments and classroom management. This teacher may find it difficult to reconcile the personal belief that students should be held to high standards of performance with the desire to be well liked by the students. An administrator with a similar pattern of need dispositions may have comparable difficulty in reprimanding teachers whose performance is unsatisfactory.

Decision-making situations often produce intrapersonal conflicts for school administrators because they force choices among values. Such choices are sometimes between two or more "goods," as in selecting one new teacher from many well-qualified applicants. Other decisions may require selecting the least harmful of several alternatives. Decisions about budget reductions often are of this type. Administrators contemplating possibilities such as eliminating art and music teachers, guidance counselors, interscholastic sports, or allocations for books and supplies may experience inner conflict as well as pressure from advocates of these activities.

Interpersonal conflict

The most common and visible type of conflict in schools as well as other organizations is interpersonal conflict. The permutations and combinations of potential conflicts involving students, teachers, administrators, and parents in a given school are many. Many of these conflicts are trivial and involve little more than a dispute between two students over some activity or adolescent insult. Others may have long histories and involve fundamental differences about priorities, activities, or associations within the school. Interpersonal conflict is not always apparent to a third party and may derive from a situation outside the organization. Thus a principal may be disappointed to learn that two very capable teachers are reluctant to work together on a curriculum project and later find out that they have been rivals in the teacher association or some other setting.

Individual-institutional conflict

Getzels and Guba formulated the concept of administration as a social process.[4] This concept is helpful in understanding the nature of conflicts between individuals and institutions. Getzels suggests that administration may be conceived structurally as the hierarchy of subordinate-superordinate relationships within a social system.

A social system includes both institutions and individuals. Institutions are characterized by certain roles and expectations which are consistent with the goals of the system. Behavior in the social system is a product of interaction between institutional demands as set forth in expectations for persons who fulfill a certain role (e.g., a teacher) and the personalities and needs of these persons as individuals. No two individuals are alike, and each brings his or her own personal needs and disposition to his or her organizational role. Thus, if one wants to know what a particular third-grade teacher does in a classroom, one must have some understanding of that teacher as a person in addition to knowing what the school as an institution expects from third-grade teachers. At times, the expectations of an organization and the needs of individuals within it will likely be in conflict.[5]

A particular type of conflict between individuals and institutions that appears in school settings is based upon differences in bureaucratic and professional orientations. Recall the discussion in Chapter 3 indicating that schools are bureaucratic organizations employing individuals who consider themselves professionals. Teachers and other staff members may resent organizational efforts to standardize and routinize their activities according to rules and regulations. For example, a requirement that teachers keep additional records or the establishment of a new evaluation system could produce conflict between teachers and the organization.

In many school districts, conflicts between the individual and the organization may escalate into conflict between the organization and the teachers or other employee group as a group. The origins of recent teacher assertiveness and activism can be attributed to their efforts to have a greater voice in decisions affecting them.[6] Teachers who have found it difficult to resist organizational directives as individuals have learned that collective action through local associations increases their power. For example, teachers' organizations have negotiated contracts that limit organizational prerogatives in such matters as establishing assignments, evaluating performance, and requiring attendance at faculty meetings.

Administrators play a critical role with respect to individual-institutional conflict. Of course, they themselves may experience conflict with the organization at times. However, the general expectation is that administrators will be mediators between the institutional and personal dimensions of organizational life. At one point, as organizational spokespersons, they will find it essential to explain, reinforce, and emphasize the school's objectives and procedures. At another point, it will be desirable to listen to members of the organization, to ascertain their feelings about certain school practices, and to try to understand why they take the position they do. When and under what conditions they do either is part of the art of administration. Clearly, there are no recipes as to when administrators behave institutionally or personally, but judgment regarding such matters may be sharpened if one knows that both kinds of behavior are appropriate. Moreover, it is well to anticipate the possibility that in serving as spokespersons for the organization, administrators will incur the hostility of those who view their interests as conflicting with the organization.

Intraorganizational conflict

Conflict may also exist among various groups within a school or school system. At a relatively simple level, conflict may exist among the members of a formal work group such as the science department at a high school. This differs from interpersonal conflict because with more than two parties involved, individuals are likely to form coalitions and deal with one another in ways designed to attract support for their interests from other group members.

A second kind of intraorganizational conflict is that which occurs between two or more units of the organization. Such conflicts may result from the efforts of both units to do the best possible job. For example, hard-working men's and women's coaching staffs have clashed over the scheduling of gymnasium facilities because each group wants to play their games at "prime time" and have as much practice time as possible. Similarly, teachers who wish to schedule field trips for their classes may encounter resistance from other teachers who teach the same students and do not want them to miss class time. Another example exists in a school system that has a series of alternative schools and programs which are very attractive to able students. Teachers and administrators in the regular programs resent these alternatives because they believe their efforts are hampered by the transfer of the best students from their classrooms.

Two units may also have a conflict when the activities of one depend upon actions of the other. Thus teachers who rely on counselors to encourage appropriately qualified students to enroll in their classes may blame the counselors for poor enrollments. Similarly, a high school faculty may notice consistent differences in the level of preparation of students from the various feeder schools. This could provide the basis for conflict between faculties at the high school and the low-achieving feeder school.

School-community conflict has become front page news in cities across the country during the past twenty-five years. Militant community leaders and their followers have confronted school officials with demands and demonstrations related to desegregation, forced busing, sex education, curriculum materials, students rights, and a host of other issues.[7] These protests have led to violence in more than one instance, and many school administrators have lost their jobs in the wake of such conflict.

School-community conflict

School-community conflict involves school officials, who are usually in the position of defending their actions or some new policy, and a range of community residents. It may stem from many kinds of events, but, according to Coleman, three conditions must be present: "The event must touch upon an important aspect of the community members' lives . . . must affect the lives of different community members differently . . . and must be one on which the community members feel that action can be taken."[8]

Conflict emanates from a variety of sources. The case studies reviewed by Coleman suggest that community conflict stems from issues dealing with economics, power or authority, cultural values or beliefs, or antagonistic attitudes toward particular persons or groups.[9] Deutsch identified a similar list of sources: control over resources, preferences and nuisances, values, beliefs, and the nature of relationships between the parties.[10] School-related conflicts can be categorized in this way.

Sources of Conflict

Conflict over resources may evolve at all levels of organizational life. An individual teacher may experience conflict about how to spend a fixed amount of money for supplies. Principals may experience conflict with one another about the number of staff assigned to their respective buildings. The board of education may disagree with community groups about the utilization of surplus school buildings. Power and authority are resources as well as money, personnel, and space. For example, teachers or administrators may be in conflict over a promotion or jurisdiction regarding some matter of interest.

Resource conflicts are likely to be most intense when they are seen as "zero-sum" or redistributive situations. A *zero-sum* situation is one in which one party is expected to win and the other to lose. A *redistributive* situation is one wherein the victory of one party is achieved by taking resources from another. School closings in response to enrollment decline may spawn such conflict. Residents and school staff in a particular neighborhood frequently resist proposals to close "their school" and redistribute the resources (e.g., students and financial support) to other schools. They often propose that other schools be closed instead, thus creating potential for widespread community conflict.

The place of preferences and nuisances in starting conflict is well known to any school principal. Students, teachers, and staff members may seek special privileges or scheduling arrangements, or react negatively to the activities of others. Food in the cafeteria, noise in the auditorium, pictures on the bulletin board, and the timing of bus routes exemplify the wide range of items that can be the source of such conflict.

Conflicts regarding values deal with opposing views of what "should be."[11] Schooling provides many occasions for such conflict. Compulsory attendance, the purposes of education, desegregation, and school prayer are some of the best-known issues of this type. School-based values conflicts often reflect changes in the broader community. In these instances, the school becomes a battleground and its policies represent a symbol of who is in control among differing community groups.[12] Conflict of this sort goes beyond the schoolhouse door to involve not only community residents and interest groups but often political actors at the state and national levels.

As discussed in Chapter 3, schools are characterized by uncertain technology. There is room for disagreement about how to teach students in most settings. Such disagreement can produce conflict rooted in different beliefs—for example, personal understandings of what is the best way to teach. Of course, people often have conflicting beliefs about less theoretical matters: students may disagree in their perception of who started a fight on the playground, or teachers and administrators may differ in their views of the consequences of assigning cafeteria supervision to teachers.

Another potential source of conflict is the relationship existing between the parties. One form of such conflict is the jurisdictional dispute in which two or more parties quarrel about who has the prerogative to influence a particular decision. For example, the assistant superintendent for personnel and the director of affirmative action may disagree about the latter's role in hiring new employees. Conflicts of this type take on importance for individuals because they raise questions about their future role in the organization. Some see jurisdictional disputes as opportunities to broaden their own sphere of influence; others fear the loss of influence. The presence of either perspective restricts the development of cooperation between organizational subunits.

Another form of conflict based upon existing relationships derives from the mutual experiences of the parties. Two principals who dislike one another as a result of previous conflicts may view each new encounter as a challenge to "get even" or achieve dominance over the other.

Most administrators are more attuned to the dysfunctions than the functions of conflict. The standard view is that conflict is unpleasant and disruptive. It leads to the disintegration of relationships and interferes with the achievement of goals. We resent the time we spend fighting with others and believe that it detracts from our real work. Relatively few administrators speak positively about the effects of conflict in their own organization. Their participation in conflict has produced painful memories and they may harbor negative feelings toward past opponents or second guess themselves for not avoiding certain issues or insisting upon particular outcomes. Their jaundiced view is fed by the knowledge that conflict has led to the firing, resignation, or premature retirement of many school administrators.

On the other hand, if one takes a more general perspective, it is clear that conflict can benefit organizations in many ways.[13] It can be the stimulus that generates new ideas, thereby helping the organization adapt to its environment. Alternatively, it can be a process through which organizational participants reaffirm the values central to the organization and strengthen their identity with and commitment to one another. Conflict with an external group is likely to build cohesion and bring forth greater effort by group members. Conflict within a group can help clarify power relationships and also reduce tensions within the group. As Coser points out,

> Conflict, which aims at a resolution of tension between antagonists, is likely to have stabilizing and integrative functions for the relationship. By permitting immediate and direct expression of rival claims, such social systems are able to readjust their structures by eliminating the sources of dissatisfaction. The multiple conflicts which they experience may serve to eliminate the causes for disassociation and to reestablish unity. Those systems avail themselves, through the toleration and institutionalization of conflict, of an important stabilizing mechanism.[14]

Note the relevance of these ideas to schools. Changes in educational policies and practices are often the product of conflict between the school and its environment or two or more factors within the school.[15] On the other hand, criticism from the community may strengthen bonds among school employees. The same teachers who criticize school practices among their colleagues in the faculty lounge may be vigorous defenders of the school in discussions with their neighbors. There is also evidence that surfacing conflicts among school personnel and dealing with these conflicts forthrightly can have stabilizing and integrative effects.[16]

Functions of Conflict

The Course of Conflict   Conflict is an episodic process with each episode involving a series of stages. For example, the conflict between a teacher and a student who refuses to comply with a teacher's request begins when one of them realizes the incompatibility of their respective positions and takes some action. An example of this is the student who does not heed the teacher's request to attend an after-school remedial session, choosing instead to report to a scheduled football practice. The other party then reacts in a way that may cause the first to reconceptualize the situation and take another action, which precipitates yet another reaction. For example, unaware that the student is a football player, the teacher may regard the student's absence from the scheduled help session as defiance or disinterest and send a strongly worded note to his parents. Surprised by this action, the student may feel the teacher is picking on him and retaliate by becoming disruptive in class. This cycle of action and reaction continues until the issue is resolved in some way—in this case, until the student is removed from the class or begins to meet the teacher's expectations. However, the outcome of the episode becomes part of the background against which both parties will assess their future relationships.

A process model   The above example is consistent with a process model of conflict developed by Kenneth Thomas[17] and presented in Figure 10–1. Although Thomas stresses that this is a model of dyadic conflict, we believe it is applicable in a general way to most school-based conflicts. From a management perspective, the key elements of this model involve the loop between conceptualization, behavior, and others' reactions. Attempts to affect the outcome of a given episode involve intervention at one of these points. Once an episode is underway, both parties are involved in the cycle of conceptualizing and behaving in response to the actions of the other. Each is influenced by a number of factors.

    Selective interpersonal perception is a central factor in this process. Each party views the situation in terms of his or her own needs, dispositions, and goals. Other similar experiences of the individuals are likely to influence the way they see this one, as will any past experiences with the current adversary. For example, the orientation of an experienced principal toward students who bring alcoholic beverages to school football games will be influenced by past encounters with such students. Moreover, the principal's conceptualizations of how to deal with any particular student in such an instance will depend upon past dealings with that student.

    Conceptualizations and actions are also influenced by the actors' preferences regarding outcomes and their concern for the welfare of the other party. Many conflicts are resolved because one party does not feel strongly about the issue and therefore withdraws or defers to the other. On the other hand, both parties may perceive an issue as a zero-sum matter of great importance. For example, the president of a teachers' association may see the group's demand to be recognized as bargaining agent for local teachers as the issue that determines whether he or she will retain the presidency of the group. The local superintendent may see the same issue as a threat to authority and job security. In this case,

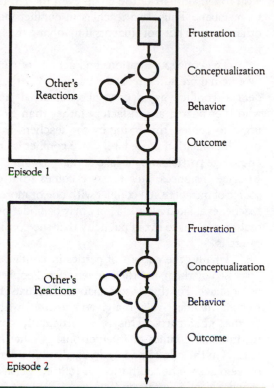

FIGURE 10–1   Process model of dyadic conflict episodes

Source: Kenneth Thomas, Process model of dyadic conflict episodes, "Conflict and Conflict Management," in Marvin D. Dunnette (Ed.), *Handbook of Industrial and Organizational Psychology.* Chicago: Rand McNally, 1976. (By permission of the editor.)

each party would have strong preferences and probably little regard for the effect of the outcome on the adversary. However, there are many situations where both parties have strong preferences regarding the outcome but are also concerned about its effect on the other party.

The setting of an episode affects the way the parties act toward one another. Individuals in a room by themselves may talk and act one way in the principal's office and another way in the teacher's classroom. The office setting is likely to make the parties more aware of the authority relationships between them.

Rules and norms can of course be a source of conflict, but they can also provide boundaries for it. Rules and norms provide guidelines for the conduct of conflict as well. For example, many organizations have formal grievance procedures for processing disputes involving students or teachers. Where formal rules are not present, the norms of the group provide an index to acceptable behavior in conflict situations. Individuals tend to comply with these norms because they wish to remain part of the group even though they are in conflict with some of its members. Thus, two teachers in conflict may discuss their differences with other teachers but not students if involving the latter would be contrary to group norms.

The conceptualizations and actions of parties in conflict are affected also by external pressures upon the parties. Whether someone even defines an incident as conflict may depend upon external pressures. For example, a teacher who is evaluated as satisfactory rather than excellent by the principal may be urged to contest this rating by the teachers' association, which objects to the overall evaluation procedure. Once conflict is underway, external pressures may encourage participants to take actions toward either escalation or deescalation. In some instances, this pressure comes from diverse sources and becomes a source of intrapersonal conflict with one or more of the parties. For example, the teacher evaluated as satisfactory may be under pressure from his wife to drop the matter in order to avoid publicity that she considers detrimental to her business interests.

Finally, the actions of parties in conflict are influenced by the resources possessed by them and their adversaries. People cannot fight with weapons they do not have. For this reason, many individuals, believing they lack the resources to compete effectively in a given situation, withdraw from the conflict or defer to the other party. This is a particularly common outcome in individual-institutional conflict or interpersonal conflict between managers and subordinates. On the other hand, individuals who enter the fray may bring a wide range of resources—the authority of office, persuasiveness, tenacity, influential friends, legal counsel, and others.

Revolts against an administration

Another description of conflict processes which involves more than two parties and which has relevance to school affairs was developed by Coleman.[18] This model, which described revolts against an administration, was based upon an analysis of community-wide controversies but it appears germane to intraorganizational revolts as well. According to Coleman, most administrations enjoy the support of a small group of ardent backers, face consistent opposition from another small group, and are regarded with acceptance or at least indifference by the large majority of the population. Conflict that engages the large passive group can be started in either of two ways:

> "(a) a change in the general climate of opinion, reinforced by national mass media and by current events, mobilizes certain basic values and dispositions . . . which the passive majority has held continuously, but which have been dormant. The current events and attendant publicity act, in effect, to create a completely new atmosphere of suspicion, where values which were well-accepted only a short time ago are liable to attack. In this atmosphere, the administration needs to commit only one tiny misstep and the suspicion will be directed against it . . . (b) The administration commits a series of blunders in matters which are of considerable importance to the members of this passive majority. . . ."[19]

This description highlights the ever-changing nature of school-community relationships. It is important for the programs and priorities of public schools to adapt to changes in community values. A recent example is the renewed emphasis on teaching basic skills in response to public enthusiasm for the "Back to Basics" movement. Another is the concern to reduce school costs. As long as school programs reflect the mainstream of community values, most residents provide at least tacit support for school officials. However, as most communities have become much more diverse, it has become increasingly difficult to assess and respond to shifting expectations. As a consequence, the incidence of school-community conflict continues to increase.

The course of destructive conflict is marked by escalating tensions and divisiveness. Destructive processes often begin with a single, relatively simple issue involving few people and expand to include multiple and more general issues involving many people. As more people become involved, the issues become personalized and feelings are intensified. It is not unusual in school affairs for participants to personify the issues by focusing on the performance of a principal or superintendent. For example, parents angered by a plan to close the school in their neighborhood may argue that the superintendent is incompetent and should by dismissed. In pressing their argument, they may incorporate any other issues that could expand their following and bring additional pressure upon the superintendent.

Destructive processes

When conflict is destructive, the participants tend to emphasize the differences that separate them. A sense of loyalty and commitment toward those who are "for us" is matched by antipathy and perhaps hatred toward those "against us." Communication between the two sides is limited, and each responds to new issues on the basis of the stereotype held about the other. Each party views the whole relationship as a conflict situation and seeks an outcome in which they will "win" by achieving dominance over the other party.

From an organizational perspective, these processes are destructive in several ways. First, they detract attention from important activities. Individuals may fail to carry out assignments because they are distracted by the conflict or because they see an opportunity to make the other side look bad. For example, a district implementing a new desegregation plan may find that some teachers who oppose the plan find subtle ways of resisting it in their classrooms. Second, conflict may injure individuals in ways that cause them to withdraw from or reduce their effectiveness in the organization. Third, destructive conflict reduces the long-range capability of the organization by destroying work relationships and impeding communication patterns.

Harlan Cleveland argues the case for constructive conflict, saying, "The wise executive . . . will deliberately induce a degree of tension within the organization; enough loud and cheerful argument among its members so that all possible outcomes are analyzed, the short-term benefits are compared with the long-run costs, the moral dilemmas are illuminated, and the public relations effects are

Constructive processes

analytically examined."[20] In contrast to destructive situations, constructive processes are marked by open communication, focused attention on specific issues, and mutual trust and respect among the participants. Administrators can increase the likelihood that organizational conflict is processed in this way by emphasizing the development of collaborative relationships and problem-solving skills throughout the organization.[21]

Even conflict that is destructive in the short run can have long-range consequences that are positive. When organizational relationships do not permit participation by and attention to the concerns of low-power groups, these groups may find that strategies of confrontation and the escalation of conflict provide the only means of addressing their concerns.[22] The most pervasive school-based example of such conflict has been the historical struggle to improve educational opportunities for minority children. Although school desegregation has been a traumatic issue in many communities, it has generally resulted in improved education and a more open society for minority citizens. However, the results have varied dramatically from one district to another. In many districts, desegregation is seen as an issue of the past and students are treated equally, but in others the tensions of discrimination remain. The differences in these situations highlight the importance of interpersonal reconciliation and reconstruction of organizational relationships in the wake of conflict.

ORIENTATIONS TO CONFLICT RESOLUTION

The first question administrators must consider in the face of a conflict situation is whether the conflict is of potential benefit to the organization. If the answer is yes, they should allow it to continue or perhaps even help intensify it while monitoring its continued development. If the conflict appears to be detrimental, they should seek a means of coping with or resolving it.[23] Efforts to resolve a conflict begin with an orientation regarding the kind of outcome to be sought. Thomas suggests that in dyadic conflicts, this orientation is based upon the extent to which a party wishes to satisfy (1) his or her concerns and (2) those of the adversary.[24] This model and the five orientations to be discussed in this section are presented in Figure 10–2.

The Thomas model has direct application when the administrator is a party to conflict. Where the administrator is an observer or potential mediator, the model describes the orientations of the participants and suggests how various forms of intervention would be received by the participants.

Neglect

One orientation for coping with conflict is to ignore or refuse to deal with it. There is a heroic school of thought suggesting that administrators should deal with all problems and confront all conflicts directly. However, we believe that it is often appropriate for administrators and others to avoid matters that are at issue with another party. This may be an appropriate orientation, for example, when the situation and possible outcomes lack clarity, when the outcome of this situation is dependent upon or will be influenced by resolution of a concurrent issue, or when other matters are of higher priority.

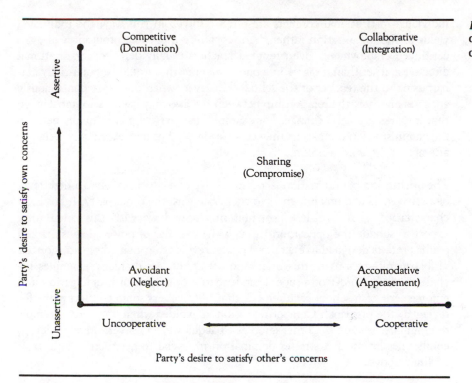

FIGURE 10–2 **Five conflict handling orientations**

Source: Kenneth Thomas, Five conflict handling orientations, "Conflict and Conflict Management," in Marvin D. Dunnette (Ed.), *Handbook of Industrial and Organizational Psychology.* Chicago: Rand McNally, 1976. (By permission of the editor.)

On the other hand, an orientation of neglect may stem from genuine indifference to an issue, distaste for the processes one sees as associated with seeking resolution of the conflict, or a sense of powerlessness. Such attitudes impede the consideration of alternatives in the organization and restrict the development of cooperative relationships. Stated more positively, we hope that faculty members and administrators care about issues of importance to their school and know about and have confidence in organizational processes to resolve differences regarding these issues. Administrators are often in a position to help others see the importance of dealing with specific issues and choose means for doing so.

Appeasement involves willingness to satisfy the other party's concern at the expense of one's own; it is "giving in" or doing what we are asked to do. Individuals are willing to appease the other party when they attach relatively little importance to the outcome of an issue, when they feel relatively powerless in the situation, or when they consider it more important to retain a good relationship with the other party than to prevail on this particular issue. Note that

Appeasement

individual-institutional conflicts are often resolved in this way; the individual yields to the organization rather than jeopardize a possible promotion or even continued employment. Even tenured teachers usually defer to organizational directives rather than disagree in a public manner that would be potentially embarrassing to the teacher or the school. However, when one party continuously appeases another, the relationship between the two may become so imbalanced that it sparks dramatic change. For example, teachers who continually defer to the administration on matters they consider important may eventually resign or attempt to organize a union.

Domination   The orientation of domination is a competitive one which involves a high level of assertiveness and unwillingness to cooperate with the other party. It has been characterized as a "win-lose" orientation. Individuals with this orientation expect to subdue the opposition through the exercise of power. Law suits and public protests designed to encourage public revolt against an administration are visible manifestations of this orientation.[25] Other less dramatic examples include the direct order of a superintendent to a principal, or promulgation and enforcement of a school requirement that all teachers submit lesson plans for review by the principal. Competition is often avoided when one party attempts to dominate because the other chooses to acquiesce. However, an approach to conflict resolution that stresses domination may lead to destructive conflict as outlined above.

Compromise   The tradition of compromise is deeply engrained in American thought. For most people, the view that disputes can be settled by giving each person a part of what they want was learned first through childhood experiences of splitting candy equally between two claimants. Subsequent courses in history stressed the skills and character of great compromisers. We have been taught compromise as a value and skill to be applied in political and organizational life. Thus we strive to understand what the other person seeks in a given situation and often try to meet him or her halfway. Compromise is apparent at all organizational levels in schools—from the playground to the board meeting. A particular form of compromise that has become increasingly important in the past twenty years is collective negotiations involving boards of education and various employee groups.

Advocacy of compromise as a solution to conflict rests on the assumption that each of the parties will be happy because they *gained* something. However, as Mary Parker Follett noted years ago, they also *lost* something, and concern over what was lost may overcome appreciation for that which was gained.[26] Thus, a compromise may well plant the seeds for subsequent conflict.

Integration   The orientation to conflict resolution which Follett considered superior to compromise was termed *integration*. More recent authors have used terms such as collaboration or "win-win" to describe this orientation, which assumes that the participants will work together for a solution that satisfies each of their concerns entirely. The initial step toward integration requires that both parties be open with one another about their respective motives and objectives. As mutual understanding of these factors increases, the parties may gain greater appreciation for each other's perspective and develop trust. The integrative solution is one that builds upon this understanding and trust to redefine the situation in a way that suggests an outcome satisfactory to both parties. Follett referred to this as obeying "the law of the situation."

Not every conflict can be resolved through collaboration. However, difficult situations are more likely to be settled in this way if one or more of the parties values this approach. Doing so requires that individuals resist the tendency to define conflict in we-they and win-lose terms and, instead, make special efforts to understand the concerns of others. It also calls for willingness and ability to view situations from different perspectives. The act of redefining a situation in a way that satisfies all participants often calls for substantial creativity.

Finally, it should be noted that the orientation of individuals to the resolution of conflict varies from situation to situation. Indeed, it may change over the course of a particular situation. For example, two teachers who are engaged in a win-lose situation about who will teach a particular course may change their orientation to collaboration or compromise as a result of skillful mediation by the principal.

ADMINISTRATIVE BEHAVIOR

To this point, we have discussed types and origins of conflict, ways in which it develops, and orientations to its resolution. We turn now to some ways in which administrators may behave in conflict situations as initiator, defendant, and mediator.

Initiating Conflict

There are times when administrators wish to initiate conflict. They will sometimes do so as a third party trying to stimulate organizational change. For example, a high school principal who believes that the science department has not kept up with recent curriculum trends may bring an outside consultant to speak to the department members in an effort to provoke debate. By encouraging individuals to pick up on ideas presented by the consultant, the principal may foster a collaborative approach to curriculum change. Another approach to the problem, in a community where parents express concern about the science program, would be for the principal to facilitate interchange between faculty members and parents. Again, the principal would probably hope for a collaborative resolution. However, it is possible that the matter would be resolved through compromise or even faculty acquiescence to citizen demands for curriculum change.

Administrators who consider initiating change by promoting conflict among others must keep in mind the potential impact of this conflict upon the organization and its members. As noted above, conflict can be either functional or dysfunctional. Those who introduce it to organizations they care about should first ascertain that the individuals and processes within the organization are capable of dealing with it.

Administrators also initiate conflict wherein they participate as advocates for their own organizational units. For example, the chairperson of an industrial arts department may conflict with school counselors over guidelines for placing students in shop courses, or the middle school and high school principals may disagree about which building should have priority in a renovation proposal to be presented to the board of education.

To be rational in the initiation of conflict, people should assess both the importance of the issue to themselves and political adversaries, and the resources each brings to the situation. An initiator is, by definition, assertive in orientation and thus initially inclined to strategies associated with dominance or integration. A preference for dominance or integration influences how the initiator deals with such matters as stating objectives, stereotyping, exercising power, and processing information. Tactics of dominance emphasize differences between the parties; thus one overstates objectives, stereotypes the opposition, emphasizes one's own coercive power, and restricts information in order to gain the tactical advantages of ambiguity. On the other hand, integrators tend to understate differences in objectives, strive to portray the opposition in accurate terms, emphasize trust rather than power, and encourage the flow of information.[27]

It is important for someone who initiates conflict to understand who is central to the desired outcome. A conflict between two parties is often resolved by a third party. In this case, the strategic objective of the initiator is not to dominate, agree, or compromise with the second party; it is to persuade the third and deciding party to act in one's favor. For example, the two principals who disagree about which building should have priority for renovation may argue publicly. However, their intentions are not to change one another's mind but to build a case that the superintendent and board of education will find convincing. The initiator of conflict in public school settings does well to remember that the ultimate arbiter is often the general public, for school issues have the potential to escalate to this level. Criticism of food served in the cafeteria, efforts to remove a football coach, challenges to Christmas assemblies, and demands to promote more women to administrative positions are examples of issues that have been initiated quietly but escalated to the point of being tried in the court of local public opinion.

Finally, administrators who initiate conflict should do so with clear goals, estimates of the costs they are likely and willing to incur by taking this course of action, and a sense of what outcomes short of total victory would be satisfactory. In addition, they should monitor the course of the conflict as objectively as possible to determine if the goals are still attainable and the projected costs within the range of acceptability. Changes in one's own resources or those of the opposition may require a change in tactics or even objectives. For example, a group of city superintendents who challenge the state funding formula for schools on the basis that it is unfair to urban areas may anticipate opposition from their rural counterparts and the legislators who represent them. However, they may also expect to prevail on the issue because they expect their own legislators to be united in their favor and they have received informal assurance that the governor supports them. If they learn during the course of the legislative session that the governor has shifted his position and now favors a compromise that some of the urban legislators find acceptable, the superintendents may wish to reconsider their original goal.

Administrators are often called upon to respond to the initiatives of others. Conflict occurs when these initiatives are incompatible with the priorities or activities of the administrator or the organization. How this conflict evolves and whether its impact is constructive or destructive depends in large measure on how the administrator responds. As already noted, the administrator's first decision is whether to respond at all, and at times this decision will be not to respond. When faced with crowded agendas or ambiguous problems, an alternative is to delay or sidetrack an issue by scheduling it for consideration at a future meeting, assigning it to a committee, or asking the initiator to assemble more supporting information. Some matters resolve themselves without further attention. However, efforts to delay or sidetrack are not without risk when issues are significant and potentially divisive. Thus, it is important for administrators to develop a sense of timing for attending to organizational and interpersonal disputes, as well as a sensitivity to their possible causes and consequences.

The Administrator as Defendant

It is human nature to personalize criticism and to react defensively in conflict situations, but such behavior encourages both sides to adopt win-lose orientations and restricts the likelihood of win-win or collaborative outcomes. Thoughtful administrators resist temptations to overreact or personalize issues. Instead, they try to understand exactly what the other party seeks and why. This is not always easy. However, trying to do so not only increases the chance of achieving a mutually satisfying resolution to the present issue but also strengthens trust and communications channels that can help in the future.

Successful conflict resolution also requires that administrators understand their own values and those of the organization. Matters others consider important may be of relatively little personal or organizational significance. In such cases, it is easy and appropriate to acquiesce. On the other hand, individuals may present issues that challenge the core values of the institution. Administrators must recognize the importance of these issues and respond in ways that preserve organizational stability. For example, administrators in many districts have been called upon to defend teacher-selected and board-approved textbooks from citizens who attack them on religious or patriotic grounds. A considered response to these citizens will take into account not only their strong beliefs but those of teachers who regard textbook selection as a professional matter and board members who think textbook approval is their prerogative as elected officials.

Many conflicts to which the administrator is a party are resolved by domination. Indeed, this is a routine occurrence in most organizations, and facilitated by traditional structures of authority. Typical of such situations are those where a student threatened with disciplinary action acquiesces to teacher direction, or the superintendent directs a principal to prepare a report that the principal considers unnecessary. The authority of office is an important resource for administrators who would dominate conflict situations. However, other forms of power are also employed. Some individuals dominate because others defer to the forcefulness or magnetism of their personality. Others dominate by marshaling facts or compelling arguments. For example, many parent-administrator conflicts are dominated by administrators who cite laws, policies, or statistics that overwhelm—but do not necessarily satisfy—the parent.

The temptation to respond to conflict by dominating the initiator is everpresent for administrators because it is generally easier and less time-consuming (at least in the short run) than collaboration or compromise. For many administrators, this response pattern has become a way of life. As already noted, however, the long-term health of the organization is more likely to benefit from emphasizing collaborative approaches, particularly with respect to matters of high salience to other participants.

We must take note of the possibility that school administrators may become defendants in community conflicts described above as revolts against an administration. There are no easy remedies for such conditions. However, Coleman's analysis does suggest two kinds of response. The first is to attempt to coopt the opposition.[28] *Cooptation* involves bringing the opposition into the decision-making structure by consulting with them informally or giving their leaders visibility as formal advisors. For example, a superintendent under community attack for failing to cut school costs could appoint a citizens' committee to advise on long-range budget planning and include cost-cutting advocates. Subsequent meetings of the committee could persuade the critics that the district actually needs to spend what it does, thereby reducing the pressure of the issue or producing some compromise acceptable to the critics.

A second tactic suggested by Coleman's analysis is to cross-pressure that segment of the public that may be attracted to the opposition's case by reminding them of other actions by the administration in which they have a stake, or by seeking public support from other groups of individuals for whom the opposition has respect.[29] Thus, the superintendent in our example might take pains to point out that school funds support special programs in which groups of citizens are interested, and seek public support from organizations that have status in the community such as labor unions and the Chamber of Commerce. The presence of such support may neutralize and ultimately dissipate the attack of the opposition.

The Administrator as Mediator   A third posture for administrators with respect to conflict is that of mediator between two or more other parties. For example, principals mediate disputes involving students, teachers, and parents. Sometimes these disputes are internal to the organization, such as those involving work relationships between two teachers. At other times, they span organizational boundaries, as in disputes involving teachers and parents. Two aspects of the mediating role must be considered. The first is a *preventive-maintenance* approach, which involves designing and structuring organizations in ways that lessen the potential for destructive conflict. The second is a *fire-fighting* approach, which involves coping with problems as they develop.

There is substantial literature regarding organizational design to promote collaboration and reduce the likelihood of disruptive conflict. Much of it deals with clarifying goals, improving communication, encouraging participation in decision making, and other organizational processes discussed in preceding chapters. Likert and Likert have described a general organizational system which incorporates these elements as System 4.[30] According to them, a System 4 organization—

> . . . is made up of interlocking work groups with a high degree of group loyalty among the members and favorable attitudes and trust among peers, superiors, and subordinates. Consideration for others and relatively high levels of skill in personal interaction, group problem solving, and other group functions also are present. These skills permit effective participation in decisions on common problems. Participation is used, for example, to establish organizational objectives which are a satisfactory integration of the needs and desires of all the members of the organization and of persons functionally related to it. Members of the organization are highly motivated to achieve the organization's goals. High levels of reciprocal influence occur and high levels of total coordinated influence are achieved in the organization. Communication is efficient and effective. There is a flow from one part of the organization to another of all the relevant information important for each decision and action. The leadership in the organization has developed a highly effective social system for interaction, problem solving, mutual influence, and organizational achievement. This leadership is technically competent and holds high performance goals.[31]

The "fire-fighting" aspect of conflict management is routine for many school administrators. For example, high school assistant principals often spend large parts of their day mediating conflicts between students and the organization, students and other students, and students and teachers. Administrators at higher levels in the system may spend less time as mediators but disputed issues that come to their attention tend to have more significance for the organization. As in other conflict situations, the first question the administrator must address is that of preferred and possible outcomes. Is the issue one that can be resolved so that all parties will be satisfied, or is it such that the best to be hoped for is the cessation of hostility and disruptive behavior? In the latter instance, the best available remedy may be one that postpones the issue or allows the parties to behave independently of one another.

The ideal resolution to a conflict is to remove its source or to help the participants reach a mutually satisfying solution. Recall that conflicts usually stem from disagreements about resources, preferences and nuisances, values, beliefs, or the nature of relationships among the parties. The formal authority of administrators sometimes permits them to alter such factors. For example, one way to resolve a conflict over limited resources is to provide additional resources, as in the case of a principal who recognizes a need to provide additional instructional supplies when teachers argue about guidelines for their use. Administrators can also use their authority to remove nuisances or to restructure formal relationships among individuals.

Administrators can also use their authority to force resolutions that are not mutually satisfying. A superintendent faced with a conflict between two principals may choose a solution that favors one and impose it upon the other. Similarly, a principal dealing with a teacher who is in violation of a particular rule may insist upon enforcing the rule. Many school conflicts are ended at least temporarily by administrator domination. Teachers or students often bring disputes to an administrator expecting the issue to be resolved and hoping that it will be in their favor. However, to some people the resolution of uncertainty and concomitant decrease in tension between the parties is a more important outcome than having the issue resolved in their favor.

Despite the fact that others may find it comforting, third-party domination has limitations as a means of conflict resolution. One danger is that of solving the wrong problems. Faced with many complex and compelling matters on their own agendas, administrators may not understand the issues between the participants or their perspectives toward them. Lacking time to familiarize themselves with these matters, administrators may impose a remedy or exact a compromise that does not deal with the true issues. A second limitation of this approach is that, if used too frequently, others will learn to expect conflicts to be resolved in this way rather than through mutual effort. Thus, participants may not develop problem-solving skills, individuals will regard their counterparts as rivals rather than colleagues, lateral communication will be guarded, and decision making will follow hierarchical patterns.

Third-party mediation is an alternative to administrator domination.[32] This approach involves the parties in conflict and explores their differences openly on an equal-power basis. The goal is to help them develop understanding of the problem as it appears to their adversary as well as to themselves and to build the commitment and trust necessary to design and implement a collaborative solution. At times, the process involves little more than bringing the parties together to discuss the issue. At other times, the mediator must first meet individually with the parties; structure a situation for them to consider their problem; participate in the discussion as a clarifier, referee, diagnostician or supporter; and help monitor implementation of the agreed-upon solution.

Finally, there are instances when the conflict between two or more parties is so fundamental that it cannot be resolved through domination or mediation. Rather than try to impose a solution that might expand the conflict or encourage valued members to leave the organization, the administration should try to establish a buffer between the combatants.[33] For example, a principal may alter room assignments or the master schedule to reduce contact between two highly competent teachers who do not get along with each other. As another example, a superintendent may transfer a young administrator whose aggressive statement of liberal views clashed with those of an established faculty group to another school where he or she can build a better relationship with the staff. Rules and regulations may also buffer conflict. For example, conflict between boys' and girls' basketball coaches about scheduling practice time in the gymnasium can be buffered by a policy statement and schedule issued by the principal. Buffering can be a strategy to postpone conflict resolution, or it can be a means for the organization to cope with conflicts that appear irresolvable.

SUMMARY

Administrative life focuses upon promoting cooperation, but administrators in schools as well as other kinds of organizations must at times deal with conflict. In some instances, administrators are direct parties to conflict; in others, they are involved only indirectly or called upon to mediate or manage conflict among others. Conflict may be intrapersonal, interpersonal, individual-institutional, intraorganizational, or school-community. Conflict is episodic and can have beneficial as well as negative consequences for individuals and organizations. How a conflict is resolved depends largely on the orientations of the participants. These may include neglect, appeasement, domination, compromise, or integration. Administrators' behavior in particular conflict situations varies according to their orientation to its resolution and whether they regard themselves as initiators, defendants, or mediators.

ENDNOTES

1. Morton Deutsch, *The Resolution of Conflict* (New Haven, Conn.: Yale University Press, 1973), p. 10.

2. Jacob W. Getzels, "Administration as a Social Process" in A.W. Halpin, ed., *Administrative Theory in Education* (Chicago: Midwest Administration Center, University of Chicago, 1958), pp. 150–165.

3. Talcott Parsons and Edward A. Shills, *Toward a General Theory of Action* (Cambridge, Mass.: Harvard University Press, 1951), p. 114.

4. Jacob W. Getzels and Egon G. Guba, "Social Behavior and the Administrative Process," *School Review* 65 (Winter 1957): 423–441. Also see Jacob W. Getzels, James M. Lipham, and Roald F. Campbell, *Educational Administration as a Social Process* (New York: Harper and Row, 1968).

5. See Chris Argyris, *Personality and Organization* (New York: Harper, 1957).

6. See Ronald G. Corwin, "Professional Persons in Public Organizations," *Educational Administration Quarterly* 1 (Autumn 1965): 1–22.

7. For discussion, see Roald F. Campbell et al., *The Organization and Control of American Schools* 4th ed. (Columbus, Ohio: Charles E. Merrill, 1980), pp. 349ff.

8. James S. Coleman, *Community Conflict* (New York: The Free Press, 1957), p. 4.

9. Coleman, *Community Conflict*, pp. 5–6.

10. Deutsch, *Resolution of Conflict*, pp. 15–17.

11. For a thoughtful discussion of the importance of values in educational administration, see

Christopher Hodgkinson, *Towards a Philosophy of Administration* (Oxford: Basil Blackwell, 1978).

12. See, for example, Scott Cummings, Richard Briggs, and James Mercy, "Preachers versus Teachers: Local Cosmopolitan Conflict over Textbook Censorship in an Application Community," *Rural Sociology* vol. 42, no. 1, (Spring 1977), pp. 7–21.

13. Lewis Coser, *The Functions of Social Conflict* (New York: The Free Press, 1956).

14. Coser, *Functions of Social Conflict*, p. 154.

15. Alan K. Gaynor, "The Study of Change in Educational Organizations: A Review of the Literature," in Luvern L. Cunningham, Walter G. Hack and Raphael O. Nystrand, eds., *Educational Administration: The Developing Decades* (Berkeley, Cal.: McCutchan Publishing, 1977), pp. 234ff.

16. See Mark Bassin and Thomas Gross, "Turning on Big City Schools: Pragmatic, Participatory Problem-Solving," in Mike M. Milstein, ed., *Schools, Conflict and Change* (New York: Teachers College Press, 1980), pp. 114–131.

17. Kenneth Thomas, "Conflict and Conflict Management," in M. D. Dunnette, ed., *Handbook of Industrial and Organizational Psychology* (Chicago: Rand McNally, 1970), pp. 889–935.

18. Coleman, *Community Conflict*, pp. 7–8.

19. Coleman, *Community Conflict*, p. 8.

20. Harlan Cleveland, *The Future Executive* (New York: Harper and Row, 1972), p. 22.

21. For assistance in this regard, see Rensis Likert and Jane Gibson Likert, *New Ways of Managing Conflict* (New York: McGraw-Hill, 1976).

22. Mark A. Chesler, James E. Crowfoot, and Bunyan I. Bryant, Jr., "Using Institutional Conflict to Achieve Change in Schools," in Mike M. Milstein, ed., *Schools, Conflict and Change* (New York: Teachers College Press, 1980), pp. 30–49.

23. For a discussion of considerations related to this choice, see James A. Conway, "Conflict and Change Strategies: The Agony of Choice," in Milstein, *Schools, Conflict, and Change*, pp. 279–296.

24. Thomas, "Conflict and Conflict Management." For another discussion of managing conflict in schools that utilizes the Thomas models, see Robert G. Owens, *Organizational Behavior in Education* 2d ed. (Englewood Cliffs, N.J.: Prentice-Hall, 1981), pp. 276–304.

25. The master theoretician of public protest was Saul Alinsky. See *Reveille for Radicals* (Chicago: University of Chicago Press, 1946).

26. See Henry C. Metcalf and L. Urwick, eds., *Dynamic Administration* (New York: Harper and Bros., 1942).

27. These ideas are adapted from Richard E. Walton, "Two Strategies of Social Change and Their Dilemmas," *Journal of Applied Behavioral Science*, vol. 1, no. 2 (Spring, 1965): 167–179.

28. Coleman, *Community Conflict*, p. 17. Also see Philip Selznick, *TVA and the Grass Roots* (Berkeley: University of California Press, 1949).

29. Coleman, *Community Conflict*, p. 22.

30. Likert and Likert, *New Ways*.

31. Likert and Likert, *New Ways*, p. 16.

32. For elaboration of this approach, see Richard E. Walton, *Interpersonal Peacemaking: Confrontations and Third Party Collaborations* (Reading, Mass.: Addison-Wesley, 1969).

33. For a discussion of buffering as strategy for dealing with organizational conflict, see Thomas L. Ruble and Richard A. Cosier, "Conflict Processes" in Don Hellreigel and John W. Slocum, Jr., eds., *Organizational Behavior* 2d ed. (St. Paul, Minn.: West, 1979), pp. 521–522.

CHAPTER 11

CHANGE

There is a mystique about leadership associating it with change. A President of the United States is expected—at least since the days of Franklin D. Roosevelt—to produce major change in the nation during the "first hundred days." An inevitable question for the newly elected superintendent of schools is "What changes are you going to make?" A retiring principal is asked, "What stamp have you put on your school?"

The implication is that an administrator enters the scene and almost immediately—through dynamic action, personal charisma, and even ruthless pruning—stamps the school or the school district as his or her own unique product. This assumption is wrong and many administrators have made major errors because they did not understand how wrong it is.

The school is subject to changes from within and the school operates in a changing environment as well. Change is a process with which the educational administrator must deal—sometimes initiating change and regularly responding to it. But neither constant nor radical change is a hallmark of effective leadership. In Chapter 5, we spoke of the ways changing situations influence the behavior—and, indeed, the success or failure—of individual administrators. In this chapter, we discuss organizational change and the role of the administrator in initiating and responding to such change.

Hawley and others point out that American public schools have become notorious for their ability to resist change and innovation.[1] If this charge is valid, it seems unnecessary to warn educational administrators against change;

perhaps we should be urging them toward ever greater change. Yet, as Boyd and Crowson demonstrate, "there have been remarkable changes in American public education."[2] Our purpose, here, then is to recognize that change will come, to understand that change is necessary, and to review the sources from which change will come and the process through which the administrator initiates and responds to change.

FORCES FOR CHANGE   An organization is constantly adjusting to new people, to new demands upon it, or to new technology. Most of these adjustments are minor in nature and have little to do with the basic purposes and programs of the organization; nor are they of real concern to organizational leadership. Several forces, however, do become of significance and concern, and may lead to the need for significant change.

Demographic   The 1970s and 1980s have seen rapid shifts in the demography—the characteristics of the population—of society, school districts, and schools. Boarded-up elementary schools that were built only twenty or twenty-five years ago bear mute and compelling testimony to changes in the birthrate in the United States. Communities that once had many young families now have a majority of families without school-age children. School districts in the southwestern part of the United States are crowded with children while districts in the northeastern region see continually declining population. The ethnic "mix" in a community may be much different today than was true just a few years ago and the "mix" within an attendance area of a community may exhibit even greater change than is true for the total community.

Demographic changes, then, affect school enrollments and ethnic mixes and can also affect the clientele—the people of the district. Economic shifts, age shifts, and other changes may, for example, lead to major changes in voters' attitudes toward school tax issues.

Structural   During the 1950s and 1960s great changes were made in the number of school districts in the United States. School consolidation—the combining of a number of smaller districts into a single district and often the joining together of elementary districts and secondary districts into so-called "unified districts"—was a major movement in education. These kinds of structural changes still take place both within and without school districts. The emergence of the middle school, the increase in busing with accompanying changes in attendance areas, and continuing school consolidation all provide structural changes to which administrative response is necessary. Many of these changes were designed to create the "perfect" setting for teaching and learning—what Tyak described as the search for the "one best system."[3] It seems clear today that no such system exists, but the search was a serious one and created many changes in school-district structure.

As school systems in many large urban areas have become larger and more complex, a variety of organizational or structural changes have been made. These changes have had major impact upon administrators. Large urban school districts have become regionalized so that in addition to the superintendent, there are area or neighborhood or (to complicate terminology) district superintendents who are to some extent chief executive officers of operating units within the overall school "corporation." Not only have these structures become complicated and extremely bureaucratic, but they have led to major changes in the roles of administrators such as principals or curriculum directors. The distance between the "central office" and the school has increased; communications problems for administrators throughout such a district are intensified; and the necessary understanding of purposes and programs have become difficult to achieve.

These structural changes are often accompanied by governance or control changes, which are discussed in a later section. The impact of these dual changes—structure and control—can be extremely great and extremely difficult with which to deal.

Curricular

Changes in society can lead to major changes in school curricula. As the Space Age began, real and imagined deficiencies in the science and mathematics preparation of American citizens led to major changes in curricular emphases and methods of teaching. Concern about the role of the United States in the world leads to periodic changes in curricular emphasis upon foreign languages and the so-called area studies programs. The introduction of new technologies—for example, the inexpensive hand-held calculator or the personal minicomputer—leads to changes in courses and methods. Concerns for equality of educational opportunity have led to both locally initiated curricula changes and changes that have been governmentally mandated.

Most of these changes are national in scope and can have the effect of nationalizing the curriculum in American schools. Campbell and Bunnell found that not only do social purposes lead to nationalizing effects in curricula, they lead to changes in guidance programs, testing programs, college admissions procedures, inservice teacher education, and school-plant planning and construction practices. What is more, they found that many people fail to recognize the impact of national programs on local schools.[4]

Curricular changes can lead to widespread changes in the school. New materials are often required, as is new space in which the materials can be used. New equipment is added while old equipment becomes outmoded, and special programs are initiated to prepare teachers to cope with curricular change. School-facility planning becomes involved, as do teacher training institutions, textbook publishers, and so forth.

Curricular changes and changes in instructional methodologies can also lead to major changes in the perceptions held by people other than those directly involved. The recent controversy surrounding the methods used in the schools to teach reading, for example, had significance well beyond what was basically conceived as a better way to teach this subject.[5] Similarly, a new philosophy of school instructional methodology can arouse feelings and lead to results well beyond those intended.[6]

Financial   Changes in financial support levels are a fairly regular occurrence in education. Changes can lead to either increased or decreased financial support. While either type of change creates tasks for the administrator, it is clear that the former change creates a much more pleasant set of tasks than does the latter.

Changes may be of several kinds. First, the taxpayers of a school district may decide by vote to either increase or decrease (usually meaning an unwillingness to increase in spite of inflationary or enrollment pressures) the level of tax support of the schools. Second, the general tax base of a school district—and thus tax receipts—may increase or decrease due to a variety of economic factors. Third, governmental support levels may change. This type of change can take two forms: either general aid (usually from the state) is increased or decreased, or support for special programs from various governmental levels is increased or decreased. While all decreases in support are difficult changes with which to deal, it is the change in support of special programs that has been particularly bothersome to local school administrators in recent years. New programs of various kinds are mandated by government with or without sufficient financial support for the programs. Each of the following statements paraphrases the requirements of recent federal legislation:

"Mainstream the handicapped."
"Bus the students."
"Respect bilingual needs."
"Meet special safety requirements in your buildings."
"Remove all architectural barriers to the handicapped."
"Remediate."

These and other mandates come flowing down to the district with or without financial commitments. Programs are started today with funding support, but are to be continued tomorrow without support.

These considerations have complicated the financial scene for schools and their administrators. Thus difficult financial times, because of general economic conditions that include inflation, are made doubly difficult by other financial considerations and changes that are in many ways beyond the control of the local administrator.

A second type of force for change involving financial matters has been court action related to state school-finance programs. A host of cases in state courts have challenged these programs on the grounds that they discriminate against children in districts with low assessed valuation per student. While the Serrano[7] and Rodriquez[8] cases attracted the most national attention, similar cases appeared in many other states. The problem became sufficiently complex as to create a number of written materials and consulting firms to aid legislators who were struggling with school finance programs and educators who were struggling to understand the changes required by these cases.[9] Thus, the issue of equality of educational opportunity became a major force for reexamination of school finance programs.

Another set of changes has been of major significance to educational administrators in recent years. Governance—as the concept operates both within and upon a school district—has undergone a number of significant changes. Within the district, some of the structural changes referred to earlier have led to districts within districts, subboards, advisory groups with some amount of authority, and other new governance mechanisms. The rapid growth of unions and collective bargaining in education have led some items that were once administrative prerogatives to become negotiable and have transferred some administrative decision making to the bargaining table.[10]

Control and Governance

The national commitment to equality of opportunity in the schools has led to a number of judicial decisions wherein federal judges have assumed direct jurisdiction over some aspects of educational administration. Greatly increased federal support of education, either directly to districts or through grants to states, has led to increased regulation of various aspects of the overall school program. And a preoccupation with the concept of accountability has added new layers of processes to the school decision-making procedures. Hearings, reports, increased audits, and other elements of accountability have materially changed the ways administrators can practice.

This catalog, not of changes, but merely of categories of changes that face the educational administrator, makes it appear as if nothing is stable in the schools. As much as that may seem to be the case to the beleaguered administrator, the school is actually a conservative institution where basic changes come slowly. In discussing change, Eiseley indicates that—

CHANGE VERSUS CONSTANCY

> over the generations, institutions slowly change but they have to have a certain amount of stability to sustain societal order. Flickering and dancing in the play of our great machines, however, and haunting our scientific establishment, is an unseen invisible elf to whose whims we are subjected in an ever-intensifying fashion—an elf we call change.[11]

If schools must deal with this elf and yet must have stability; and if, as we said in the introductory remarks of the chapter, change is not necessarily a sign of administrator effectiveness, and yet is inevitable, it is important to examine the change-constancy dichotomy to see where the school generally lies along that continuum.

We spoke earlier of the decline in the "grades" earned by the public schools as a result of the American public assessing their performance. But there are a number of other events and reports revealing that the public schools are not held in high regard. In 1981, both *Time* and *Newsweek* ran series on the failures of the public schools. Efforts to provide some form of tax support for attendance at private schools continue to be pursued by many. A new and controversial study comparing the performance of public and private schools awards a clear victory to the latter.[12] In spite of studies showing that public schools must move from one crisis to another,[13] these times do not reflect a strong faith in the schools. In several states, schools have actually closed because of the unwillingness of voters to provide funds to keep them open.

On the other hand, a variety of court cases seeking access to schools for children, some form of education for almost everyone, and particularly the availability of postsecondary, adult, and continuing education demonstrate the American people's deep and continuing faith in education. They may not believe that it should cost as much as it does; they may not believe in the necessity or even the moral rightness of each element of the curriculum; they may not believe that a current group of teachers is "good" or support a current administrative or school board team; and they may not agree with a given form of "schooling," but the American people do continue to believe in education.

A second unchanging element is the personal contact between teacher and learner. Technologies may come and go but the act of teaching always involves the cybernetic interaction between a responsive teacher and a responsive learner. Technology is essential in support of teachers and learners, but this dyad cannot be replaced by it.

A third and often overlooked unchanging element is that the school does indeed influence values, character, and beliefs whether educators or lay citizens are willing to admit it or not. The school as an institution—as an entity greater than the sum of its parts—has always had a significant impact upon the character of its students. Much of the current discussion about the impact of schooling upon value formation relates to the degree to which specific values can and should be taught. While this discussion is a significant one, the existence of so many parochial school systems in the United States illustrates the persistent belief that schools and schooling are expected to shape value systems and character. Of course, the school is certainly not the only educative force in a society, but the school is a comprehensive and complete educative force rather than something in which the impact is restricted only to prescribed curricula and lesson plans.[14]

A fourth unchanging element is the heart of the curriculum—those courses and subjects that assist in the creation of individuals who can function in their society. Reading, writing, and arithmetic are at the heart of today's curriculum just as they were in the schools of ancient Greece. Methods of teaching these subjects change, but the subjects themselves remain crucial.

Finally, regardless of how they are expressed, the purposes of the schools in

America remain fairly constant. As Ward Reeder wrote in 1930, "Suffice it to say that from the time of the founding of the first settlements in America, education of the proper type and amount has been regarded as the bulwark of a democratic government, as the best guarantee of a progressing society, and as an open sesame to the individual for the realization of his potentialities."[15]

Surely this statement would serve as well at the end of the twentieth century as it did in the early decades. Bulwark of democracy, means for societal progress, and realization of individual potential are certainly purposes that have remained constant.

To clarify the constancy of purpose in education, Goodlad makes an important distinction between its aims and goals. He points out that aims are direction-oriented—the effort to move from a present condition to a better condition—while goals are generally descriptions of ways to move toward aims. In other words,

> Educational aims, then, potentially provide for stability in schooling. They speak to things worth sustaining, calling continuously for fresh interpretation of individual welfare, social justice, and what is good for humankind. School goals speak to needed changes, usually calling for correcting some imbalance between individual welfare and the common good.[16]

What Reeder is speaking about above are aims, and it is within these and similar statements of aims that constancy is found. It is in the role of the school to provide nutritious lunches, or the exact nature of schooling as opposed to education, or the relative importance of music and science for the "good life" that we find change. Thus, the ways schools help individuals realize their potential do vary, but the aim of accomplishing that realization remains strong and constant.

One other element of constancy should be mentioned. The American people have always believed that the governmental agencies that exercise control over the public schools should be local ones. For many years it has been stronger as a belief than a fact in the real world.[17] It continues, however, to be a strong belief in spite of substantial state responsibility and federal funding and controls. Because the belief regularly surfaces to affect various aspects of school functions—from a review of books in the library and a concern for attendance-area boundary lines to arguments about school closings—it is one that deserves recognition by administrators today.

THE ADMINISTRATOR AS MODERATING AGENT

The school, then, is basically a conservative institution in our society, and radical and sudden changes have never characterized education. But obviously the school cannot survive if it is unable to adapt to changes in the society in which it exists. Thus one of the primary tasks of leadership is to determine when change is necessary and when it is not. Most of this determination should be made in an anticipatory way; i.e., the leader should attempt to see societal changes coming before they arrive, and consider responses (if any) in advance of the absolute necessity to respond. The administrator, however, will face conflicting pressures for change from various groups: teachers asking for fewer student contact hours and more time for preparation; employers asking for more curricular elements that prepare people for the world of work; universities asking for increased preparation in foreign languages or in sciences; and so on. Each group usually presents its needs in forceful and dramatic ways, indicating that nothing short of major overhaul will suffice. Students, on the other hand, seek some stability—they need programs started this year to continue on next year. The educational leader becomes the moderator, the one who recognizes the need for change, but recognizes also the need for continuity and stability in any institution of learning. It is the administrator who must preserve the focus upon the basic purposes of the schools and other elements of constancy described above. It is the administrator who must determine when change will insure faithfulness to those elements and when it will constitute an attack upon them.

This role is often an uncomfortable one. It is a fact of physics that heat is created by a brake, and anyone who is viewed as resistant to movement (change) will experience "heat" from various constituents. Nonetheless, the role—and probably the heat—is an integral part of school leadership.

THE CHANGE　There are a variety of ways in which the change or adaptive process can be de-
PROCESS　scribed. As we indicated earlier, it is unlikely that any one model will fit a given situation exactly. Nonetheless, it is useful to be aware of change-process models, and some of them will be reviewed here.

Several models focus on the interaction between an organization and its environment. An early concept of this type is Thompson's idea of "boundary spanning."[18] The boundary-spanner works not only to adapt the organization to meet changing environmental demands, but to change, interpret, or dampen the impact of environmental factors upon the organization. Hence the boundary-spanner deals with at least two environmental situations simultaneously. Research indicates that this concept is particularly valuable in describing the role of a school principal.[19]

Another description, which expands upon the boundary-spanning concept, is called the process of mutual adaptation.[20] This model posits that innovation or change is developed to respond to a problem or to anticipate and to avoid a problem, but then must be adapted to fit the needs, preferences, and abilities of the personnel who are to put the change into practice. Occasionally, the adaptation is so great that the innovation is no longer responsive to the problem for which it was designed. The balance between the requirements of a change and the requirements of the personnel who must make change happen is a delicate one, and the mutual adaptation model describes an important set of issues for leadership.

The continuous nature of change is the emphasis of a number of researchers who describe it using negotiated-order theory.[21] Here, the change process is not something that is initiated and then concluded, but rather a constant negotiation toward equilibrium. The addition of a substitute teacher or the introduction of a new technology influences equilibrium and thus will lead to negotiations to "restore order." Change, then, is not normally a major event; it is, rather, an incremental and ongoing process that is so regular as to be unnoticed. Presumably the educational administrator is a major participant in this ongoing process, but the theory assumes that all parts of an organization are involved with only occasional need for prompting.

The negotiated-order concept differs greatly from the common view of a stable bureaucracy where change is a major event. However, both are views of stability: in one stability is maintained by constant change, and in the other stability is maintained by protection from constant change.[22] As is often the case, how organizations actually change probably lies somewhere between the two concepts.

Several other change models are based upon concepts of growth and development. In these models, organizations or their personnel react to changing situations in the same way that human beings grow and develop in their environment. One such model which has received a great deal of attention is called *organization development* or OD. Change through OD involves planned and sustained effort with the continuous assistance of outside consultants using behavioral science theory as a foundation. The school, in this case, is viewed as an individual that grows under the attentive care of a "family" and professionals from outside of the "family." Growth (change) is continuous in these models too, but based on behavioral science principles rather than negotiation.[23]

Each model of the change process posits an organization within an environment, affected by the environment, and seeking stability. We have said that the aims of schools are fairly constant, thus the purpose of change (regardless of the process employed) is to enable the school to be persistent and effective in achieving those unchanging aims. In addition, all theories of change in organizations recognize an "organizational need" for equilibrium. This recognition is given in spite of the fact that there is no formal proof that an organization meets the physical laws of equilibrium. It is clear, however, that a radical change in an organization—a loss of equilibrium—is resisted, and if successful, results in a new and different organization. The continuing existence of an organization is viewed by those in it as requiring a state of equilibrium. Hence change is a means through which a lost or threatened equilibrium can be regained or simply maintained.[24]

The initiation of change is an activity that follows the classic decision-making pattern (discussed in Chapter 6). The critical aspects of decisions about change are (1) the identification of the purpose or purposes of a change proposed by others, and (2) the anticipation and identification of problems or opportunities

INITIATING CHANGE

that may require change. As is true for all decisions, decisions to make major changes lead to both products and to byproducts—and both need to be anticipated as change is considered.

To illustrate, let us assume that the school system in a medium-size city has been experiencing rapid growth because of the annexation of territory by the city (which automatically leads to its inclusion in the city school district) and because of new industry in the city. Growth in this case is not only in numbers, but in complexity because new ethnic groups, of a socioeconomic makeup different from what existed before, are being introduced to the schools and neighborhoods. What was a fairly homogeneous city, in which a school board of five members could be said to be quite representative, has become a heterogeneous community in which representation is difficult. The schools have always been supported well by the city, and they are of very high quality, but continued growth will bring with it the need for more operating and capital funds as well as other changes.

What changes in this community have created the need for change in the schools? What constants need to be protected from change?

Obviously, both the high quality of the schools and the high level of community support need to be maintained, but rapid growth and increased heterogeneity in the community can threaten both. Thus, the school district needs to initiate certain actions, including:

1. New means of establishing two-way communication channels between the schools and both the new and old elements of the community. The board may no longer understand the needs of the whole community and it must be made aware of this possibility.
2. Increased appraisal in the schools to test whether existing curriculum methodologies are suited to the new elements of the student body. Are there language problems? Is the educational environment of the home and the community changing?
3. Analysis of employment opportunities and students' goals to insure that the content of the curriculum still fits the needs of the community. Will new vocational programs be required? Will there be new opportunities for cooperative programs involving the schools and local businesses and industries?
4. New attention to attendance areas. Are emerging housing patterns in the community likely to create any problems in the schools with regard to desegregation efforts?

Each of these areas of concern (and others) may or may not reveal problems that require immediate change. In some cases, too, no change will be needed, while in others, change may be needed but not immediately. In some instances changes may be required, but only after other things are done first. In the areas of concern listed above, probably increased communication is the highest priority because through that means will come data and insights related to the other areas.

The key point is that the educational administrator—if he or she is to be a leader—cannot simply sit passively and try to be prepared to respond to new situations after they occur. The administrator can help shape the new situation, attempt to assist the community to avoid crises, and try to insure that the schools really do respond to today's (rather than to yesterday's) needs and environment.

In playing this active role, one crucial consideration for the administrator is *where* change must be made, if change is indeed necessary. Goodlad points out that much of our literature on change in education uses *military* terminology and the school is usually the target of change.[25] Little effort is made to determine whether the social environment outside of the school is an appropriate place for change, and little effort is spent to consider small adjustments within the school, as opposed to major overhaul. It is not enough, then, for the administrator simply to conclude that change is or is not warranted by a set of circumstances: it is also necessary to contemplate changes both within and without a school system or a school.

If, for example, levels of reading ability are a persistent problem in a school system, one solution may lie outside the reading classroom. To some extent, successful reading depends upon an interest in reading and the opportunities a young person has to develop and to pursue that interest. National programs such as RIF (Reading Is Fundamental) have worked to provide youngsters with their own books—the beginning of a personal library—to support the opportunity to develop reading as a hobby. Perhaps broadened support of a community library system, too, could create changes in a community that would enhance interest in reading. There may also be new ways whereby the school board, a library board, and perhaps book dealers in a community could cooperate to create an environment in which reading ability is more sought after than is currently the case.

The administrator must not rush into proposing change before it is needed, however. It may be, for example, that in a growing city such as the one described above, some curricular changes are necessary. But before changes are proposed, it is necessary to gather facts. A change in the socio-economic mix of the community does not automatically require a whole new remedial education program. Likewise, the addition of a few new students from new ethnic backgrounds does not necessarily justify a massive new bilingual education program. As we indicated in Chapter 10, initiating change can have the result of initiating conflict as well and this is something the administrator must keep in mind.

Change should obviously be appropriate to the problem; thus the problem must be clearly understood. Without the latter, the former cannot really take place except through extraordinary good luck. While educational leaders do occasionally experience good luck, a pattern of administrative leadership based upon the regular expectation of good luck is doomed to failure.

To continue with the example of the city described above, neighborhood school boards may propose that they take on some of the authority vested in the board of the school district. They may see these proposals as necessary solutions to the new communication problems. In considering them, however, the administrator should ask the following questions:

Do they resolve or intensify communications problems?

Does the school district become a federation of independent neighborhood school units?

Is responsibility as well as authority clearly (and legally) delegated?

What do the proposals have to do with quality of education and with community support of schools?

Are these proposals the only way to deal with the problems they are supposed to solve?

Thus the administrator, to be an active participant in change, must determine not only whether change is needed, where it is needed, and how much is needed, but what specific solutions are most appropriate to the problems.

RESPONDING TO CHANGE   It would be pleasant if all changes in a school or school system were initiated by educational administrators as solutions to—and in anticipation of—well-understood problems. Unfortunately, such is not the case. Often, in spite of the best foresight of the administrator, unanticipated changes arise and must be dealt with. Some of these changes are emergencies: a teacher dies, a school building burns, a major industry suddenly leaves town. Others have simply come without warning, evidence that even the best leader cannot always see into the future. (It is a truism, however, that everyone is 100 percent accurate in hindsight.)

A situation that looms up suddenly and appears to require change should be viewed as an opportunity, even if it is not always a welcome one. The administrator must take the time to consider alternative responses even when time pressures do not permit exhaustive creation or consideration of responses. To the extent possible, the immediate response should be one that does not eliminate the possibility of second thoughts, alterations, even completely different responses later.

The heroic figure who stands on the still-smoldering ruins of a school building and announces with finality, "We shall begin tomorrow to rebuild this building on this very site," may well be making a number of mistakes. Even more important, he or she may be missing an opportunity to respond to other problems or changes besides the current one.

As with decision making, it is important in considering responses to change to study whether any response at all is necessary. And certainly, administrators usually have the option of determining the timing of their responses.

Immediacy is not necessarily the determining factor in evaluating the quality of a response.

Aside from how the impetus for change comes about, change varies primarily in terms of time frame rather than the basic process. Analysis of the problem, consideration of various ways to address it, anticipation of the results of each alternative, deciding upon a response, and following through with the response are the elements of instituting change, whether dealing with a slowly evolving demographic change or an immediate personnel crisis.

Regardless of whether the administrator is initiating change, responding to change, or resisting change, a number of the studies we have cited earlier indicate that there are specific kinds of administrative structures and administrative behavior that influence the change process. A formal organizational structure, with levels of responsibility, written position descriptions, and well-understood reward systems, is a powerful force for stability. Earlier we spoke of a situation where reading problems might be approached through a change in the relationships between the schools and the community library system. If such changes are perceived as threatening the positions of the teachers, or school library staff, or jeopardizing the financial support of the school libraries, then the changes would be resisted. Griffiths describes a school organization as an open system in which a set of internal components achieve a balance among themselves and in which this balanced group also achieves a balance with the external environment. Because any change requires the establishment of new balances within the system, it is resisted and relatively infrequent. In a sense, a highly organized system is like a gyroscope—once set in motion, any change in direction is strongly resisted.

Based upon this concept of the open system, Griffiths constructed a series of propositions related to changes in organizations, paraphrased as follows:

ADMINISTRATIVE STRUCTURE AND CHANGE

1. The major impetus for change is from the outside.
2. The degree and direction of change is directly proportional to the intensity of the external stimulus.
3. Change resulting from a change of the chief administrative officer is more likely if the new officer comes from outside the organization.
4. If external stress on the organization continuously increases, the organization first lags in response, then overresponds, and then collapses.
5. The number of innovations introduced is inversely proportional to the tenure of the chief administrator.
6. The more hierarchical the organization, the less the possibility of change.
7. Change in an organization tends to occur from the top down.
8. The more functional the interplay of internal subsystems (the more sound the balance among subsystems), the less the tendency for organizational change.[26]

This theory speaks not only to the resistance to change in organizations but also to the importance of the administrator as a change agent.[27] It is clear that the administrator needs to be a moderating agent, to resist unnecessary and too-frequent change; it is also clear, however, that the administrator can become a barrier to necessary change. If, as Griffith contends, change tends to occur from the top down and innovation is inversely proportional to administrator tenure, then there is a need to consider the degree to which the top administrator has become too set in his or her ways. The administrator with long experience in a school district runs the danger of responding to new problems only within the framework of old experience. Experience is a valuable asset, but it can become an inhibitor of action if it is not a continually growing asset. The difference between "twenty years of experience" and "one year's experience twenty times" is a good picture of two possible approaches to administrative life.

Both organizational structure and administrators themselves, then, are major factors in change. What Griffiths describes as balance could also be described as comfort; and it is not wise for either school systems or the administrators in them to become too comfortable.

SUMMARY[28]

The school is essentially a conservative institution, but because of change in both the internal and external environments, educational leaders must at times initiate change and other times respond to it. The role of leadership in the area of change is essentially as decision-maker. A special characteristic of decision making as it relates to change is the element of anticipation: it is advisable to anticipate—to develop information sources that will help the administrator deal with situations before they become problems or crises. But it is also important to understand that the teaching-learning process—the basic task of the schools—takes place most effectively in a stable environment. Evolution, rather than revolution, is most supportive of teaching and learning. For most educational leaders, the maintenance of quality programs and their support is the primary task rather than crises in which quality and support must be created. "Is this change really necessary?" is a question that the administrator should ask regularly, and one to which the positive answer should require a strong burden of proof.

ENDNOTES

1. W.D. Hawley, "Dealing with Organizational Rigidity in Public Schools" in Frederick M. Wirt, ed., *The Polity of the School* (Lexington, Mass: D.C. Heath, 1975), pp. 220–240.
2. William L. Boyd and Robert L. Crowson, "The Changing Conception and Practice of Public School Administration" in David C. Berliner, ed., *Review of Research in Education* (Washington, D.C.: American Educational Research Association, 1981), pp. 311–373.
3. D.B. Tyak, *The One Best System* (Cambridge, Mass.: Harvard University Press, 1974).
4. Roald F. Campbell and Robert A. Bunnell, eds., *Nationalizing Influences in Secondary Education* (Chicago: Midwest Administration Center, 1963).
5. For a good example of the way in which a teaching-method change aroused much broader criticism, see Rudolph Flesch, *Why Johnny Can't Read* (New York: Harper, 1955).

6. See Louis M. Smith and Pat M. Keith, *Anatomy of Educational Innovation: An Organizational Analysis of an Elementary School* (New York: John Wiley and Sons, 1971).

7. Serrano v. Priest, 5 Cal. 3rd 584, 487 P.2d 1241 (1971) and Serrano v. Priest II, 135 Cal. Rptr. 345 (December 30, 1976).

8. Rodriquez v. San Antonio Independent School District, 337 F. Supp. 280 (W.W. Texas, 1971), rev'd 411 U.S. 1 (1973).

9. For example, see J. Pincus, "The Serrano Case: Policy for Education or for Public Finance?" *Phi Delta Kappan* 59 (November 1977): 173.

10. For an excellent review of various views on the impact of collective bargaining upon schools, see *Phi Delta Kappan* 63 (December 1981): 231–251.

11. Loren C. Eiseley, "Alternatives to Technology" in Aaron W. Warner et al., eds., *The Environment of Change* (New York: Columbia University Press, 1969), pp. 175–176.

12. James Coleman et al., *Public and Private Schools: A Report to the National Center for Education Statistics by the National Opinion Research Center* (Chicago: University of Chicago Press, 1981).

13. Michael Kirst and D. Walker, "An Analysis of Curriculum Policy Making," *Review of Educational Research* 41 (1971): 479–509.

14. For a fuller discussion of this point, see W. Brookover et al., *School Social Systems and Student Achievement: Schools Can Make a Difference* (New York: Praeger, 1979) and M. Rutter et al., *Fifteen Thousand Hours* (Cambridge, Mass.: Harvard University Press, 1979).

15. Ward G. Reeder, *The Fundamentals of Public School Administration* (New York: Macmillan, 1930), p. 3.

16. John I. Goodlad, *The Dynamics of Educational Change: Toward Responsive Schools* (New York: McGraw-Hill, 1975), p. 7.

17. See Roald F. Campbell et al., *The Organization and Control of American Schools* 4th ed. (Columbus, Ohio: Charles E. Merrill, 1980).

18. J. D. Thompson, *Organizations in Action* (New York: McGraw-Hill, 1967).

19. M. T. Moore, *The Boundary-Spanning Role of the Urban School Principal.* Doctoral dissertation, University of California at Los Angeles, 1975.

20. See D. Mann, ed., *Making Change Happen?* (New York: Teachers College Press, 1978).

21. See, for example, Arnold Strauss et al., "The Hospital and Its Negotiated Order," in E. Friedson, ed., *The Hospital in Modern Society* (New York: Free Press of Glencoe, 1963), pp. 147–169.

22. The classic description of the bureaucratic model is Max Weber, *The Theory of Social and Economic Organization*, trans. A.M. Henderson and Talcott Parsons (Glencoe, Ill.: Free Press, 1947).

23. See Richard A. Schmuck and Mathew B. Miles, *Organization Development in Schools* (Palo Alto, Cal.: National Press Books, 1971).

24. For an excellent summary of concepts of change see S. Ranson et al., "The Structuring of Organizational Structures," *Administrative Science Quarterly* 25 (1980): 1–17.

25. Goodlad, *Dynamics of Educational Change*, pp. 14–15.

26. Daniel E. Griffiths, "Administrative Theory and Change in Organizations," in Matthew B. Miles, ed., *Innovation in Education* (New York: Teachers College Bureau of Publications, 1964), pp. 428–435.

27. For a complete discussion of the change-agent role, see Kenneth A. Tye and Jerrold M. Novotney, *Schools in Transition: The Practitioner As Change Agent* (New York: McGraw-Hill, 1975).

28. Lillian K. Drag has prepared an excellent annotated bibliography on educational change that appears in Goodlad, *Dynamics*, pp. 223–247.

CHAPTER 12

APPRAISAL

In simple terms, school programs need to be planned, implemented, and then appraised. As is true of people generally, school administrators seem to do rather well with planning, not quite so well with implementation, and appraisal is frequently neglected. Recent events have given renewed emphasis to the need for appraisal: many federal programs, for instance, have appraisal or evaluation stipulations written into the legislation. There has also been a call by a number of scholars in educational administration for research in the field to give much more attention to student outcomes.[1]

Just what do we mean by appraisal? In some of the early literature on administration the word *control* seemed to connote much of what we now call appraisal.[2] For the last decade or two the National Assessment of Educational Progress, an extensive program testing student achievement, has brought the word *assessment* into frequent use. The term *evaluation* is also commonly used to describe efforts to find out how effective educational programs have been. Indeed, evaluation has become a separate subfield in education, with its own theories, methodologies, and advocates. Since evaluation, for many, has taken on a rather formal meaning, we have chosen to call our efforts here appraisal. We shall, to be sure, make reference to many of the concepts used in evaluation. Appraisal, as we see it, gives attention to the purpose of a program, to the evidence indicating how well the program is meeting its purpose, and to the judgment of whether the outcomes are good or bad. In short, appraisal is the process by which we describe how well we are doing.

APPROACHES TO
APPRAISAL

A number of approaches to appraisal have been developed. We shall consider here a few of the formal evaluation approaches and then suggest a few less formal approaches.

Formal Evaluation

While evaluation of educational programs is as old as education itself, the formal evaluation movement in education is largely a product of the last half-century. Ralph W. Tyler was a notable pioneer in the movement. In 1935 Tyler contributed a chapter to the NSSE yearbook entitled "Elements of Diagnosis,"[3] setting forth what he called problems involved in evaluation. They were: "(1) defining the behavior to be evaluated, (2) selecting the test situations, or determining the situations in which the behavior is expressed, (3) developing a record of the behavior that takes place in these situations, and (4) evaluating the behavior recorded."[4] This simple formulation has influenced the work of many scholars and a number of major evaluation studies since then.[5]

Tyler's formulation required evaluators to begin with their purposes, which then had to be defined in behavioral terms. For instance, teachers could no longer simply say they were teaching critical thinking; they now had measures of observable behavior that would suggest to what extent students were engaged in critical thinking. The behavior then had to be recorded in some objective form, and might include a wide range of things, such as scores on a formal test or an anecdotal description. Finally, from the data recorded inferences had to be made about the extent to which the purposes initially set forth had been attained. If the evidence suggested that the results had been less than satisfactory, those concerned could then ask why. For instance, were the purposes unrealistic? Were the behavioral definitions inadequate? Was the instruction appropriate? Was the data-gathering sufficient? Or might other inferences be drawn from the results? Answers to these questions suggested another round of instruction and evaluation, modified to be more effective than the first.

Clearly, the process set forth above is not a precise formula; at many points judgments and inferences have to be made. The process does stress, however, that these be informed judgments. Moreover, the process emphasizes that those who are concerned with teaching must give thought to what they are doing. In addition, the process emphasizes that those who evaluate teaching should make their judgments on the basis of evidence secured on the basis of explicit criteria.

Tyler's approach to evaluation has another limitation: it seems doubtful that all learning outcomes can be reduced to descriptions of observable behavior for which evidence can be objectively recorded. Moral and aesthetic objectives, for example, would be particularly difficult to observe and measure. Even so, the early evaluation movement stressed a number of important concepts. Emphasis was placed on outcomes and not merely on intentions. Evidence (as opposed to guessing) was stressed. Perhaps of even greater importance, the question of purpose came to be applied to the examination of any program. In short, teachers and administrators more frequently came to ask *why* they engaged in any particular activity.

One of the more recent formulations of evaluation grew out of a national study sponsored by Phi Delt Kappa and represents the work of a panel of scholars chaired by Daniel L. Stufflebeam.[6] Stufflebeam and his colleagues define educational evaluation as "the process of delineating, obtaining, and providing useful information for judging decision alternatives,"[7] and delineate four types of evaluation in their model: context evaluation, input evaluation, process evaluation, and product evaluation. Context evaluation is the most basic type, and its purpose is to provide a rationale for the determination of objectives.[8] To achieve that end the relevant environment—the actual conditions, the problems that exist—is to be examined and judgments made as to how it could be altered to achieve desired ends. Input evaluation is concerned with how to use resources to meet program goals. It might involve assessing the capabilities of an agency, the strategies for achieving program goals, and designs for implementing a strategy.[9] Process evaluation is concerned with periodic feedback, particularly to detect defects in the procedures as they are used to implement programs.[10] Product evaluation is the measurement of results, not only at the end of a program but as often as is necessary during a program.[11] A flow chart depicting these four types of evaluation and the activities and decisions necessary for their application to any program is also part of the model.[12]

There is no doubt that the CIPP model, as it is called, is a more comprehensive approach to evaluation than were earlier efforts in the field. Even if context evaluation is called by another name (e.g., an environmental study), the idea of giving attention to current conditions before setting out on a program of improvement is an important one. Likewise, input evaluation can also be called the assessment of organizational capability, but in any case such an assessment is important to program improvement. Particularly significant are the concepts of both process and product evaluation: we need to be cognizant not only of the outcomes of a program but of the processes that are being employed along the way.

As useful as these four types of evaluation are, their application to all or even many programs in a school or school district may require a commitment of time, staff, and money that is not feasible. To perform course evaluations, for instance, a school district could have eight or ten subjects at ten to twelve grade levels, for a total of eighty to 120 evaluations. Clearly, that many complete evaluations in any one year would not be possible. Nevertheless, the CIPP model provides a way of thinking about programs, decision making, and evaluation. When such thinking becomes part of the professional repertoire of school workers they can frequently make informed judgments about the context and input aspects of evaluation in particular, even if full-blown studies cannot be done. Then, too, the model gives specific direction to the development of more formal approaches to the evaluation of programs demanding the most careful scrutiny.

As noted above, evaluation has become an important subfield in education, commanding the attention of many scholars. Worthen and Sanders,[13] for example, have compared seven different evaluation models in terms of twelve selected characteristics.[14] One of the twelve concerns the unique characteristics of each of the frameworks. In the judgment of Worthen and Sanders, one of the notable contributions of the Robert Stake model is its systematic method for arranging descriptive and judgmental data, thus emphasizing the relations between them. One of the contributions of the Michael Scriven model, Worthen and Sanders believe, is his distinction between formative (ongoing) and summative (end) evaluation, and indeed, those two terms have become common in the evaluation literature. A major contribution of the Malcolm Provus model is its emphasis on continuous communication between program and evaluation staff through feedback loops.

In a recent treatment of evaluation, however, Guba and Lincoln[15] level fundamental criticism at the field. They state that the consistent failure to use evaluation findings is almost a national scandal, and explain:

> Often such failure is laid to ignorance, laziness, or political sidestepping by responsible decision makers. We are more inclined to feel, however, that such failure simply illustrates the poverty of traditional evaluations, which are likely to fail precisely because they do not begin with the concerns and issues of their actual audiences and because they produce information that, while perhaps statistically significant, does not generate truly worthwhile knowledge. Given their general level of triviality, it is probably a good thing that evaluation results have *not* been more widely used.[16]

Guba and Lincoln then develop a new approach to evaluation that gives major attention to what they call responsive evaluation and use of a naturalistic approach. By *responsive evaluation* they mean an attempt to provide information of concern to the stakeholding audiences. By the *naturalistic approach* they mean making greater use of situational data employing methods drawn from ethnography, anthropology, and sociological field studies.

This is not the place to deal extensively with formal evaluation approaches; suffice it to say that there are more approaches available than are mentioned here. These approaches differ somewhat in their detail but in many ways each tends to complement the others. When formal evaluation is needed one or more of them can be useful for planning it. But keep in mind that current evaluation practices could be improved. Worthen and Sanders, for instance, suggest that an evaluation plan should be included from the beginning of any program,[17] and in many cases this is not done today.

General Approaches   We agree that any program worth doing should also be evaluated. As mentioned earlier, however, time, staff, and money may not permit a full-blown formal evaluation of every program. In the actual operation of schools and school districts general approaches to appraisal are often more feasible. For instance, formal evaluation approaches usually assume that the program to be evaluated is a new one, and hence the evaluation component can be built in from the beginning. Actually, most school programs are not new; they are ongoing. In a particular school a first grade reading program may have remained much the same for a decade or two. Under these circumstances questions pertaining to process and outcomes may be appropriate. Only if the answers to appraisal queries were unsatisfactory would it be appropriate to raise questions about context or input.

Formal evaluation programs were also developed, for the most part, to deal with instructional programs. Important as instruction is, it is by no means the only activity or condition that needs appraisal. We need to deal not only with course effectiveness but also with student achievement, personnel performance, and the other arrangements and procedures in schools.

We also find that formal evaluation approaches sometimes ignore data that are commonly generated and readily available from ongoing programs. Attendance data, for instance, might be most useful. A consideration of excessive absence might say important things about administrative procedures, teaching, the community, and other matters. Hunches derived from such speculation could be checked and might lead to one of two courses of action: acceptance of the situation, or a plan for improving those factors under school control.

Frequently, follow-up data on graduates from a high school are available or can be made available. Did the students go to college? Which colleges? How long did they remain? Or did the students go to work? What kinds of work? What training programs were there on the job? Once the procedures for securing follow-up data are set up they can be continued easily from year to year.

Results from national testing programs of student achievement are also readily available. Many high schools, for example, administer the Scholastic Aptitude Test (SAT) to their high school seniors. While socio-economic factors have to be taken into account if meaningful comparisons are to be made with national averages, the performance of students in any high school, particularly over a period of years, can provide useful appraisal data. Some schools and school districts are also giving tests developed as part of the National Assessment of Educational Progress. Again, comparisons with national norms have to be made with some caution, but the data themselves can provoke important questions about local practices.

Still another example of useful data available in school operation and often overlooked in formal evaluation programs has to do with cost. School people are often asked not only how effective a particular course may be but also the per-pupil-hour cost of instruction. We are not necessarily advocates of cost-effectiveness analysis; however, in a world of scarce resources some attention must be paid to alternative ways of spending the school dollar.

General approaches to appraisal should deal with the following concerns: purpose, evidence, and meaning. Perhaps we are just building another model, but let us explore each of these. For the purpose, the appraiser can consider the objectives of a new program—or an ongoing program, for that matter. Moreover, the consideration of purpose can apply to a course of instruction, an organizational arrangement, or a business procedure. The question of why we are doing or want to do something has universal application to any kind of appraisal.

Our second general concern is evidence. More specifically, how can we get evidence that would suggest how well we have achieved our purpose? This obviously leads to what we mean by evidence. Test results? Anecdotal descriptions of behavior? Extent of paper work? A related concern is where and how we collect the evidence. In the classroom? In the faculty meeting? In the school board meeting? In parent-teacher conferences? In the audit report? Here we have to give some attention to objectivity, validity, and reliability, all time-honored concepts in testing and measurment.[18] But in simple terms, evidence can be framed, "How do you know?"

Questions to be asked about meaning are: Is the purpose worthwhile? Is the evidence appropriate? Is it compelling? Is the cost reasonable? Might there be better approaches? Should the activity be continued? If an activity is not continued, what would be the repercussions? Can these repercussions be dealt with? Is there a greater need for the money elsewhere? Where? Obviously, this aspect of appraisal is one of attaching value: valuing one purpose above another; valuing the evidence generated; or valuing as reflected in the allocation of resources. School workers, particularly principals and superintendents, are expected to make such value judgments. They will be subjective, but two conditions can at least help to make them more palatable to others: (1) the judgments can be informed, as suggested by our emphasis on evidence; and (2) the criteria employed in arriving at the judgments can usually be made public.

APPRAISAL OF
COURSE
EFFECTIVENESS

APPRAISAL OF COURSE EFFECTIVENESS

School workers frequently find it desirable to appraise the effectiveness of a course, a unit within a course, or some other segment of an instructional program. Let us apply the general appraisal process described above to an instructional program and then examine the questions that such an appraisal might raise.

The Appraisal Process

Let us suppose that the teachers and principal of a high school are considering the inclusion of a unit on energy in a high school course in science or consumer economics. The first consideration is the purpose of the unit. Presumably, one purpose is the extension of understanding about energy in general—sources of energy, location of the sources, U.S. dependence on other countries, the development of alternative sources, and so forth. A second purpose might deal with the conservation of energy—short- and long-term prospects of energy reserves, ways of conserving energy, and related matters. A third purpose might be the support of certain attitudes—a disposition to change one's habits in the use of energy and to encourage others to do likewise.

These purposes for a new unit have to be considered in light of competing demands. Questions such as the following must be answered: Is there real need for such a unit? If this unit is offered what other unit or units will be eliminated or reduced? Is a member of the staff competent to teach such a unit? If not, how can a staff member become competent to do so? Are appropriate instructional materials available or can they be made available? If and when these and related questions are answered satisfactorily the decision is made to install the new unit.

The next concern in the appraisal process is evidence. Here, at least some of the knowledge and attitudes that are the purposes of the program need to be spelled out in more specific terms. Only when the understandings sought are quite specific can teachers (or others) decide what kinds of evidence can indicate the extent to which the understandings have been achieved. Once the objectives are in hand, it is then possible for the teacher to construct a test, perhaps a combination of short answer and essay questions, with which the understandings of students can be ascertained. It might even be desirable to give the test early in the unit as well as at the end. Results on the early test would show where there is lack of understanding, and these areas could then be given particular emphasis by the teacher. To assess student attitudes, useful evidence could come from observing class discussions, or from student reports on conversations they have had with their parents and other adults about energy conservation.

With test evidence, anecdotal evidence, and report evidence in hand, teachers and principal then turn to the question of meaning. Let us suppose that about half the students did not acquire the expected understanding or change their attitudes toward energy conservation. These outcomes would provoke a number of questions: Have the purposes been realistic? Is the evidence of achievement valid? Are the materials adequate? Are the methods appropriate? Was the teacher's attitude positive? Was the group too large? Were some of the students slow readers? The answers to these questions would permit the principal and teachers to decide what to do about the program. For instance, they might decide to repeat the unit, but to reduce class size, supplement the written materials with some field trips where energy-saving devices were being installed, and arrange to have each student serve for a few days as a member of a crew of workers on energy-conservation projects. After the unit was given for the second time, then the appraisal procedures could be repeated and the outcomes compared with those obtained the first time.

Implications of the Appraisal

While the above has been a hypothetical case, the appraisal procedures involved could, with appropriate adaptation, be applied to many real situations. Moreover, such procedures might be applied to ongoing programs of instruction as well as new ones. The same questions of purpose, evidence, and meaning could be raised about the teaching of arithmetic at any grade level of the elementary school, or for that matter, about the entire arithmetic curriculum. Such appraisal would be particularly appropriate if new text books for arithmetic were under consideration.

Closely related to the appraisal of course effectiveness is appraisal of student achievement. The difference between the two is essentially one of focus: in one case the emphasis is on the course and teaching procedures and in the other the emphasis is on student learning or outcomes.

APPRAISAL OF STUDENT ACHIEVEMENT

**Many Purposes,
Much Learning**

Schools have no monopoly on expectations held for children and youth: society at large has expectations, both implicit and explicit, for its young people, and parents certainly have expectations for their children. Some of these concern understandings, some attitudes, and some skills. In a homogeneous culture there is considerable agreement about expectations, but in a pluralistic culture such as ours securing agreement is often difficult and sometimes impossible. Even in the area of knowledge or "truth" there is controversy, as indicated by the current disagreement over scientific evolution and biblical creationism in the public schools. In the realm of attitudes, arriving at consensus on expectations held for the young may be even more difficult. We are reminded daily by the media, for example, how attitudes toward abortion differ among our citizens. In the skills arena we have our differences as well. Some would have us go "back to basics" with great emphasis on reading, writing, and arithmetic. Others contend that these skills are not enough: children must also have opportunities for self-expression, for making independent judgments, and becoming self-reliant human beings. Some also insist that high school students learn work skills that permit them to compete in the labor market. Others believe that for most students such work skills should be learned at the post-high school level, either in a community college or in industry.

Despite these differences, schools are faced with the need to establish purposes or expectations for students. The expectations should represent what schools are prepared to do well, such as teaching literacy. It is also necessary that such expectations be supported by a working consensus in the larger society. Public schools in many American communities cannot expect unanimous support for the expectations they set up for students. But these schools must have the support of most of the people in their communities or they cannot continue to operate. Those who differ sharply with what the public school expects to do can in many instances place their children in a private school of some kind.

Whatever the set of purposes or expectations established, schools must recognize that student mastery of those expectations is not a product of schools alone. For most people, the home is still the most important teacher; for many, the church is another important one. The attitudes of the young, particularly, are influenced by home and church. Other types of learning, especially economic, are influenced most by the community and the job. As a back drop to all of this learning is the ever-present influence of the media, notably television. In our view, the school can and does play an important role in the instruction of the young (in some cases becoming the place of last resort when other agencies fail) but learning goes on in many places, and many agencies, advertently or inadvertently, shape its nature.

Thus schools cannot take full credit for high student achievement nor full blame for the lack of it. Despite this fact, however, schools do have the obligation to appraise student achievement and to be guided by the evidence generated in the process.

Again we use the three major concepts we ascribed to appraisal—purpose, evidence, and meaning—to look at student achievement. Let us be more specific and consider the appraisal of student achievement in reading. Our first step is to determine the purposes of reading. For example, do we need word recognition, reading for meaning, or both? Do we want children and youth to read for information? Or, do we want to appraise the extent to which students read for pleasure and evaluate what they read for this purpose? And at what grade levels do we wish to collect evidence on student achievement in reading? Is our purpose to secure evidence on group performance? Or are we also interested in evidence on individual performance that might permit a diagnosis of individual difficulties? In short, a consideration of purpose gets at the heart of why reading instruction is offered, and then gives us direction for the nature of the procedures and instruments to be used in the appraisal. The program should determine the test and not vice versa.

For purposes of illustration, let us suppose that a particular school district decides to test comprehensive reading achievement, particularly on a group basis. Let us suppose further that the district decides to administer the tests in grades 1, 4, 8, and 12; and that a standardized reading test is suitable for the purpose and commercially available. The use of such a test is one way of collecting evidence on group reading achievement in that school district.

In addition, the district may wish to make use of the tests developed by the National Assessment of Educational Progress for ages 9, 13, and 17 (corresponding roughly with grade levels 4, 8, and 12). From the use of the National Assessment tests as well as the commercial, standardized tests group achievement in that particular school district could be compared with both national and regional norms. School district variations could also be noted.

Information on group achievement, however, does little to pinpoint reading difficulties experienced by individual students. The school district, then, decides to address that problem by developing diagnostic testing programs in reading that can be given to individual students. Particular emphasis in this program is placed on grades 2, 5, and 9. The diagnostic testing of individual achievement would have direct implications for not only improving the regular teaching of reading but for suggesting the magnitude of the remedial program needed in the school district.

Though the scenario above is hypothetical, the point remains that administrators, teachers, and (in this case) reading specialists should consider first their purposes and then what kinds of evidence to collect to indicate how well the purposes are being achieved. We favor collecting evidence of many kinds, so long as it appears to be relevant to the purposes of the reading program. We certainly would not ignore standardized achievement tests as long as they appeared to be valid and fairly reliable instruments, particularly since no other aspect of educational practice has been developed with the care and expertise that has gone into the testing movement, beginning with J.M. Rice and his spelling scale in 1897.[19]

To continue with the example cited above, the scores of student performance on the standardized achievement test would permit both school people and
citizens of the community to see how students in grades 1, 4, 8, and 12 of their
district compared with the national norms established for the test. Since the test
was comprehensive, the results on certain aspects of reading, such as word recognition or paragraph meaning, could also be ascertained. It would also be possible
to examine achievement in each of the schools of the district. By making comparisons with national norms or comparing one school in the district to another
local factors should be taken into account. For example, students from homes of
high socio-economic status ordinarily earn better-than-average scores on standardized tests; thus, schools with many students from such homes should do better
than national norms. It would be unfortunate if a district or school with many
students of this kind were to be satisfied with average achievement. It would be
just as unfortunate if a school with many students from homes of low socio-
economic status were to be compared (unfavorably) with schools very different
from it socially or economically.

A standardized test such as the one referred to above is called a *norm-
referenced test*. This means that the scale is based on the average performance of
selected persons—a national sample of fourth graders, for example. Some people
find such standards objectionable, and in the last decade or so considerable effort has gone into the development of *criterion-referenced tests*. Indeed, the tests
used in the National Assessment of Educational Progress are criterion-
referenced. In criterion-referenced tests the score is usually based on the extrem-
ities of the scale, with a score at the top indicating complete mastery of some
defined ability and a score at the bottom indicating complete lack of that ability.[20] In spite of diagreement over the merit of the two types of test, we believe
that certain meanings can be derived from each and thus we included both in
our illustration above.

While the relative standing of a school or a school district in reading
achievement is of some use, information to help reconstruct a teaching program
in reading would more likely come from the development and use of individual
tests. These instruments can ascertain individual achievement on specific skills
and understanding. From the results teachers can determine not only what procedures are appropriate for the entire class but those special techniques that are
needed by individuals in the class. If a school district has to choose, it might be
wise to go with less survey or group data on reading achievement and more on
the achievement of individual students, using the information to improve teaching procedures.

Other Areas and   Our treatment of reading achievement above should not obscure the fact that
Other Evidence   student achievement in many other areas should also be appraised. Indeed, we
think that both formal and informal instruction should be appraised. We mean
by *formal instruction* those aspects of the instructional program that are organized
into specific courses, units, or other subdivisions; for which time allocations are

made; and to which teaching personnel are assigned. For many elementary students the formal program includes not only reading but language usage, mathematics, science, social studies, and other subjects. By *informal instruction* we refer to the learning that comes from the regimen of the school and the relationships among students and faculty. We suspect that values such as honesty, respect for others, and trust, for instance, are learned more from these relationships than through programs of direct instruction. If that is true, the nature of school relationships should also be appraised.

At this point we want to emphasize that our use of tests as evidence in the example above does not mean that we see tests (standardized or teacher-designed) as the only kinds of appraisal evidence. Indeed, for some informal instruction simple observation of student behavior in the classroom and corridors, on the playground, and other places may reveal whether or not students seem to be learning. Check sheets can sometimes be developed to facilitate the recording of informal behavior; frequently, however, no evidence is more appropriate than a descriptive (or anecdotal) record. Writing anecdotal records may take some practice in order to separate descriptions of behavior from judgments about it, but teachers, parents, and other observers can certainly learn how to do it. As with other evidence, it requires interpretation for meaning once it has been collected.

Nor would we rule out interview data. Teachers and principals frequently find that students (even those in some difficulty), when approached on a one-to-one basis, will reveal many things about themselves, how they perceive others, and how they perceive their school. Personal perceptions are valid to the person expressing them and they should not be taken lightly. In such perceptions school workers may find many clues that help them to understand school operation and even improve it. In short, our concern with the appraisal of student achievement is a broad one and we advocate the use of many kinds of evidence in such a quest.

APPRAISAL OF PERSONNEL PERFORMANCE

Few question the need to appraise course effectiveness and student achievement. When we turn to the appraisal of personnel performance, however, we enter a "thorny wicket" with more questions and more reservations. Even so, we are convinced that the performance of teachers, administrators, and other personnel in schools and school systems should appraised. There are two major reasons for the appraisal of personnel performance: (1) the improvement of performance and (2) the facilitation of administrative decisions, such as reemployment, promotion, and dismissal. Some educators believe the improvement and the administrative purposes should be kept separate, but we see no practical way of doing so; hence the following discussion should be assumed to apply to both.

Teacher Performance

The appraisal of teacher performance has long elicited the attention of scholars and practitioners. Much of the research and experience in this area has been synthesized by Bolton in the *Selection and Evaluation of Teachers*,[21] a volume providing detail beyond what can be presented here. For our purposes, the three appraisal concepts used above—purpose, evidence, and meaning—still suffice. Purpose in this instance takes a somewhat different form than before. It is necessary to begin with a definition of *effective teacher performance;* thus, if appraisal of teacher performance is to occur we have to establish a set of criteria against which performance can be examined. Any set of criteria for effective teaching reflects the values held by those who establish them, and values differ from place to place; hence the criteria also differ. The criteria we suggest here reflect our own values and should be considered illustrative only.

In recent years much attention has been given to competency-based teacher education programs, formulations that usually include definitions of what is meant by effective teaching.[22] We certainly have no quarrel with competence, but some of the competency-based programs have placed great emphasis on overt behavior and behavior that can easily be measured. The reflective aspects of teaching have not been dealt with adequately in the competency-based formulations developed to date. These formulations have also focused on preservice teachers and we are concerned here with inservice appraisal. In any case, we do not choose to get caught up in the specifics of competency-based teacher education programs.

At times, other "easy" approaches to the appraisal of teaching have been offered. Some advocate testing student achievement at the beginning and end of the school year and ascribing the gain, if any, to the teacher who had the students during the school term. For some specialized courses, such as advanced French or advanced mathematics, this approach may have some merit. In these instances, there are probably few learning opportunities outside the formal classroom. In many other instances, however, it is most difficult to isolate the instruction received from a particular teacher from all of the other learning opportunities available to a student. For instance, progress in reading in grade 4 may depend in large measure on the foundation laid in grade 3. Or, progress in music in grade 8 may depend in large part on private instruction and not on instruction in the school. In short, learning goes on in many places, so achievement cannot be assumed to be the result of the school instructional program only.

In view of this problem, it seems more useful and valid to establish intermediate criteria based on behavior of the teacher, rather than that of the student. We suggest two major criteria. The first is the degree to which teachers "know their stuff." If they are teaching mathematics, they must know something about mathematics. They should also know something about children and youth and how they learn. In short, they must have both content and pedagogical know-how. The second criterion is the ability to relate constructively to students. This means that teachers hold high expectations for students, and motivate them to do their best; that student performance is monitored and when reteaching is needed it is given; and that a work-like atmosphere is created in the classroom. It is helpful if teachers also maintain amicable relationships with their colleagues, if they willingly assume their share of the extra duties in every school, and if they are adroit in relationships with parents, but performance in these areas is of secondary importance.

Our next task is collecting evidence regarding these two criteria. The college transcript of a teacher will give some indication of how knowledgeable he or she is about content and pedagogy. There are also standardized tests that purport to measure knowledge in these areas and, if necessary, such tests can be administered to teachers. Considerable evidence about the knowledge of teachers can also be gleaned from professional conferences between a teacher and principal or teacher and supervisor. Still further evidence of knowlegability might be secured from observing teacher participation on curriculum committees. To be useful in appraising teacher performance, records of professional conferences and observations of teacher participation on curriculum committees must be prepared. Here, as with anecdotal records on student performance, care must be taken to distinguish between description and judgment.

Evidence of teacher relationships with students can also be secured. Perhaps the most direct evidence comes from classroom visitation. A principal or supervisor can tell whether students are at work, whether exchanges among students and between students and teacher are relevant and respectful, and whether there is some excitement in the classroom. Again, some care must be exercised in recording these impressions. Further evidence on student relationships can be secured by using a rating scale in which students are asked to describe different aspects of their work environment. As a supplement to observations by superordinates and student ratings, test results of student achievement can also be secured. (It can be argued that there is some relationship between constructive student relationships in the classroom and progress in student achievement as shown by test results.) Another form of evidence regarding teacher performance comes from students' and parents' comments to administrators. Although such comments are not necesarily valid, they can certainly be considered hypotheses which conscientious administrators should use as a basis for gathering additional information.

Teachers and teachers' organizations sometimes contend that principals are unable to collect adequate appraisal data on teachers. There are indeed some principals who are unable or unwilling to do so. We believe, however, that principals should be helped to become more skillful in this area, or they should be replaced by those who have the necessary skill and disposition. In short, we think principals must take major responsibility for the appraisal of teachers in the schools under their jurisdiction. Principals may—and often should—solicit help in this process. A director of personnel or a subject-matter supervisor from the central office can frequently be helpful.

Turning to the meaning of the evidence collected, we should first examine the adequacy and consistency of the data. Is there enough evidence? If not, what might be done to secure additional evidence? Is the evidence consistent or is it conflicting? If conflicting, what might be the reasons? For instance, did the principal and the supervisor see different things when they visited a teacher's classroom? If so, perhaps other visits should be made.

Once questions of adequacy and consistency are settled, improvement of performance can be considered. If a teacher lacks sufficient knowledge in a content area, an extension or summer school course might be a remedy. If classroom discipline is difficult for a teacher to maintain, a program of visits to other teachers strong in that area could be arranged. Clearly, the means leading to improvement must be discussed by the principal and teacher and, to be useful, must in the end make sense to the teacher.

Adequate performance and prospects of improvement normally suggest that a teacher continue in the present assignment. In some instances, however, a reassignment may permit the teacher to be more effective and an appraisal can point out the wisdom of doing so. For instance, a teacher with a strong science background who does not maintain the best of relationships with primary grade children might be better placed in a position where science teaching is more important and relationships with young children less so—in upper grades, perhaps. Obviously, a teacher should be continued in the current assignment or shifted to a new one only after he or she has been consulted and finds the plan acceptable.

At times, appraisal of teacher performance can lead to dismissal or the decision not to renew a teacher's contract. In these instances, much more evidence may be needed. The administrator must also show that reasonable steps toward improvement have been tried and have apparently not been successful. Dismissal of a teacher is never a pleasant task, but the onus of such a task is somewhat reduced when a school system has a regular appraisal system that has been well implemented. It should also be mentioned that when principals and other administrative officers participate in dismissal procedures they do so as representatives of the organization; thus they should exercise the courage, compassion, and professionalism congruent with their positions.

We should emphasize at this point that the appraisal of teacher performance can also lead to teacher promotion. Outstanding teachers can be recommended for positions in supervision or administration. They might also be supported in securing additional graduate work and becoming college professors in their areas of expertise. While these and other promotions may mean that capable teachers are lost (at least temporarily), for the wellbeing of both teachers and education in general such promotions are desirable.

Administrator Performance   Important as is the appraisal of teacher performance, the appraisal of administrator performance may be even more important, since a school administrator can affect—for good or ill—the lives of many teachers and even larger numbers of students and parents.[23] In this discussion we will focus on school principals but keep in mind that what we say applies to other administrative officers as well. In appraising the performance of school principals, the superintendent of schools is the major actor in most school systems, though in very large systems responsibility for the appraisal might be delegated to one or more members of the superintendent's staff. The steps in appraising the performance of principals are much the same as those used to appraise the performance of teachers. Concern with purpose must lead to the establishment of criteria against which principal performance can be judged. With criteria established, attention must then be directed to evidence and its meaning.

We included in Chapter 1 a list of six distinctive functions that should be performed by school administrators, and these can easily be used as criteria for appraising the effectiveness of principals.

The first criterion is knowledge about both pedagogy and organizational behavior. Under the heading of pedagogy we might include areas such as the purpose and nature of the school curriculum and instruction, and conditions conducive to effective teaching and learning. Some of the evidence of the principal's knowledge about these areas can be found in his or her college transcript. In addition, there are standardized tests covering education that could be administered. Where he or she is already employed by the school system, however, probably the most relevant picture of the principal's knowledge would come from conferences with the superintendent in which education topics are discussed. Following such conferences the superintendent should record what the principal has said and perhaps also express an opinion as to what these responses mean.

Evidence about the knowledge of a principal in the area of organizational behavior could be collected similarly. Clearly, principals should have some understanding of how organizations work internally—what motivates people and what tends to turn them off. They should also recognize the external constraints within which organizations work—the school system itself and the influence of parents and patrons in the community. Here again, conferences with the superintendent will reveal a principal's understanding, after which a summary of what transpired should be compiled.

The second criterion is the degree to which the principal exemplifies a sense of purpose for the school, and this criterion can be broken down into three parts. First, the principal should have a sense of purpose for the school. Second, he or she should articulate that purpose to teachers, students, parents, and others. Third, in this articulation an attitude of caring should be conveyed. In short, we think principals, as the official leaders of the schools, should transmit their feelings, their concern with direction, their excitement about the enterprise, to others. The best evidence of these attitudes and convictions comes from personal conferences with principals, reports of those who work with them, and written documents prepared by them for teachers, students, parents, and others.

The third criterion for principal effectiveness is skill in interpersonal relations. Much of what we have in mind has already been discussed in earlier chapters, particularly Chapter 7 (Leadership) and Chapter 8 (Communication), but we mention it again here to emphasize how crucial it is. Principals are engaged in getting others to do things that contribute to effective teaching and to effective learning. Only as these others—teachers, students, parents—sense a common purpose with the principal can this mobilization of effort be fully effective. We do not mean to imply that only principals have a sense of direction for the school; we do suggest, however, that principals should be skillful in conveying their sense of direction to others. We also suggest that principals should be perceptive about what others believe and think would be best for the school. The evidence for this kind of skill would probably come most easily from observations of the principal at work, particularly if an appropriate record were made immediately afterward. If necessary, additional evidence could be obtained from reports of those with whom the principal works.

As always, once the evidence has been collected, it must be examined for meaning. If the superintendent concludes that the principal is deficient in knowledge about education or organizations, the problem might be corrected by attending an inservice program within the school district or at a nearby university. If, however, the problem is the principal's attitude about the school and its direction, or skill in interpersonal relationships, a remedy is neither obvious nor easily implemented. Studying appropriate attitudes and skills may or may not contribute to their improvement. If not, the superintendent is faced with the replacement of a principal.

In the consideration of meaning, however, the superintendent should do his or her best to understand why a principal has seemed to perform inadequately. The principal's own explanation of the situation should be given full consideration. The principal may have personal problems that are temporary, he or she may prefer an assignment to a different type of school, or teaching to administrative work. In the end, however, when the principal's performance is not adequate, when he or she has had the opportunity to improve and does not seem able to do so, and when alternative arrangements have been exhausted, the superintendent should have the courage to make a suitable replacement.

The Performance of Others

There are many others who work in schools and school systems whose performance should also be appraised. Some of these are professionals, such as the central office staff (not excluding the superintendent); others are clerical and secreterial staff, maintenance and janitorial workers, bus drivers, and cafeteria workers. In each case, a set of criteria against which to judge performance should be established; evidence bearing on performance should be collected; the evidence interpreted; and the implications for improved performance, separation, or promotion decided.

APPRAISAL OF OTHER PROGRAMS

We have to this point dealt with the appraisal of course effectiveness, student achievement, and personnel performance. We will now discuss the appraisal of two other programs or systems found in schools and school districts: organizational arrangements and business procedures.

Organizational arrangements can mean many things. The term can mean how the schools in a district are organized, as in a K–6–3–3 or a K–5–3–4 system. Or the term might refer to how teachers are assigned to classrooms. Is the plan essentially a self-contained system or basically a departmental one? The term also covers how a central office is organized. Are assistant superintendencies established by levels, such as elementary and secondary, or by functions, such as instruction and business? These and many other organizational arrangements can be and should be appraised, both before they are installed and after they have been operating for a period of time.

To illustrate in more detail, let us suppose that the superintendent and others in a school system have decided that the administrative structure should be decentralized; that more autonomy be given to individual schools, and that less direction emanate from the central office. The first question concerns purpose: why is such a change desirable? Obviously, the anticipated long-term effects of such a change are improved learning or better student outcomes of some kind. Since there is no way this objective can be verified immediately, some intermediate criteria need to be established. It could be argued that more building autonomy would produce the following outcomes: a more responsive curriculum, better staff morale, innovative use of resources, and better parent support. It could be assumed that these outcomes would eventually lead to a more appropriate or a higher level of student learning. Organizational changes should not be undertaken unless the explicit purposes, as well as the long-range or ultimate purposes, make such changes defensible.

The explicit purposes should be used in the next few years as the bases for gathering evidence. When principals and teachers are given the green light to exercise some control over the curriculum, do they set up responsive curriculum changes? If so, what changes and how are they working out? To measure changes in staff morale, we can collect data on such things as teacher absence and tenure stability. Is teacher absence going down? Is turnover decreasing? In terms of resources, we can ask what innovations, if any, are being attempted. Parent support can be ascertained by asking parents to respond to some kind of survey. This is by no means a complete list of the appropriate evidence that can be gathered on these issues; our point is that some of the evidence should be fairly objective, and that the "hard" data should be supplemented by the informed judgments of teachers and administrators.

When it comes time to look at the meaning of the evidence it is helpful to ask the following questions: What do the responses of teachers, students, and parents to curriculum changes mean? If the changes have not worked well, could it be that the new purposes were unrealistic? Might teachers have been asked to do things for which they were not prepared? Should the new program be continued or dropped? If continued, should it be in its present form or with some revision?

If teacher attendance and teacher stability have improved, are there other indications of staff morale (such as willingness to contribute to the total school

Organizational Arrangements

program) that have also improved? If not, are there other indications that can measure morale with greater validity and reliabililty?

What have been innovations in the use of resources? What are the reasons for such innovations? If there have been no innovations, why not? Is tradition so well ingrained that the staff or the principal (or both) are fearful about making changes? Could it be that with scarce resources there seem to be no viable alternatives for their distribution?

What do the results from the parent survey mean? Even if most parents express firm support of school programs, are there some who express dissatisfaction? Which parents? About what? Is there anything that can be done about these dissatisfactions? If so, what? If many parents express a lack of support for the school what are the reasons behind this? Could interviews with selected parent help to get at the sources of the apparent dissatisfactions? Ultimately, how can the results of this appraisal lead on to further attempts at organizational improvement?

Business Procedures

To this point we have dealt with appraisal largely as to how it applies to educational programs or activities. But schools and school systems also engage in many business activities, and these also need to be appraised.

As noted in our discussion of resources in Chapter 9, school operation consists of a number of business procedures in both the procurement of revenues and the expenditure of funds. Revenues from local, state, national, and private sources must be calculated, and this involves (among other things) intimate knowledge of tax provisions, legislative appropriations, and the allocation procedures of the administrative agencies. Procedures for making purchases, payrolls, and other expenditures must be established. An accounting system for both revenues and expenditures must be set up and maintained to assist in long-term planning as well as to provide current information on the financial status of the organization. In this day of automation there is also the issue of how machines can and should be used to implement these procedures.

In addition to current operation, most school districts engage at times in capital improvement programs such as the erection of new buildings or the renovation of old ones. Projects such as these require a number of additional business procedures such as developing plans and specifications, advertising for bids and awarding contracts, the sale and amortization of school bonds, and many others. Frequently, there is an assistant superintendent for business or a business manager who is directly responsible for the implementation of the capital improvement program as well as the business procedures related to the day-to-day operations of the school district.

Clearly, every business procedure of a school district should be appraised. It is as appropriate to ask questions about the purpose of alternative accounting systems as it is to raise questions of purpose about alternative reading programs. With respect to evidence, it is as appropriate to inquire about the advantages of one machine over another as it is to deal with the merits of one teaching methodology over another. In terms of meaning, it is fully as appropriate to examine why the plans and specifications of a particular architect seem useful as it is to ponder why a particular school principal seems effective in securing the cooperative effort of teachers and parents. In short, appraisal is a way of thinking and thus it ought to be applied to business procedures as well as to educational activities.

Much has been written in the last decade or so about cost effectiveness, which can be simply defined as the relationship between what something costs and how effective it is. An analysis of cost effectiveness consists of the following essential steps:

1. Specification of objectives
2. Identification of alternative means to reach objectives
3. Generation of a model of the problem under study
4. Computation of costs (disadvantages) for each alternative means to an objective
5. Determination of effectiveness (advantages) for each alternative
6. Computation of the relationship between cost and effectiveness for each alternative (usually expressed as a ratio)
7. Agreement on a criterion (that is, a rule or standard) to be used for ranking and selecting alternative means to an objective
8. Recognition of the importance of the iterative process for continuing refinement of the analysis [24]

The application of such an analysis to our discussion is clear: the determination of the relationship between cost and effectiveness for each of the many programs operated by the school. With respect to certain school programs this analysis is a straightforward and useful approach. For instance, the cost effectiveness of centralized school cafeterias versus lunch kitchens in each of the schools could easily be ascertained. Such a method, too, might be applicable to the transportation of pupils, by computing the cost effectiveness of each alternative way of routing school buses. In many cases, however, applying cost-effectiveness procedures to school operation runs into a serious snag in trying to secure agreement on a criterion or standard to be used in ranking one alternative against another. In short, cost-effectiveness analysis rests on the assumptions that all programs are rational, that evidence regarding their achievement is objective, and that interpretation of the evidence is value-free.

In actual situations all of these assumptions may be in error. For instance, a large school district with a growing population recently sought passage of a $21 million bond levy to build new school plants. The secretary of the state taxpayers' organization spoke out against the proposal. His contention was that the district could institute a year-round school program and thereby accommodate an increased enrollment of as much as 33 percent. Such a plan would obviously increase the cost effectiveness of the school building; the secretary's thinking was completely rational. But despite the secretary's objection, the electors subsequently voted by a large majority in favor of the bond issue. Not only were parents negative about year-round school in general, but in this case they also seemed to resent outside advice from a state organization about what they viewed as a local problem. Thus, values and feelings can be overriding factors in a decision, and cost-effectiveness analysis does not take them into account.

There is another potential weakness in the cost-effectiveness approach. If each of the steps listed above were followed in detail, the process might break down of its own weight; it is a time-consuming one, probably too lengthy for many school appraisals. Nevertheless, it is a valid approach to appraisal for certain types of programs, particularly those where data are fairly objective and values play little part.

For those programs and systems where evidence is subjective, and as interpretation requires sensitive and informed judgment, however, administrators would do better to use purpose, evidence, and meaning as key concepts in their appraisals.

SUMMARY   Just as programs in schools and school districts should be planned and implemented, so should they be appraised. Appraisal has been formalized in the evaluation movement; indeed, it has become an important subfield in education, with its own concepts and methodologies. In the day-to-day operation of schools, however, less formal approaches to appraisal are also needed. Informal approaches to appraisal should be guided by the key concepts of purpose, evidence, and meaning. We used these three concepts to examine how to appraise course effectiveness, student achievement, personnel performance, and other programs and systems found in schools. While appraisal should lead, whenever possible, to improved performance, it should also serve administrative purposes such as decision making concerning reemployment, promotion, or dismissal. Appraisal is not only a process to be followed but a useful way of thinking for the school administrator.

ENDNOTES

1. For instance, see Donald A. Erickson, "Research on Educational Administration: The State of the Art," *Educational Researcher* 8(March 1979): 9–14; and Glen L. Immegart and William L. Boyd, *Problem Finding in Educational Administration* (Lexington, Mass.: D.C. Heath, 1979), Ch. 14.
2. Henri Fayol, *General and Industrial Management* (London: Issac Pitman and Sons, 1949).
3. Ralph W. Tyler, "Elements of Diagnosis," *Educational Diagnosis, 34th Yearbook of the National Society for the Study of Education* (Bloomington, Ill.: Public School Publishing, 1935), Ch. 7.
4. Tyler, "Elements of Diagnosis," p. 114.
5. For instance, see Wilford M. Aikin, *The Story of the Eight-Year Study* (New York: Harper and Bros., 1942).
6. Daniel L. Stufflebeam et al., *Educational Evaluation and Decision Making*, PDK Committee on Evaluation (Itasca, Ill.: F.E. Peacock Publishers, 1971).
7. Ibid., p. 40.
8. Ibid, p. 218.
9. Ibid., pp. 222–223.
10. Ibid., p. 229.

11. Ibid., p. 232.
12. Ibid., p. 236.
13. Blaine R. Worthen and James R. Sanders, *Educational Evaluation: Theory and Practice* (Worthington, Ohio: Charles A. Jones, 1973).
14. Worthen and Sanders, *Educational Evaluation*, pp. 210–215.
15. Egon G. Guba and Yvonna S. Lincoln, *Effective Evaluation* (San Francisco: Jossey-Bass, 1981).
16. Guba and Lincoln, *Effective Evaluation*, p. ix.
17. Worthen and Sanders, *Educational Evaluation*, p. 345.
18. For instance, see Robert L. Ebel, *Practical Problems in Educational Measurement* (Lexington, Mass.: D.C. Heath, 1980).
19. See John A. Green, *Introduction to Measurement and Evaluation* (New York: Dodd, Mead, 1970), Ch. 2.
20. Ebel, *Practical Problems*, Ch. 11.
21. Dale L. Bolton, *Selection and Evaluation of Teachers* (Berkeley, Cal.: McCutchan, 1973).
22. For example, see W. Robert Houston and Robert B. Howsam, eds., *Competency Based Teacher Education* (Chicago: Science Research Associates, 1972).
23. For more information on the evaluation of administrative personnel, see Dale L. Bolton, *Evaluating Administrative Personnel in School Systems* (New York: Columbia University Teachers College Press, 1980).
24. Stephen J. Knezevich, *Program Budgeting* (Berkeley, Cal.: McCutchan, 1973), p. 185.

CHAPTER 13

CHALLENGES OF ADMINISTRATION

As we reflect upon what we have said in the earlier chapters, we feel some need to present and amplify the challenges inherent in educational administration. This chapter, perhaps more than any other, is our credo.

We take the position that a particular kind of educative process, open to all, is necessary in a society that aspires to a democratic way of life. In like manner we see a public school system characterized by certain values and practices as an essential part of the educative process. And we take the position that administrative leaders who meet certain requirements occupy critical roles in the public school. Let us amplify each of these beliefs.

We believe that sustaining the democratic way of life is the primary challenge for educational administration. To be sure, this is a challenge for all the citizens of our nation, but we think that it is a challenge that holds unique meaning for the school administrator. As stated in the Preamble to the 1982 Platform of the American Association of School Administrators (AASA),

THE DEMOCRATIC WAY OF LIFE

> We cherish our heritage of freedom and government under law. Respect for the individual is the basis of our heritage and human rights. We believe that education in America should rest on a firm commitment to the recognition

of the dignity and worth of each individual, preeminence of enlightenment and reason over force and coercion, and government by consent of the governed. Further, we believe that free public education serves society by providing the principal means for the achievement of these ends.[1]

A Great Experiment

Democracy was and is a great experiment. The movement to free the common man found fertile soil in America, where, first, tradition was not a binding force; and second, free land was available, for almost three hundred years, to any who would settle upon it and begin its cultivation. Economic opportunity went hand in hand with the development of social and political democracy.

But from its inception the idea of a democratic way of life was a radical one. The thought that all men could and should read and interpret the scriptures for themselves, as advocated by Luther, was in direct contradiction to the established order of the Roman Catholic Church. Locke's ideas of the sovereignty of the people ran counter to centuries of governmental practice. Most of the people in today's world are governed by systems that still do not incorporate these ideas, yet many of them have been put into practice in America. What success they will ultimately have we cannot yet say: their impact is still being determined; the experiment goes on. The capacity of the common people to rise to such a role is fraught with difficulties. For common people who are also ethnic, racial, or social minorities the difficulties appear to be even greater. But the excitement of participating in a great experiment can be experienced by any who will.

It can be argued that our words, as reflected in constitutions, laws, and court decisions, are better than our deeds. They are. But we keep at it, and our deeds seem to improve. It can be argued that ours is essentially a political democracy, and that our social democracy has not kept pace with it. Again, that is true, but we submit that political democracy is essential if social democracy is to be achieved. It can also be argued that the right to vote assumes that accurate information is available to the voter, a condition many attempt to subvert. To be sure, this is one of our difficulties, but it constitutes part of the challenge we face. In other words, what has been done and what remains to be done constitute two parts of the great experiment.

Operational Agreements

Although our society is far from expressing unanimity on many values, we do seem to have reached certain operational agreements.

John Gardner has observed that some consensus regarding values is essential for a society to function effectively.[2] The absence of such a consensus would encourage chaos and jeopardize personal freedom. The historic values that are fundamental to American society are at what Gardner terms a middle level—neither dealing with trivialities nor forcing agreement on matters of a deep philosophical or religious nature.

At that level, in our case, one finds the ideals of freedom, equality of opportunity, the conception of the worth and dignity of the individual, the idea of justice, the dream of brotherhood. The fact that we are not always faithful to these shared values does not indicate confusion nor a failure of the consensus. *We know the values to which we are being unfaithful.* One might ask, "What difference does it make that we agree on our values if we aren't faithful to them?" The answer is that if one is concerned about therapy, it always makes a difference what the patient is suffering from. This society is suffering not from confusion but from infidelity.[3]

Reference to *Goals for Americans,*[4] the report of the President's Commission on National Goals in 1960, is also illuminating. This commission emphasized that opportunity for individual development must remain a primary concern; that discrimination on the basis of religion, sex, or race is morally wrong; that the degree of *effective* liberty available to the people is the ultimate test of liberty; and that the development of the individual and the nation demands that education at every level be improved.

It is possible to arrive at the values stated above from different philosophical orientations. For that reason, we stress here our operational agreements rather than our philosophical differences. This we must do (in any culture as diversified as that in America) if there is to be a common ground for action.

In light of this approach, we can set forth the values we think underlie what we have been calling the democratic way of life. First, there is a belief in people. This is much harder to live with than to say, as we have already indicated. Nevertheless, our overall history suggests that most of us place people above institutions. For most of us this means *all* people, without regard to race, color, religion, sex, economic circumstance, or national background. In particular, we believe that educational opportunity should not be denied to any person.

A second value characteristic of the democratic way of life is a belief in cooperation for the common good. True, some cry out against the idea of a welfare state, but when the nation has been threatened, even as early as the days of the Mayflower Compact, we have been willing to join together and to submerge individual desires when necessary in order to foster the welfare of the group. This tendency received special impetus during the era of the New Deal, but it is noteworthy that subsequent administrations have repealed little of the New Deal legislation. Actually, both political parties have acted this way because we as a people adhere to this principle.

Third, our nation believes in freedom of the press, speech, and religious expression. Again, we have abridgment and abuses of these rights, but in the end our courts and the public stand up for these freedoms. To be sure, we have had to learn that freedom is a relative matter and that it must be accompanied by responsibility. The relative nature of freedom means that none of us is free to pursue his or her own interests to the detriment of the group. A balance between personal freedom and the social good is what we are working to achieve.

Finally, our people accept the method of rational thinking as an approach to problem solving. Some of us, as Broudy[5] has suggested, may be temporarily enamored with the new humanism which seems to stress feeling more than thought. Yet there seems to be a conviction on the part of most Americans that we can, with intelligent thinking, solve many of the problems with which we are faced. Moreover, we have a conviction that this ability to think is not the possession of the few, but the heritage of the many.

There are both challenges *to* and challenges *of* the democratic way of life. Let us discuss each of these in more detail.

Challenges to the Democratic Way

The challenges to the democratic way can be categorized as external and internal challenges. The chief outside challenge, as is clear to most of us, is world communism. Communism as a political system is a far cry from what Karl Marx, its founder, visualized. Marx advocated a militant movement, but the ends he sought seem to many to be in keeping with the Judeo-Christian ethic to which we ourselves subscribe. He wanted an abundant life for the individual, the elimination of human exploitation, and the establishment of a worldwide regime of peace and brotherhood.

It has now become clear that communism in practice exalts the state above the individual, that the ruling hierarchy is straining to perpetuate autocracy, and that any challenge to the system will be quelled by force. It may have taken such events as the Hungarian rebellion of 1956, the invasion of Czechoslovakia in 1968, the Russian aggression in Afghanistan in 1980, or the labor uprisings and imposition of martial law in Poland in 1981 to convince many people, but most of us now see world communism for what it is. Clearly, we do not wish to be dominated by such a system.

There is also a challenge to democracy from within. In spite of our optimism about what we believe to be long-term gains in the achievement of the democratic way, there are definite "schizophrenic symptoms" in our culture. Brameld has listed them as follows:

> Self-interest versus social interest.
> Inequality versus equality.
> Planlessness versus planning.
> Nationalism versus internationalism.
> Absolutism versus experimentalism.
> Man against himself versus man for himself.[6]

An examination of each of these issues will convince anyone that at both the verbal and the operational levels of American life there are adherents to each of the contrasting values. Unfortunately, emphasis on the dichotomies obscures the point that, in many cases, none of them is an either-or proposition. There may be, for instance, enlightened self-interest that is consistent with social interest.

The tension related to these values may well increase as our nation comes to grips with a population that is older, natural resources that are increasingly limited, and prospects for economic growth that are not as great as in previous years. The decade of the eighties is likely to be characterized by the politics of scarcity and increasing dependence upon other parts of the world. Most of our present population has not lived through a comparable experience before and will thus be called upon to deal with these old issues in a new context.

Our cultural conflicts suggest that our society is a dynamic one, that its direction may not always be clear, and that in the arena of ideas a good many battles are still ahead of us. This struggle is the internal challenge to the democratic way.

There are also challenges *of* the democratic way of life. One of these is the challenge of accurate information. If average citizens are to participate in the nation's economic, social, or political destiny, they must be informed. This has always been a difficult expectation. In our early history the immediate need was to teach people to read and understand; the next to make written documents widely available.

Challenges of the Democratic Way

In recent decades the process of informing has been complicated by the tremendous development of the mass media, notably radio and television, and the evolution of the great competition for influence on human opinion—advertising. As a matter of fact, the money spent annually on advertising in this country approximates that spent for the operation of all the schools and colleges in the nation. In advertising, of course, the motive is not primarily to inform but rather to sell.

The effect of advertising on conscious decisions seems serious enough, but with the recent development of motivation research (M-R), the planned, large-scale appeal to the human subconscious is coming into play as well.[7] The application of M-R to the selling of automobiles may seem somewhat trivial, but when the same techniques are applied to presidential elections, as they have been in recent campaigns, it is not difficult to become cynical about the "information" made available to the average elector.

Another aspect of the challenge of informing has to do with the amount of information available and how it can be transmitted to the public. The problem is perhaps clearest in scientific areas where the amount of new knowledge expands very rapidly. But it also exists in other fields. For example, it is very difficult for individual citizens to keep track of all actions in their state legislatures, to understand the range of foreign policy issues that confront the nation, or even to be knowledgeable about the scope of consumer choices available to them. The inevitable result is to rely upon the media, which necessarily choose what news to present and how to present it. In turn, the "ratings" pressures upon the media sometimes lead them to focus on stories that are more sensational than significant. Thus, citizens are sometimes inundated with "noise" that masquerades as news but actually is not helpful.

The growth of special-audience newsletters and magazines has made it easier for individuals to receive information in areas of special interest, often from an ideological perspective they find attractive. The expansion of cable television channels and the potential for home microcomputers with telephone access to many news services may further increase the extent to which individuals can "choose their news." Thus, society faces two information problems. On the one hand, it is impossible for everyone to be aware of all important matters. On the other, individuals can now be so selective about the information they receive that it may reinforce existing biases, thereby limiting their openness and ability to interact with those who differ with them.

A second challenge of the democratic way is interest or concern about public affairs. A number of studies suggest that in most communities, about 50 percent of the people are uninformed and apathetic about public questions. Some social critics go so far as to suggest that this indifference indicates the twilight period for our political system.[8] In any case, this condition represents two potential dangers. First is the possibility that actions of the leadership of a community will go unchecked. Such a course of action may mean that the leaders cease in time to represent the values and programs of their constituents. The second danger inherent in apathy is the possibility that citizens with no facts at hand may become prey to those who seek personal advantage and who do not hesitate to use emotional and biased approaches. In both of these dangers the challenge of how to create concern in people is clearly exemplified.

Along with the challenges of providing information and creating concern, there is the challenge of action. How Americans exercise their voting privileges serves to illustrate our point. In recent presidential elections little more than half of the people of voting age cast ballots. If voting is indicative of a general concern for the common good (and we fear it is), it is little wonder that organized efforts to thwart projects fostering the general welfare can succeed.

THE EDUCATIVE PROCESS

The second challenge to educational administration is to facilitate the educative process. Without an educative process of the kind we describe, the democratic way is an impossibility. In other words, if the great experiment to which we have alluded is to succeed, a genuine opportunity for learning must be available to all.

Meaning of the Educative Process

The educative process is much broader than schooling. Much of what we learn is not acquired in school. Our schooling, for example, seems to have relatively little to do with how we vote, how we spend our leisure, and the ways in which many of us make our living. Without in any sense deprecating the school, it sharpens our discussion to recognize that education and schooling are not synonymous.

It is clear that the whole culture is involved in teaching and learning. Perhaps we can see this more easily in cultures other than our own, as described by anthropologists.[9] Benedict, for instance, spoke of the Zuni Indians as a ceremonious people. She reported that grown men spent most of their waking hours in ceremonial observance for which a staggering amount of word-perfect ritual had to be memorized.

The teaching-learning potential of our own culture has been dealt with in dramatic terms by Bloom.[10] After a comprehensive synthesis of the research in human development, he concludes that, with the exception of achievement in school, the period of most rapid development is the first five years of life. Thus, physical growth, intelligence, language development, and other characteristics are more than 50 percent determined by the home and its surrounding culture by the time the child enters school.

How does this educative process, or cultural adaptation, occur? As we see it, there are three steps: (1) acquiring of a feeling of being at home in one's culture, (2) learning about one's culture, and (3) contributing to one's culture.

Coming to feel at home in one's culture appears to be largely emotional in character. The affection extended to the new baby by the parents and other members of the family are part of it. The trial and error behavior of age-mates as they learn to play together, whether in a nursery school or on the street, are an important factor in the process. The great need for peer approval of most adolescents, and the need of all of us for recognition from other adults are also involved. We must feel that we belong somehow.

But we must feel that we belong to the larger culture, not merely to some specific group within it. This point has particular relevance for those who grow up in the ghettos of our cities, but alienation is not found only there. We see manifestations of alienation among privileged youth in our high schools and on our college campuses.

Keniston has argued that alienation from American society is fostered by stresses flowing from the unquestioned primacy of technology in our society.[11] According to his analysis, the supremacy of technology deemphasizes human values and needs and creates conditions such as chronic social change, fragmentation in society, discontinuities between childhood and adulthood, and value conflicts, which alienate us all to some extent, and totally alienate certain especially sensitized individuals. We cannot pass from this topic without noting that another source of alienation among our youth in recent years has been the increasingly obvious contradictions between our society's ideals and its practices.

The educative process cannot stop with belonging; there is also the necessity for understanding. This places great demands upon all of us. How can we learn about the social and physical world in which we live? Much can be gained from observation, but we soon find a need for trained observation, for observation without reference to some conceptual scheme is relatively pointless. Regardless of the field of study, we soon learn that we need to consider the observations, the feelings, and the reflections of others. This process constitutes the beginning of scholarship, whether it takes place in or outside of an organized school.

Feeling at home in and knowing about one's culture ought to lead one to contribute to that culture, the third step of the educative process. Contributions, to be sure, will vary greatly in nature and in quality; and ways of contributing improvements to the culture will be apparent only to those who have the capacity to examine critically the cultural beliefs and practices now extant.

The challenge of the educative process to equip people to reflect critically about the conditions of life around them and to project possible improvements is, we believe, the aspect of the educative process most important to the survival of the democratic idea. Unfortunately, those who attempt to examine our way of life critically, in an attempt to make improvements, are often misunderstood and sometimes even called subversive.

Many Institutions Contribute

Many institutions make contributions to the educative process. The home, despite the suggestion of some that it has reached a point of declining influence, still seems to be the most important educative agency we have. Our basic personality characteristics, including matters such as friendliness or distrust, are in large part a product of the home. Our attitudes toward religion, government, sex, and learning itself reflect the home environment. To be sure, the home also tends to reflect the biases of the culture of which it is a part. The home, as any social worker or psychiatrist can testify, is a signficant influence on whatever a person learns.

For most people the church, too, is an important agency in the educative process. The segment of our population that affiliates with a church and participates in church activities is subject to an educative influence of considerable magnitude. For instance, the attitudes of these people toward marriage, child-bearing, authority, and social behavior are greatly influenced by the church. For those people who belong to no church, the influence of the church may be less direct, but it is nonetheless significant: all of us are affected by the Judeo-Christian tradition as it has found expression in our ethics and our law.

Also important is the street corner or the play group of one's peers. Beginning at about eight or ten years and continuing through adolescence, most young people feel great need for acceptance by their peers. Often it takes expression in the clothes that are worn. If designer blue jeans are the thing, then designer blue jeans there must be. Woe to any parent who has the temerity to suggest that there is a satisfactory substitute. Many times status with one's fellows is acquired by doing those things that the group has decided to do. Anyone not joining in the activity is labeled "out of it." Clearly, these peer groups have great influence with young people and are thus potent educative influences.

Nor should we stop with young people. Riesman made the point some time ago that our culture is becoming more and more other-directed.[12] In other words, the sanctions one feels, which influence one's behavior, have their origins in the group to which one belongs rather than in one's upbringing as reflected in one's conscience. Whyte makes a similar point when he describes the "organization man."[13] For all of us, the group or groups with which we affiliate, particularly in our work, seem to be decisive forces in determining our family life, our goals for educating our children, our dress, our leisure, and our values in general. All of this gives some support to Jencks, who contends that family background is the most important determinant of educational attainment.[14]

Even if we accept this point, we should not overlook the fact that the school has a unique role in the educative process. An educative process that is comprehensive, understanding, and permissive within limits is essential to the democratic way of life. This means that the educative role of many institutions in our society should be recognized. It means, too, that each institution should exercise its role with some recognition that other influences and agencies are and must be at work in our kind of society. Finally, it means that class barriers should be sufficiently flexible so that one's place and position in society can be altered through the educative process.

THE PUBLIC SCHOOL

The third challenge to education administration is found in the public school itself. Despite the breadth of the educative process, we hold that the public school has a unique—indeed an indispensable—part to play in that process. Let us examine this idea.

Characteristics

About 90 percent of the children and youth who attend school in this country attend public schools.[15] Although this percentage has remained roughly constant in recent decades, it masks a growing disenchantment of the public with the public schools.[16] This disenchantment is manifested in public opinion surveys[17] and recent legislation in several states that requires minimum-competency tests for both teachers and students. It is fed by reports of violence and disruption in schools and evidence that student performance on college aptitude tests has declined steadily in recent years. It is also fueled by some specific concerns of parents: some do not want their children bused to schools, some want more rigor and emphasis on basic skills, others object to the use of particular materials, and still others prefer that their children be educated from a particular religious or philosophical perspective.

Criticism of public schools is by no means a new phenomenon. What sets the present groups of critics apart from their predecessors is that so many of them prefer to renounce the public schools rather than reform them. The solution that many advocate is a voucher system or tax-credit legislation that would make public funds available to private schools. Powerful intellectual support for such a policy was provided by a highly controversial report by James Coleman and his colleagues, which asserted that both the quality and equality of educational opportunity in private schools is superior to that in public schools.[18] Efforts to enact voucher or tax-credit legislation have not so far been successful, and if any such legislation is passed it is likely to be challenged on constitutional grounds. The possibility of tax-credit legislation remains an issue for the future. As long as it is unresolved, it will probably be a deterrent to increased public funding for public schools.

But the tax-credit issue symbolizes a more fundamental problem for American education. Since the time of Thomas Jefferson, Americans have supported public education on the premise that an educated citizenry is in the best interest of the nation. We have willingly paid taxes to educate our neighbors' children as well as our own. Today it appears that many citizens question this historic premise. They continue to believe that education is vital for their own children or grandchildren, but they are less willing to be taxed to provide education for the children of others. As our society grows older and the percentage of citizens who have school-age children continues to decline, the financial problems of the public school will become even more severe unless faith in its public importance is restored.

Decline in public support for schools is a corollary to unanticipated consequences of education reforms prominent during the 1960s and 1970s.[19] These reforms stressed the equalization of educational opportunity through school desegregation, special provisions for the handicapped, and fiscal policies. Policy-making processes were modified to permit greater participation by teachers and citizens, and curricula were expanded to incorporate the requests of many different advocates. Desegregation and implementation of provisions for the handicapped have been costly. Fiscal equalization has required state agencies to reduce previous imbalances in school expenditures between affluent suburbs and less wealthy urban or rural areas. Dissatisfaction with such reallocations has led many upper-middle-class parents to seek private school alternatives for their children.

Broader participation in policy making has contributed to the politicization of schools and, in some locales, public resentment of teacher strikes and other political actions. It has also led to curricula dealing with a broad range of mandated subjects such as driver education, drug and alcohol abuse, citizenship education, sex education, ethnic studies, and creationism. Many citizens are reluctant to vote additional school taxes to provide increased pay for militant teachers or to support instruction in newer curricular areas. Moreover, time spent teaching the expanded curriculum has reduced the emphasis upon traditional academic subjects, thus contributing to the declining tests scores that citizens find objectionable.

Despite these conditions, a strong case can be made for the strength of the American school as a public institution.[20] Our society is now better educated and more prosperous than at any time in our history. In the past thirty years, high school completion rates have risen from approximately 50 percent for whites and 25 percent for blacks to 85 percent for whites and 75 percent for blacks. More than half of these high school graduates (compared with 10 to 20 percent in 1950) now enter post-secondary education. Despite the fact that American schools provide education for a much larger part of the population than is the case in other nations, "the top 5 percent of U.S. young people attain the same high scores reached in nations where advanced schooling is reserved for an elite."[21]

The pupil populations of the public schools tend, by and large, to be more heterogeneous than the pupil populations of the private schools. Although this circumstance has its problems, it also provides opportunities, for the public school becomes a prototype of society itself. The diversity of our nation is well reflected in the public school.

We do not wish to overdo this matter. We are well aware that many individual public schools, particularly in urban and suburban areas, have pupil populations with less diversity than suggested above. Indeed, some exclusive suburban communities have schools whose enrollment is comparable to the most elite private schools, and central cities often have some schools comprised primarily of disadvantaged or minority students. It now seems clear that there must be deliberate social planning of both housing and school attendance areas if many youngsters in the public schools are going to have the opportunity to find out "how the other half lives."

In diversity, once common but now harder to attain, the public school pupils have an opportunity to acquire a sense of realism as to what people are like; they can see the variety of contributions that its various members make to the group; and they can learn much about relating to many kinds of people. These skills are essential to our kind of culture.

The public school has still another opportunity. More than any other nonschool community agency, and possibly more than most private schools, the public school can be the most impartial institution in our culture. Business, labor, and farm organizations have great difficulty in viewing all sides of a controversial issue, particularly if the issue affects them in any way. Most churches must approach problems within a particular framework. Thus, useful as these organizations are for some purposes, they cannot alone adequately nurture the person with an inquiring mind who wishes to weigh the evidence on all sides of a tough problem and come to his or her own decision. We recognize that some teachers in the public schools are not adequately prepared to guide objective inquiry, but we still maintain that the opportunity for such inquiry is present in the public school and that it is being admirably exploited in some instances.

The School's Unique Role

It is a difficult task to describe the unique role of the public school, for over the years it has gradually taken on more and more functions, usually as a result of public demand. Moral education on one hand, and driver training on the other, are two cases in point. Sometimes it seems that relatively little examination of the appropriateness of the new functions being placed in the public school has been made by either the public or school officials. In some cases there are probably other agencies in society that are better equipped to meet these new demands than is the school. The transfer of certain child-rearing functions from the home to the school is a good example.

Another reason it is difficult to delimit the public school's role is the concomitant character of learning. As children learn to read and write, they are also learning many other things. They may be learning to like or dislike school. They may be learning to like or dislike teachers. They may find in acquiring skill with words that the doors of ideas have been unlocked, or they may find reading a wearisome task, never to be pursued except under duress. We cannot ignore or be unconcerned about these reactions.

Our concern is that the public school recognize some priorities in what it does, so that those things that are essential to the democratic way of life and to the educative process shall not be left undone. We are not offering objection to the fact that other functions can and, in many cases, should be performed. Moreover, we recognize that the school shares with other institutions responsibility for helping the young acquire constructive beliefs and attitudes. As the demands placed upon the public school have increased, however, the financial resources to meet such demands have not always been increased proportionately.

The first task we would place upon the public school is teaching for literacy. To read, to write, and to figure are old, old expectations of what the school is to prepare individuals to do. With the advent of mass media, reading has come to seem relatively unimportant to some people. Moreover, literacy alone may simply make people prey to those who control what is to be read. However, this is an unlikely result of literacy in a free country, and it is clear that all citizens of a nation such as ours need skills in reading, writing, and numbers.

The fact that literacy is a matter of acquiring certain skills—skills that are helpful in developing certain understandings and appreciations—might lead some to suggest that the understandings and appreciations are the sine qua non of education, and the skills only instrumental. We still think that there are practical reasons for the public school to consider its first indispensable task to be teaching for literacy.

If the public school does not do the job of teaching for literacy, it will not be done. The private school can do it for only a few. Few parents are equipped to do it. Other agencies in society are even less able to step into such a role. The literacy of most of our citizens is indispensable to our way of life, and the public school is indispensable to providing it.

The teaching of critical thinking is, we think, the second unique task of the public school. This is really the purpose that the founders of our public schools had in mind when they spoke of the need for intelligence on the part of all people. As Caleb Mills said to the legislature of Indiana in 1846, "The true glory of a people consists in the intelligence and virtue of its individual members, and no more important duty can devolve upon its representatives in their legislative capacity than the devising and perfecting of a wise, liberal, and efficient system of popular education . . ."[22]

Mills and others may not have appreciated fully what it takes to get people to behave intelligently, but there was no question in their minds about the need for such behavior. Nor did the early champions of the public school foresee the age of propaganda, the rise of mass media, or the sophistication of modern advertising techniques. Yet the objective they had for public education is still a worthy one, even though its achievement has been beset with new difficulties.

What do we mean by critical thinking? We mean, simply, the ability to define a problem, seek the relevant facts about it, weigh the evidence, and make decisions based upon the evidence. In short, we are talking of problem solving or the scientific method. Literacy, as we have discussed it above, is a necessary tool to most problem solving, but literacy alone is not enough. Also necessary are the ability to suspend judgment until the evidence is in, and the ability to analyze the evidence so as to detect when personal bias or privileged position has obscured, slanted, or selected the facts. There is, finally, the courage to accept the position supported by the evidence even in face of preconceived notions.

This is a big order. The capacity of individuals to learn critical thinking, even with the best of tutelage, varies just as it does with other kinds of learning, but the public school must exploit its objectivity to provide opportunity and encouragement for it.

How can this actually be done? According to Thelen,

> Inquiry involves firsthand activity in real situations. I want the student to transact his business directly with the work and the work environment; I want him to discover that there are realities outside of his own personal desire or those of "authorities," for it is only within such a stable framework of action that his own behavior can be assessed unequivocally by himself. It is only thus that he can discover and learn to depend on his abilities and that he can face up to weaknesses, because they cannot be blamed on other persons.[23]

The White House Conference on Education in 1956 highlighted the third unique task of the public school: the facilitation of social mobility. One conclusion in the Conference report is that "the schools have become a major tool for creating a Nation without rigid class barriers. *It is primarily the schools which allow no man's failure to prevent the success of his son.*" (italics in original)[24] To be sure, other institutions in our society contribute to social mobility. For some the ladder is supplied by business, for others by the military, and for others by the church. But the schools seem to be the chief agency in society that can and should accept the responsibility for providing the opportunity for the upward (or downward) mobility of its students. When the school accepts this as one of its major functions, those who live "across the tracks" have an opportunity to rise in the world.

The need for social mobility and the role of the public school in such a process take on new urgency in a technological society. Workers are needed in most skilled and professional occupations. A major source of these workers could be the unskilled workers and the children of unskilled workers. If these children are to enter new jobs and acquire new social status, they must of course have more schooling than their forebears. For most people the extent of upward mobility in a single generation is probably limited, but the need for such mobility and the role of the school in the process should be clear.

The fourth task we would assign to the public schools is the development of understanding and appreciation of our Western cultural heritage along with a sense of other cultures.[26] This goal requires attention to the humanities and the sciences and is essential if young people are to comprehend their opportunities and responsibilities in our complex society. In recent years, too, our search for additional energy sources and fluctuations in our economy have demonstrated the increasing importance of international relationships. Accordingly, it is important for the schools to provide information about values and practices of other cultures.

In sum, as the school performs the four functions discussed above it also serves as one of the most powerful instruments of social policy. The basic purposes of the school are continually under examination and as society changes the school's unique and supporting roles may also change.[27]

ADMINISTRATIVE LEADERSHIP

The fourth challenge, perhaps the pivotal one as far as this book is concerned, is the challenge confronting administrative leaders in the public schools. When we speak of administrative leaders we refer to appointed or official leaders in the school system, such as principals, supervisors, directors, and superintendents. We do not wish to minimize the roles played by classroom teachers; at the same time, teachers and researchers alike have repeatedly indicated that a good part of what any school does is dependent upon its administrative leadership. The principal, for instance, has a key role in setting the tone, establishing the conditions, and providing stimulation for living and learning in his or her school.

Each administrator relates to certain major reference groups, and in each of these relationships there are challenges. Let us examine the nature of challenges with respect to the community, the board of education, the teaching staff, and the pupils.

The Community Challenge

Obviously the public or the community is a major reference group with which any school administrator must work. Most people understand that this applies to the superintendent of schools; for the school principal, however, such recognition is not as general. As a matter of fact, some principals have almost no relationship with the citizens of their respective attendance areas. This condition seems most undesirable to us. We think every superintendent and every principal in the public schools must deal extensively with the public. While supervisors and directors may deal less with the public, we are convinced that they, too, must be involved in some public relationships.

The public is not monolithic in nature—in fact, there are many publics. And school officials may stand alone among administrators in the great number of publics to whom they feel responsible. Moreover, these publics are more than local in nature. Often decisions affecting local school districts are made at county, state, and national levels. Administrators must ascertain for their schools or school districts who these publics are and how they believe and act with respect to school matters.

Communication with the many publics of a school community must be a two-way process. The old business of selling, telling, or interpreting the schools just will not suffice. Just as the problems, the achievements, and the shortcomings of the public schools must be explained, the feelings, beliefs, and aspirations of the people who make up the various publics must also be ascertained. There is, then, the need for listening as well as telling; the need for assessment as well as projection. Hearing what people say in our pluralistic society is no simple task. There are many conflicting voices and some of the voices once submerged are now loud and vociferous.

The real challenge to the administrative leader in dealing with the many publics of the school community is dealing with the feelings, beliefs, and aspirations of the people. Ordinarily, the data alone cannot be accepted as the basis for charting courses of action, any more than professional values can be imposed on a community without consideration of the many factors comprising that particular situation. In other words, administrators find out what people think, what they value, and what they want in order to determine where to begin, or what are the reasonable limits beyond which action cannot go.

The excitement comes from finding and helping to arrange ways for people to get new ideas, gradually accept new values, and come to have more realistic expectations of the public school. In the diversity of ideas and aspirations among the publics of a school community, sometimes ways can be found to reach a greater degree of agreement so that the course of school operation can go forward with renewed enthusiasm and direction.

We are not suggesting that administrators can be all-wise in this situation. Administrators are probably no wiser than other leaders in the school community, and they would do well to relate to people so as to learn from them as well as influence them. We do suggest, however, that administrators have professional knowledge as well as the convictions that the democratic way of life is important and that the public school has a significant role to play in its realization. With these values as a prime motivation, they can retain their focus without offending others by insisting upon patterned behavior.

In the end, the community must take action for public education, through the selection of wise school-board members, the passage of bond issues, and the approval of operating levies. Important and necessary as these acts are, the continuous voice of the community as it gives expression to what schools ought to be, and as it reacts both favorably and unfavorably to what schools are, may be even more indicative as to how well the community challenge is being met.

The Board Challenge

Public schools in America are controlled through legally constituted boards of education. These boards have been given broad grants of power by the respective state legislatures. In most states the board members are publicly elected to their offices, and while they are assumed to be representative of the people of the school district, the courts have actually declared them to be officers of the state.

School-board members are usually selected from the professional and managerial groups of society (though in rural areas they are often farm owners). This fact has caused some to conclude that boards are strong defenders of the status quo. Studies of board performance, however, indicate that this interpretation is too simple and, in many cases, not warranted. Most board members are seriously concerned with their responsibility and welcome professional help in interpreting and implementing this responsibility.

Clearly, the board of education is the major reference group with which the superintendent must deal. On occasion superintendents involve other administrators in the board relationship; and board opinions, board action, and board policies are always significant to all administrators.

Superintendents have two major roles to play to meet the challenge of working with the board of education. First, they are the chief executive officers of the board. As such, they help a board decide what its legislative and judicial functions are, and what their own executive functions are. Even after such definition there may be the continuing necessity of clarifying the board-superintendent relationship, particularly when new members join the board.

Assuming that reasonable agreement concerning the board-superintendent relationship can be reached, superintendents still have the challenge of the executive function. Can the superintendent and his or her staff develop an adequate instructional program? Can they secure competent personnel and mold them into an effective organization? Can they accurately project the financial needs of the district? Can they efficiently expend the available funds and accurately account for them? Can they appraise effectiveness and assure efficiency in the use of resources? Can they effectively represent the schools to others? These represent some of the major expectations most boards of education hold for their superintendents.

In addition to being the chief executive officers of the board of education, superintendents have a second role as chief educational advisers to the board. In this role superintendents help the board form basic policy for school district operation, and broaden the understanding of board members so that they function with greater intelligence as the chief policy-makers for a school district. Zeigler[28] contends that board members not only expect their superintendents to implement board decisions, but they have permitted superintendents to become the chief policy-makers as well, a position that probably underplays the board role.

For the superintendent to serve as chief educational adviser to the board, certain conditions are necessary. As in the case of the community, the superintendent must bring professional understanding and convictions. He or she will find it necessary to work closely with the staff so as to reflect the best possible insights to the board of education at a particular time and place. The superintendent also must have a deep understanding of community values and expectations in order to help the board assess the feasibility of policy alternatives. Finally, he or she must be able to work with the board as a group in ways that generate mutual respect and appreciation for the significance of their shared responsibilities.

Another major reference group for any school administrator is the school staff. We use the word *staff* here to designate all certificated personnel within a school system, including teachers, pupil personnel workers, and administrators. Much of what we say about these personnel also applies, of course, to the noncertificated personnel of a school system.

The Staff Challenge

The first challenge is that of building and maintaining a staff that is thoroughly equipped to do the job of the public schools. If the district is a sizable one, there must be a staff for the central office. For any school district, there is the necessity of building the staff for each school building, whether there is one or a hundred. Building a staff is the obligation of the chief administrator assisted by the entire administrative staff, including each of the building principals.

We want to emphasize again the critical nature of each staff selection. School systems sometimes work years with relatively incompetent teachers in order to help them reach a better level of performance. A better selection in the first place could have saved the principals and supervisors hundreds of hours of effort. The selection of an inadequate principal may mean that for years the program and atmosphere of an entire building, often with hundreds of youngsters involved, is seriously handicapped. To secure for each position the most competent available person is a continuing challenge to administrative leadership.

Assuming the administrators of a school system have been able to build a competent staff, there remains the challenge of keeping the staff productive. In too many school systems there are teachers, administrators, and supervisory personnel who, once vigorous, stimulating, and effective people, have now settled into a dull routine of doing only what has to be done, with no zest for the task. The factors contributing to such a situation are undoubtedly complex. They may include low salaries, which force many teachers to take a second job and thus divide their energies. They may include a perceived lack of opportunity for promotion, particularly within the teaching ranks. But we suspect that there are other factors of importance lying within the direct control of administrators, and these constitute a part of the challenge to their leadership.

Maintaining and improving staff productivity depends on (1) establishing procedures to assess effectiveness and (2) providing appropriate experiences to remedy weaknesses; that is, teacher evaluation and in-service education. As we discussed in Chapter 12, past approaches to both of these matters have often been ritualistic and ineffective. However, change seems likely. Public concerns about school effectiveness have focused new attention on evaluation. In addition to locally initiated programs, some states have mandated new practices in this area.[29] Teachers have been among the severest critics of in-service programs, which too often appear designed only to fill time and fail to provide the kinds of help teachers have requested. Working with staff members to implement evaluation procedures that are fair and effective and providing staff development programs that are helpful have always been important challenges. This is especially so at a time when schools face widespread criticism and economic and demographic factors contribute to low turnover in teaching positions.

As further challenge to administrators, teachers and other staff members have become increasingly militant in recent years. Teachers' organizations are no longer willing to be treated paternalistically by the superintendent or the board of education, no matter how benevolent such action might be. Increasingly, school managers are faced with annual negotiations with teachers wherein procedures developed in private industry are being adapted to the schools. Principals as well as central-office administrators are called upon to administer their units in accord with the agreements set forth in the master contract. This has been especially difficult for administrators who resent these limits upon administrative discretion. Others have found it possible to work harmoniously and respectfully with their staff in similar settings.

Human-relations skills are important to administrators; personal concern for each member of the staff is necessary and appropriate. However, the evidence clearly suggests that it is not enough for an administrator to be concerned with human relations only. In addition, the administrator must be able to help a staff develop goals and a plan of action, to help each staff member make a particular contribution to the total effort, and to stimulate each staff member to make the best contribution possible.

Another aspect of the staff challenge is to contribute to the profession at large. Individual administrators can do this by sharing their time and ideas with professional organizations, by assisting promising young people to become administrators, and by speaking out on issues of importance to the profession. Regional, state, and national meetings of administrators' organizations provide opportunities to share ideas about common problems and effective practices. Participation in such meetings enables individuals to stay abreast of current trends, to share ideas of interest, and to help the organization chart policy positions regarding state and national issues. No issue is more important to the future of the profession than encouraging able, young people to enter it. Established administrators are in an ideal position to do this and have done so for many years through mentoring relationships. Of particular importance in the future is assuring that capable minorities and women have opportunities to advance in educational administration. Finally, administrators can help the profession by serving as knowledgeable and responsible spokepersons on education issues. The general public will judge all school administrators by the few they meet; thus all should be mindful of their responsibilities to the profession as well as to themselves and to their community.

The Pupil Challenge   Another major reference group with which administrators must deal is the children and youth who are enrolled in school. In a sense, all challenges to administrative leadership converge to focus here, because the pupils are the immediate consumers of the school programs. School-community agreements, school-board action, and staff efforts all culminate in what happens to youngsters. These more remote and instrumental programs, no matter how pretty they appear on paper, are of no avail unless they make a difference in the programs of instruction and services to pupils. This is the whole purpose of educational administration, as emphasized throughout this book.

Of all administrators and supervisors within a school system, the building principal is nearest to the teaching-learning situation. His or her influence in that situation is a strategic one. What central office people can do to influence instruction must, for the most part, be expressed through the building principal. The principal, more than any other person, can see that teacher assignments are appropriate, that necessary pupil personnel services are available, and that extra-class activities are significant experiences for youngsters.

The principals of most school buildings want some direct contact with pupils, but there are limits to how much they can do this. Effective principals recognize that their chief work group is the faculty, and that most of their influence with pupils will be expressed through the faculty and the programs of the school. Several studies during the past decade have emphasized the importance of the principal in promoting school effectiveness as measured by student achievement. Shoemaker and Fraser, after reviewing these studies, concluded that principals can enhance teaching and learning if they provide "1) assertive, achievement-oriented leadership; 2) orderly, purposeful, and peaceful school climate; 3) high expectations for staff and pupils; and 4) well-designed instructional objectives and evaluation systems."[30]

In working with the staff to build and implement a school program the principal must recognize its four aspects: classroom instruction, pupil personnel services, extra-class activities, and daily regimen. In addition, attention must be paid to how each of these parts should fit together into the whole offering. There is the continual need to keep classroom instruction stimulating and challenging. In the case of extra-class activities, particularly at the secondary level, there is the need for keeping them educative and not exploitative or simply commercial. With respect to pupil services, there is the need to provide health, guidance, and other services that will contribute to the total development of each youngster or the ability to go on more effectively. Trying to provide the best possible program for each pupil enrolled is the tremendous challenge to public education. An essential integrating element is the school regimen, which establishes and communicates expectations for achievement, initiative, and personal responsibility in an orderly and caring environment.

SUMMARY

We began this chapter by presenting challenges to educational administration. Our first challenge is sustaining the democratic way of life, which is dependent upon an educative process open to all, to which contributions are made by many agencies. Thus the educative process is much broader than any program provided by the public schools, but public schools perform a role that is an indispensable part of it.

For public schools to perform well their administrative leaders must give appropriate direction to the enterprise. If they can visualize the crucial place of the public schools, if they can bring understanding and skill to their task, then public schools can contribute substantially to the development of the people's capacity to think critically about their world. People with this capacity can (and we think will) take steps to preserve that which should be preserved in our culture, and to change that which needs to be improved. Working through numerous community agencies, their efforts will reinforce and complement the goals of the public schools. Together, they can perpetuate and extend the democratic way of life. To the educational administrator is given the privilege of participating significantly in this endeavor.

ENDNOTES

1. 1982 AASA Platform and Resolutions, *AASA Convention Reporter* (Arlington, Va.: American Association of School Administrators, 1982), p. 33.

2. John W. Gardner, *Self-Renewal* (New York: Harper and Row, 1965), pp. 115ff. A similar perspective, which focuses upon schools, is M. Donald Thomas, "The Limits of Pluralism," *Phi Delta Kappan* 68 (April 1981): 589, 591–592.

3. Gardner, *Self-Renewal*, p. 118.

4. Reports of the President's Commission on National Goals, *Goals for Americans* (Englewood Cliffs, N.J.: Prentice-Hall, 1960), pp. 3–6.

5. See Harry S. Broudy, *The Real World of the Public Schools* (New York: Harcourt Brace Jovanovich, 1972), p. 75.

6. Theodore Brameld, *Philosophies of Education in Cultural Perspective* (New York: Dryden Press, 1955), pp. 53–62.

7. See Vance Packard, *The Hidden Persuaders* (New York: David McKay, 1957). See also Joe McGinniss, *The Selling of the President, 1968* (New York: Trident Press, 1969).

8. For instance, see Robert Nisbet, "The Decline of Academic Nationalism," *Change* (Summer 1974).

9. For example, see Margaret Mead, *Coming of Age in Samoa* (New York: W. Morrow, 1928) and Ruth Benedict, *Patterns of Culture* (Boston: Houghton Mifflin, 1934).

10. Benjamin S. Bloom, *Stability and Change in Human Characteristics* (New York: Wiley, 1964).

11. Kenneth Keniston, *The Uncommitted: Alienated Youth in American Society* (New York: Dell Publishing, 1965).

12. David Riesman et al., *The Lonely Crowd* (New Haven, Conn.: Yale University Press, 1950).

13. William H. Whyte, Jr., *The Organization Man* (New York: Simon & Schuster, 1956), Ch. 3.

14. Christopher Jencks et al., *Inequality: A Reassessment of the Effect of Family and Schooling in America* (New York: Basic Books, 1972), p. 158.

15. W. Vance Grant, "The Demographics of Education," *American Education* 17 (Aug.-Sept. 1981): 8–9.

16. See, for example, "Why Public Schools Fail," *Newsweek*, 20 April 1981, pp. 62–65.

17. For example, see the responses to questions about "What grade would give you the public schools?" in the poll conducted by George H. Gallup and published in each September issue of *Phi Delta Kappan*.

18. James S. Coleman, Thomas Hoffer, and Sally Kilgore, *Achievement in High School: Public and Private Schools Compared* (New York: Basic Books, 1982). Also see the article by Coleman and responses in *Phi Delta Kappan* 63 (November 1981): 159 ff.

19. For discussion of the decline in public support for schools, see Stephen K. Bailey, "Political Coalitions for Public Education" and Michael Kirst, "Loss of Support for Public Secondary Schools: Some Causes and Solutions," *Daedalus* 111 (Summer 1981): 27–68.

20. See Harold Hodgkinson, "What's Right With Education?" *Phi Delta Kappan* 61 (November 1979): 159–162. Also David K. Cohen and Barbara Neufeld, "The Failure of High Schools and the Progress of Education," *Daedalus* 111 (Summer 1981): 69–89.

21. Ralph W. Tyler, Jr., "The U.S. vs. the World: A Comparison of Educational Performance," *Phi Delta Kappan* 62 (January 1981): 307.
22. Quoted in Ellwood P. Cubberley, "Reading in Public Education in the United States" (Boston: Houghton Mifflin, 1934), p. 192.
23. Herbert A. Thelen, *Education and the Human Quest* (New York: Harper & Brothers, 1960), p. 107.
24. The committee for the White House Conference on Education, "A Report to the President" (Washington: U.S. Government Printing Office, 1956), p. 9.
25. Jencks et al., *Inequality*.
26. Roald F. Campbell et al., "The Purpose and Nature of the Public Schools." Report of Task Force #3 to the Utah Statewide Planning Commission of Education, Salt Lake City, 1981.
27. For instance, see James S. Coleman et al., *Youth: Transition to Adulthood* (Chicago: University of Chicago Press, 1974).
28. L.H. Zeigler et al., *Governing American Schools* (North Scituate, Mass.: Duxbury Press, 1974).
29. See for example, Paul F. Kleine and Richard Wisniewski, "Bill 1706: A Forward Step for Oklahoma" and Thomas R. McDaniel, "South Carolina's Education Improvement Act: Portent of the Super School Board?" *Phi Delta Kappan* 63 (October 1981): 115–119.
30. Joan Shoemaker and Hugh W. Fraser, "What Principals Can Do: Some Implications from Studies of Effective Schooling," *Phi Delta Kappan* 63 (November 1981): 178–182.

INDEX

continued